The Archetypal Artist is a long-awaited offering to the fields of creativity and depth psychology. Scholars, students, artists, ecologists, and activists will find revelation here – it's an accessible yet intricately woven map of Jungian and archetypal concepts and their relationship to artistic expression. Dr Mary Wood at once honors the great mystery within the soul of every artist while leaving no stone unturned in the pursuit of deeper understanding.

Kim Krans, *Artist and NY Times Bestselling Author of The Wild Unknown Tarot*

Mary Wood's fine book, carefully researched and presented, draws on her talents as artist, depth psychologist, and scholar. With a keen historical sense and marshalling a wide range of sources, it leads us to recover and reconceptualize the high purpose and calling of the artist as a conduit for the creative depths of the psyche and the expression of soul.

Dr Keiron Le Grice, *Professor of Depth Psychology at Pacifica Graduate Institute, California*

Dr Mary Wood's creative vision that inspires *The Archetypal Artist* is fiercely and delightfully expansive and deep, measured, but not without a tincture of wildness. Her calling to re-vision the creative spirit in each of us implies that creativity is a spiritual practice – a way of being enthused to sense the world's sacredness anew.

Dennis Patrick Slattery, *PhD, Author, Poet, and Distinguished Professor Emeritus in Mythology at Pacifica Graduate Institute*

In an exciting and provocative transformation of Jungian and Archetypal Studies, *The Archetypal Artist* shifts the center of gravity of depth psychology to the artist rather than the therapist. For surely those conducting images into being through artmaking are individuating for the world as well as themselves? By bringing Jung, post-Jungians, Hillman, soul-making, and myth into depth psychology's re-connection of shaman to artist, Wood restores art to its ancestral homes in medicine, religion, divination, and magic. Modernity split the psyche, so reducing art into soul-less artifacts. *The Archetypal Artist* restores the art of life. It shows artworks as a living medium for the soul. This book is soul-juice for anyone who wants to find authenticity in the urge to create. It is essential reading for all who seek for the art of living, as well as for those driven to fashion life into the in-spirited matter of art.

Susan Rowland, *PhD, Depth Psychology, Creativity, and Humanities Professor at Pacifica Graduate Institute*

Wood has created a magnificent homage to James Hillman; reminding us of his vibrant mind and presence and simultaneously she introduces new generations to a true genius whose creativity continues to evolve in ways that are timeless. Her superbly researched volume unfolds, in very readable ways, a comparative study of the meaning of the soul in the world, an idea much needed in our time of loss and disorientation. She helps clinicians bring to the foreground the profound value of art, aesthetics, and creativity as the combined essence of healing. This book provides the backdrop for understanding the "depth" of "depth psychology."

Linda Carter *MSN, Jungian Analyst, CS, IAAP*

The Archetypal Artist: Reimagining Creativity and the Call to Create

In this thoughtful and revelatory book, Wood explores enduring and powerful theories on art, creativity, and what Jung called the "creative spirit" in order to illuminate how artists can truly understand what it means to be a creator.

By bringing together insights on creativity from some of depth psychology's most iconic thinkers, such as C.G. Jung, James Hillman, and Joseph Campbell, as well as featuring a selection of creators who have been influenced by these ideas, such as Martha Graham, Mary Oliver, Stanley Kunitz, and Ursula K. Le Guin, this book explores archetypal thought and the role of the artist in society. This unique approach emphasizes the foundational need to understand and work with the unconscious forces that underpin a creative calling, deepening our understanding of the transformational power of creativity, and the vital role of the artist in the modern world.

Acting as a touchstone for inquiries into the nature of creativity, and of the soul, this enlightening book is perfect for artists and creators of all types, as well as Jungian analysts and therapists, and academics interested in the intersection of the arts, humanities, and depth psychology.

Mary Antonia Wood, PhD, is Chair and Professor for the Depth Psychology and Creativity program at Pacifica Graduate Institute, USA. She is a visual artist who works in a variety of media and the founder of Talisman Creative Mentoring.

The Archetypal Artist

Reimagining Creativity and the
Call to Create

Mary Antonia Wood

LONDON AND NEW YORK

Cover image: "The Sorceress," Mary Antonia Wood

First published 2022
by Routledge
4 Park Square, Milton Park, Abingdon, Oxon OX14 4RN

and by Routledge
605 Third Avenue, New York, NY 10158

Routledge is an imprint of the Taylor & Francis Group, an informa business

© 2022 Mary Antonia Wood

The right of Mary Antonia Wood to be identified as author of this work has been asserted in accordance with sections 77 and 78 of the Copyright, Designs and Patents Act 1988.

All rights reserved. No part of this book may be reprinted or reproduced or utilized in any form or by any electronic, mechanical, or other means, now known or hereafter invented, including photocopying and recording, or in any information storage or retrieval system, without permission in writing from the publishers.

Trademark notice: Product or corporate names may be trademarks or registered trademarks, and are used only for identification and explanation without intent to infringe.

British Library Cataloguing-in-Publication Data
A catalogue record for this book is available from the British Library

Library of Congress Cataloging-in-Publication Data
A catalog record for this book has been requested

ISBN: 978-0-367-17796-6 (hbk)
ISBN: 978-0-367-17797-3 (pbk)
ISBN: 978-0-429-05772-4 (ebk)

DOI: 10.4324/9780429057724

Typeset in Times New Roman
by Apex CoVantage, LLC

Contents

	Dedication and Grateful Acknowledgments	viii
	Introduction	1
1	An Archaeology of Soul, Creativity, and Transformation	16
2	C.G. Jung: Reluctant Artist, Servant of the Creative Spirit	37
3	A Thousand Voices: Inflections and Interpretations of Jung's Creative Vision	62
4	Archetypal Creativity: Image, Imagination, and Instinct	83
5	Image Making and Soul-Making	100
6	Mythopoesis: The Archetypal Ancestors of the Modern Creator	120
7	The Soul, the Creative, and the Archetypal Artist	142
	Epilogue as Testament and Talisman	157
	Index	158

Dedication and Grateful Acknowledgments

This act of *bricolage*, of combining and recombining dusty treasures with newly found jewels of insight, is dedicated to my husband, Marcus – a devoted creator, *bricoleur*, and lifelong initiate of the imagination.

This book would not have come into being without the many opportunities for deep engagement with the mysteries of creativity and the soul offered by my mentors, colleagues, and students at Pacifica Graduate Institute in Santa Barbara, California; a *temenos* of ideas and experiences where psyche is honored through study, creative practice, ritual, and community. In particular, I thank Susan Rowland and Dennis Patrick Slattery for their inspiring scholarship, generous mentoring, and marvelous friendship. In addition, I extend my deep gratitude to Susannah Frearson and Alexis O'Brien at Routledge for their very kind and very patient support for this project.

Introduction

Creativity and the soul

Creativity is a mystery, an enigma. Like other enigmas such as "soul" and "imagination," creativity cannot be located, measured, or summoned at will. The depths of creativity, like those of the soul, are beyond our ability to completely know and describe – yet creativity, like soul, animates our lives. It may seem odd to begin a book on creativity by so quickly revealing the limitations of human curiosity when attempting to explore and ultimately understand both the origins and essential nature of creativity. However, rather than offering a surrender, this book will approach creativity as one might approach a wild animal in the forest – with a sense of reverent awe, combined with a dose of humility. To approach creativity is itself a creative act; one that includes the same type of patience and attentiveness necessary for catching a glimpse of any wild thing, including the soul.

Creativity and soul are very much alike in that neither of them is a thing, substance, or possession. In their ambiguity, both soul and creativity are better approached and imagined as symbols, perspectives, happenings, experiences, ways of being – or even *as beings* themselves. In fact, the word "creativity," with its exclusive and aspirational connotations, occludes more than it reveals. To reimagine creativity begins by reimagining it as "the creative," as something alive and autonomous. Breaking out of the pattern of thinking of creativity as a possession is not easy, so the terms "creativity" and "the creative" will be used interchangeably due to the former's prominence in contemporary thought. As will become clear, this book is not an explication of terms but rather an *invitation* to enter into a renewed relationship with both the creative and the soul – ultimately, they are one and the same.

Before the reunion, however, it is worthwhile to consider creativity and the soul individually. Our Western notions of the soul have been shaped by a myriad of sources: from early Mediterranean shamanic traditions to the pre-Socratic philosophers of Greece; from India to the Far East; from Plato to the Renaissance Neoplatonists; from Christian theologians to Romantic poets; from medical doctors to the pioneers of psychology; and on to today's philosophers, artists, spiritual guides, and neuroscientists.

DOI: 10.4324/9780429057724-1

2 Introduction

C.G. Jung described soul, or psyche, as an imaginative process, an imaginer, and as a "picturing of vital activities."[1] Soul, according to archetypal psychologist James Hillman, is closer to a symbol than a concept. Like all true symbols, it is "deliberately ambiguous," even as it acts as a "root metaphor" of human thought.[2] Both symbols and metaphors form bridges between distinct territories such as inner and outer, conscious and unconscious, material and spiritual, known and unknown. Soul acts as just such a bridge – a mediatrix, *psychopomp*, and connecting guide situated in the middle, yet connected to each side of a polarity. From an archetypal perspective, soul is both creative and creator in that it is synonymous with the "imaginative possibility in our natures, the experiencing through reflective speculation, dream, image, and fantasy – that mode which recognizes all realities as primarily symbolic or metaphorical."[3] Soul cannot be seen in a literal sense, but soul can be sensed, felt, longed for, and lived. As a mediating symbol, soul is oftentimes illuminated most clearly when our lives seem darkened, obscured, and out of focus.[4] Our human connection to soul is clarified precisely at those times when we sense its absence; we may feel barren, depressed, blocked, or simply disconnected with no bridge in sight.

Similarly, we recognize the vital power of creativity most clearly when we feel that it is missing from our lives – that somehow it has abandoned us, or perhaps that it has passed us by altogether. There is also the troubling possibility that it is *we* who have abandoned creativity – what poet, essayist, and critic Sir Herbert Read called "turning one's back on the muse."[5] Muse is an ancient term that has at times been thought of as synonymous with other guiding forces, such as the daimon, genius, *mana*, or soul. Poet Mary Oliver settled on "the Miraculous," as the best term for a force that calls for attention, devotion, and creative action:

> The Miraculous swerves at us. . . . [and] my loyalty is to the inner vision, whenever and howsoever it may arrive. . . . There is no other way work of artistic worth can be done. . . . The most regretful people on earth are those who felt the call to creative work, who felt their own creative power restive and uprising, and gave to it neither power nor time.[6]

The "Miraculous" requires relationship and the regret that Oliver described stems in large part from our dominant, yet profoundly limiting, contemporary Western notions of creativity and imagination. As a root metaphor, perspective, or psychic symbol, creativity is not the exclusive birthright of those individuals whom we call "artists." While individuals in every culture have always stood out as exemplary models of creative expression, creativity and artistic ability *are not* synonymous, as will become clear.

What is an artist?

The question of whether the creative individual is somehow inherently different from others has been argued for centuries. This book will consider a range of

Introduction 3

arguments, both *for* and *against* exceptionality, with a realization that an "either/or" question is limiting from the start. Creators are shape-shifters – as varied as the works that they create. For this reason, no one term encompasses their inherent multiplicity. The term "artist" is loaded with centuries of meanings; it implies a sense of recognition, gratitude, and dedication to one's gifts, but its lofty and exclusive overtones have also stifled creative yearnings in many who are not comfortable with claiming the title. This book will utilize many terms for those who create including creator, maker, creative individual, and artist. Multiple terms will assist in amplifying the figure of the creator beyond the prevailing and limiting divisions of artist versus non-artist, professional versus amateur, full-time versus part-time, fine artist versus commercial artist, and so forth. As a starting point, let us say that an "artist" is one who feels a need to "make" beyond necessity, to recombine what is given into new forms, and to create something extraordinary out of the ordinary. The Greeks called this *poesis*; a type of making, or bringing forth, that implies a heightened sense of devotion to a creative potential, and service to what Jung called the "creative spirit."

Some creators have described their calling as a chronic nudging or disturbance, others have likened it to being driven by a daimon or an angel, and still others as something akin to possession by a force that has at various times been called fate or destiny. Modern dance pioneer, Martha Graham described living with a constant "queer divine dissatisfaction" and a "blessed unrest" that propelled her creative output. Echoing some of Jung's sentiments on the exceptionality of creators, she stated that the artist, while rarely satisfied, was also more alive than non-artists.[7]

The call to create is not an easy thing to accept; the sacrifices required are not so different from those associated with the call to spiritual service. This affinity was articulated by Jean Erdman Campbell, who led her own company after years of dancing with Graham. Erdman Campbell's sensitive appraisals of the artist's life influenced her husband, the mythologist Joseph Campbell:

> One day when we were talking [Jean said], "The way of the mystic and the way of the artist are very much alike, except that the mystic doesn't have a craft." I use that as the key for paralleling the two ways of the mystical life and the artist's life. The artist with a craft remains in touch with the world; the mystic can spin off and lose touch and frequently does. And so it seems to me that art is the higher form.[8]

One of the key ideas that will appear in various forms throughout this book is precisely what Campbell observed: that artists, even while surrendering to inspiration, do not completely lose themselves in the experience. They return from their descents into the unconscious – or what non-Western cultures have sometimes called journeys into the spirit world – with boons of insight for the collective, which they craft into experiences and objects to be shared. What this describes is the eternal and universal path of the magician, the alchemist, the healer, and the shaman – the archetypal ancestors of the artist.[9]

Longing for the creative

Far from a frivolous pastime, the desire to create may have evolved as a selective and beneficial human behavior – one that contributed to the flourishing of humankind. Researcher and evolutionary biologist Ellen Dissanayake developed the phrase, "making special" to encompass her theories on the evolution of human creative expression – not as "art" as we generally know it but as a generative act closely related to play and ritual. All of these activities elaborate upon reality or what is considered to be reality. They transform with intent or deliberateness, adding value or "specialness" – what has also been called "magic or beauty or spiritual power or significance." Both the maker(s) and the collective are renewed and refreshed through these activities.[10] Our longings for creative expression (including play and ritual) have not diminished even in an era mostly bereft of ritual and suspicious of play; an era defined by rationality, specialization, and marketplace supremacy.

Jung believed that creativity held a central role in human life. Along with the instincts of hunger, sexuality, the drive for activity, and the need for reflection, he added a fifth factor: a "psychological creative drive" that propels the flowering of each human life. If, as he insisted, creativity is akin to a vital human instinct, then our prevailing notions of creativity begin to seem less exclusive, less linked to certain types of artistic abilities.[11]

"Creativity as instinct" allows for a vast range of creative expression while also recognizing that certain creative outcomes have always stood out as particularly powerful or visionary. In addition, there have always been individual differences in both the intensity and the circumstances related to the call to create. Jung's ideas on the creative instinct were furthered by Hillman, who argued that creativity was not a gift or special grace nor an ability or talent: "Rather it is that immense energy coming from beyond man's psyche which pushes one to self-dedication. . . . Creativity impels devotion to one's person" even as it "brings with it a sense of helplessness and increasing awareness of its numinous power."[12]

As will become clear, creativity or "the creative" has many faces. While we all share in the immense energies that drive the opus of each human life, these same energies also urge many of us toward a type of *psychopoesis*, or soul-making, that necessitates the actual making of things and experiences. This heightened calling longs to be realized – it is in fact *made of longing* – for the time, inspiration, opportunities, skills, clarity, and especially the courage to answer this vital call. As Hillman said, "tell me for what you yearn and I shall tell you who you are."[13] We are what we long for.

Creativity at a crossroads

These enduring longings for deeper connections to the creative imagination fuel an industry of books, classes, conferences, workshops, lectures, videos, and the like. Most contemporary approaches tend to rest upon assumptions that overemphasize personal willpower, control, and performance optimization while deemphasizing or dismissing what Jung called "the collective unconscious" as the transpersonal realm of creativity and imagination. This is not surprising, since American culture, as described by cultural historian Jackson Lears is "a culture of control" built upon long-standing assumptions regarding the primacy of the individual human being and the efficacy of human agency over the vast collection of unseen forces that interact with our conscious intentions and which were once called "fate."[14]

Answering the call of those restive urges that Oliver described has never been easy. It is tempting to look for ways to control or maximize the creative process. In our heroic quests to awaken what we are told is "our dormant creativity," and "unleash our constricted imaginations," we miss the fact that these psychic forces *have always* been awake and unbound. Theories of creativity that offer formulas for "harnessing" the creative process can never offer creators what they yearn for as they miss half of the equation: the autonomous, collective depths of the psyche, which are resistant to all manner of harnessing. Regardless of the multitude of terms used over the centuries to describe these depths, they are all synonymous with imagination, a mystery that is always awake and always creating – *it is we* who must awaken and renew our bonds to this ever-creating force.

Contributing to our slumber is the fact that creativity has become commoditized: We strive to "get" creative as a means to an end, as a tool for success. Recognizing this pressure and the outsized role of the marketplace, however, is not meant to set up an either/or situation where commercial success and authenticity are mutually exclusive. The situation is much more complex as commercially successful creative projects of many kinds (films, novels, songs, plays, paintings, concerts, videos, and even advertisements) are oftentimes deeply meaningful, soulful, healing, and transformative. In addition, many well-known creators have continued to express a humble and authentic sense of awe about the mysteries and duties of their calling long after achieving commercial success. The insights of creators such as Stanley Kunitz, Mary Oliver, D.H. Lawrence, Ursula K. Le Guin, John Lennon, Octavio Paz, Louise Glück, Martha Graham, Franz Kakfa, Brittany Howard, Lin Manuel Miranda, Anaïs Nin, and Amanda Gorman are tremendously valuable and will be woven through the following chapters.

As a universal psychic dynamism, creativity's restive callings do not recognize boundaries between professionals and amateurs, and we are impoverished both individually and culturally when creative expression is encouraged and supported in only a select few. Depth psychological approaches to creativity can act as much-needed correctives for this limiting structure. One of the most valuable aspects of depth psychology's multifaceted relationship with creativity is the fact that this relationship simultaneously – and convincingly – honors the soul's appearance in renowned acts of creative expression *along with* its appearance in anonymous, modest, quiet, and even secretive expressions of creativity. As we are reminded each night through our dreams: The soul longs to display itself to us and *to itself.*

An intersection of ideas

Poet Stanley Kunitz intuited that there is "something happening behind your life that is yours and not yours at the same time."[15] This revelation led him to ask, "How could you be an artist if you don't explore your inner life?"[16] This type of exploration is what depth psychology has been doing for over a century and what this book hopes to reimagine for creators in the present era.

Depth psychology is a term that has been applied to a variety of schools or psychological approaches, including at least three distinct areas of emphasis: analytical/Jungian psychology (associated with C.G. Jung), archetypal psychology (associated with James Hillman), and psychoanalysis (associated with Sigmund Freud). Put simply, these disciplines have concerned themselves with the phenomenon of the unconscious and its relationship to human consciousness.[17] Put poetically, a "depth" psychology values the "deeper meanings of the soul."[18]

In approaching creativity, imagination, and the creative calling, depth psychology balances on a fascinating edge – it can both position the artist as one set apart, a visionary or prophet – while arguing that imagination and creativity are embedded in *every* human life. The enduring bond between depth psychology and creativity is not surprising in that the origins of depth psychology are rooted in the arts and humanities, particularly philosophy, literature, and mythology. Sir Herbert Read argued that the artist has been exploring the unconscious for a considerably longer time than the scientist and that the material for a theory of the unconscious is drawn from the experiences of the poet and the painter.[19]

The familial bonds between artist, philosopher, and psychologist lead back to the very beginnings of human culture when shaman-like healers dealt in "magic, mythmaking, protophilosophy, song, and poetry," long before the evolution of the specialized professions of physician, artist, and philosopher.[20] Contemporary philosophers, such as Alva Noë, continue to see the affinities between art and philosophy as they "share a common aim: self-transformation and the achievement of understandings."[21] Depth psychology shares these same aims. To reimagine creativity is to recognize that artists, healers, scientists, and philosophers are not as distinct as a worldview based on specialization would have us believe.

Jung insisted that creativity was the very nature of the psyche, and that psyche itself was nature. He described psyche as an image, as an imaginer that pictured our realities: The autonomous activity of the psyche is "like every vital process, a continually creative act. The psyche creates reality every day."[22] Regardless of whether or not we engage in a recognizable artistic practice, the imaginative psyche, in which we are participants, is constantly creating. Jung, along with colleagues, such as Erich Neumann, oftentimes elevated artists, setting them apart from others as "great individuals."[23] However, regardless of their exceptionality, Jung insisted that creative individuals acted as servants to the objects and experiences that sought to be crafted and manifested through them.[24] Jung positioned "the artist" as an exceptional and driven individual, while at the very same time insisting that a type of primal creativity is available to all – a vital creative

Introduction 7

connection to the unconscious that included the actual crafting of images and experiences.[25] An examination of this paradox is at the heart of this book's intent.

Like Jung, Hillman wrote extensively about artists and creators, oftentimes examining their complex lives against the backdrop of his theories on the nature of soul, calling, and "soul-making." Hillman's description of "soul-making" as a type of essential creativity will be fully explored in the coming chapters.[26] Viewing one's life as an opus, as a living artwork, and as the ultimate venue for creativity is a perspective that Hillman developed via archetypal psychology's explicit alignment with the arts and humanities.[27] In contrast to Jung, Hillman situated the artist fully within the human community: Artists are not exceptions to "normal" individuals; rather they are craftspersons or *bricoleurs*. Hillman also utilized the term "*artifex*" to describe the artist as one who may indeed possess great gifts but who also humbly recognizes a sense of duty and destiny in their calling.[28]

Recently, Jungian analyst and scholar Joseph Cambray has demonstrated the affinities between creativity, synchronicity, and complexity theory, or "emergence," while Susan Rowland's work moves with a transdisciplinary flair between depth psychology, the arts and humanities, and arts-based research.[29] Transdisciplinarity breaks down hierarchies of knowledge and allows for a porous blending of subject and object, of rationality and the irrational/intuitive, of ancient wisdom traditions (including ritual, religious practice, divination, and artmaking), and contemporary science. The implications for creative individuals are profound as transdisciplinarity actively seeks to rebalance modernity's valorization of science and diminishment of the arts and artmaking. Transdisciplinarity always includes a "hidden third" between polarities, which is revealed when disciplines merge into each other via the bridging symbol of creativity.[30]

In addition to Cambray and Rowland, many outstanding contemporary thinkers have advanced both Jung's and Hillman's theories on imagination and creativity in directions that are vital for the twenty-first century. The following chapters will bring together enduring and powerful theories on creativity, imagination, and the call to create from scholars such as Erich Neumann, Marie-Louise von Franz, Sir Herbert Read, Henry Corbin, Rosemary Gordon, James Hollis, Ginette Paris, Roberts Avens, Howard McConeghey, Rollo May, and Richard Tarnas, among others.

Along with the arts, disciplines known as the humanities, such as philosophy, mythological studies, and religious studies have influenced, and have themselves been influenced by, depth psychological thought. This cross-fertilization is quite clear in the work of twentieth- and twenty-first-century scholars such as Mircea Eliade, Joseph Campbell, Thomas McEvilley, Camille Paglia, Yuval Noah Harari, Dennis Patrick Slattery, and Karen Armstrong, among others whose insights will be featured in later chapters. Depth psychology's debt to philosophical and spiritual thought across the centuries will also become clear as the insights of Heraclitus, Lao Tzu, Plato, Plotinus, Eckhart, Ficino, Vico, Kant, Nietzsche, Bachelard, and Barfield, along with many others, have been recognized as contributing to depth psychology's emergence and continued expansion.

An archetypal model

Ideas around archetypes are enjoying a resurgence in popular consciousness as both artists and scholars continue to advance archetypal theory while offering exciting and meaningful ways of working with archetypes in our own lives.[31] This is all the more reason to return to Jung, and to those thinkers and creators (both ancient and modern) who have known archetypes to be dynamic potentials, and not a set of rigid stereotypes or character traits. An archetypal approach to creativity considers Jung's archetypes of the collective unconscious as primordial and thematic shaping energies – dynamos with the power to generate enactments in the physical world, including the artist's response to "the call to create." Ultimately, "archetypes were, and still are, living psychic forces that demand to be taken seriously . . . they have a strange way of making sure of their effect."[32]

An archetypal approach considers Hillman's reassessment of Jungian archetypes as a precursor for the development of his archetypal psychology – a psychology well suited for the artist as it is rooted in imagination itself. For Hillman, archetypes, along with soul, imagination, and creativity are root metaphors that "can never adequately be circumscribed" even as they "govern the perspectives that we have of ourselves and the world."[33] He preferred the word "archetypal" as it refers *to a way of seeing and sensing* rather than the thing seen or sensed. As an adjective, "archetypal" does not "point at something, it points *to* something, and this is *value*." Additionally and importantly, "archetypal" refers to "a move that one makes, rather than to a thing that is [seen]."[34] For both Jung and Hillman, it is the "archetypal image" that initiates our phenomenological encounters with the primal shaping energies of the psyche. These images may come forward in many ways, especially through our dreams, through the work of artists, and through myths from every culture.

An archetypal approach to creativity considers myth to be of primary importance. Jung described myths and fairytales as bridging symbols and as the "supraordinate third" that "give expression to unconscious processes . . . their retelling causes these processes to come alive again and be recollected, thereby re-establishing the connection between conscious and unconscious."[35] Through myth we also find archetypal models for the artist as the quintessential shape-shifter with multiple archetypal manifestations: trickster, alchemist and magician, creator and destroyer, lover and hermaphrodite, mother, father, and wounded healer. These manifestations include the Egyptian Isis, Nut, and Geb; the Greek Hermes, Dionysus, Eros, and Asclepius; the East Indian Shiva, Parvati, Ardhanarisha, and Kali; the Native American Coyote, Raven, and Changing Woman; and the African Legba and Eshu.[36]

An archetypal approach recognizes that this book itself is an act of *bricolage* – an arrangement of disparate, and in some cases half-forgotten, perspectives, which were encountered, noticed, and crafted into a unique conversation at a particular intersection of time and place. Following Hillman's model of "restatement" when working with images, certain key insights will be restated and reconsidered in various chapters, as their value is inexhaustible. Finally, an archetypal approach to reimagining creativity is also an *epistrophé*; a spiraling back to ancient and not so ancient insights that may serve anew in our contemporary world. As Jung affirmed, "To give birth to the ancient in a new time is creation."[37]

The *sourcier*, the shaman, and the artist

In a journal entry from 1946, essayist and diarist, Anaïs Nin imagined herself, and all creators, as akin to ancient water diviners: as *sourciers* always attentively searching for the primal and endlessly creative underground sources of life. She described the hidden reservoir of the unconscious as interdependent with the upper world of reality and action: "Dreams pass into the reality of action. From the action stems the dream again, and this interdependence produces the highest form of living. I have been able to make these transitions. I have passed from one to the other."[38]

The two-way journeying that Nin accomplished is the characteristic movement of both the artist and the shaman. As *psychopomps*, or guides of souls, they can traverse the depths with the aim of returning with the water and fire of life necessary for recharging every age. Woven throughout this book is a connecting thread that has at various times been called the shamanic spirit, shamanic sensibility, or shamanic personality. Ecotheologian, Thomas Berry, witnessed the shamanic spirit at work in those who risk the "journey into the cosmic mystery" in order to bring back "the vision and the power needed by the community at the most elementary level."[39] He insisted that this role was not exclusive to the traditional shaman per se but was shared by many who have always been called to rebalance the world at times of imbalance:

> In moments of confusion such as the present, we are not left simply to our own rational contrivances. We are supported by the ultimate powers of the universe as they make themselves present to us through the spontaneities within our own beings. . . . The shamanic insight is especially important just now when history is being made not primarily within nations or between nations but between humans and the earth, with all its living creatures.[40]

The shamanic sensibility is a call to service; it unites all those who intuit that their participation as image makers and storytellers is necessary if the world is to survive.[41] This assertion is not an exaggeration; on the contrary, personal as well as shared narratives drive human actions, for better and worse. Contemporary philosopher Yuval Noah Harari has described this phenomenon as living by means of "imagined orders" and has made the point (as Jung did a century earlier) that fictions (our shared myths) organize our relationships to each other and to the planet.[42] As to the role of art, cultural critic Camille Paglia insisted that art has the power to re-story (and restore) a world out of balance: Art serves as "the voice of liberty, requiring nurture without intrusion. Art unites the spiritual and material

10 Introduction

realms. In an age of alluring, magical machines, a society that forgets art risks losing its soul."[43]

Contemporary creators are our mythmakers and our guides in this project of re-storying. As Jungian analyst James Hollis has suggested:

> The artist is often the carrier of the mythological project, the one who, from the intersection of conscious intent and unconscious patterning, makes the myth of the age – mythopoesis. If we are, in Karl Jaspers' phrase, to "read the ciphers" of our time, to decipher the mythic texture that lies just beneath the surface, we are obliged to attend to the artistic voices around us.[44]

Attending to and honoring these voices is what this book is about. Reimagining creativity reveals that our quest for the creative needs to be reversed: Creativity is alive and well – *it is we* who are the sleepwalkers who must be awakened and brought into a renewed relationship with this vital living power. As Franz Kafka knew, art is akin to prayer; it is a hand outstretched, longing to be transformed into a hand that bestows gifts.[45]

Reading this book

The reader who is new to Jungian and archetypal thought might want to enter the forest at the beginning and meet each guide, each concept, and each insight as they appear. The seasoned scholar, analyst, or creator may want to plunge directly into territory where new connections between seemingly disparate disciplines and thinkers have been discovered. The list of references at the end of each chapter will direct both kinds of readers to critical primary and auxiliary sources.

Chapter 1 details how both Jungian and archetypal psychologies share a lineage that may be traced back in time to the healer-artists of antiquity. Attending to "soul" is the focus of both Jungian and archetypal psychologies, and their aesthetically rich therapeutic methods and philosophical orientations reveal striking similarities to ancient and contemporary shamanic practices, which have always been concerned with the souls of individuals and the world soul or *anima mundi*. In addition, both Jungian and archetypal psychologies were built upon preexisting foundations from across the arts, literature, philosophy, religion, and world mythology – particularly the myths and early philosophies of ancient Greece. Both disciplines offer a wealth of revitalizing perspectives on creativity and the role of the creative individual due in no small part to their own deep roots within those earlier practices and disciplines known collectively as the arts and humanities.

Chapter 2 focuses on C.G. Jung's groundbreaking contributions toward an understanding of the creative process and the vital role of the artist/creative individual in any society. Many of Jung's signature theories hold immense value for a creative life, including his conception of the collective unconscious and the function of symbols, complexes, archetypes, and archetypal images. These will be explored, along with Jung's notions of the daimon, his delineation between psychological versus visionary art, and the role of the artist as "servant" to autonomous psychic forces. By focusing on C.G. Jung as both a reluctant artist and a devoted servant to what he called the "creative spirit," this chapter also addresses the persistent question of whether creativity is the exclusive province of artists or whether it is equally available to all. As illuminated by Jung's personal example, a paradox emerges where creativity is *both* a type of universal instinct *and* a unique daimonic calling, which bestows what Jung called "the gift of creative fire." As is clear in Jung's own life, this gift mirrors the shamanic pattern of initiation, descent, return/rebirth, and communal service as it beacons creative individuals to a more than personal duty and destiny.

Chapter 3 highlights the contributions of four prominent Jungian scholars and practitioners who have critiqued, amplified, and re-visioned Jung's insights into the creative process. In addition to their fluency with Jung's ideas, Erich Neumann and Sir Herbert Read (Jung's contemporaries), along with the post-Jungian scholars Rosemary Gordon and Susan Rowland, have each skillfully introduced their own unique perspectives on the nature of creativity and the call to create into broader conversations across disciplines and into the twenty-first century. This chapter illuminates Neumann's articulation of the numinous within creative practice, Read's notions of "vitalism" as the driving archetypal force of creativity and his connection of anima to muse, Gordon's work with the concepts of "symbolization" and "bridging" as keys to the creative process, along with Rowland's ideas on alchemy, magic, creativity, and the power of the synchronous symbol to mend the great splits of modernity.

Chapter 4 introduces the archetypal psychologist, James Hillman, with special attention to his advancement of Jung's declaration that "image *is* psyche." This chapter traces the development of archetypal psychology – which was deliberately aligned from its inception with the arts and humanities – while illuminating its relevance for today's creators, specifically with regard to the idea of "creativity as instinct" and the need to differentiate creativity from artistry. In addition, this chapter highlights Hillman's passionate allegiance to imagination and image, which was matched by his allegiance to artists and makers of all types; this union informed and enriched his stirring insights into the creative process, the call to create, and the nature of psyche itself as the quintessential artist. In addition, this chapter will highlight several of the most influential sources of archetypal thought as developed by James Hillman, including the Platonists and Neoplatonists, the Romantic poets, Henry Corbin, and C.G. Jung. Moreover, this chapter will examine Hillman's move away from the traditional Jungian notions of archetype and symbol to a broader definition of "the archetypal" as expressed through images and experiences.

Chapter 5 revolves around Hillman's conception of "soul-making" beginning with his insights into the nature of soul/anima/psyche itself. Hillman's passionate writing on art includes his assertion that art is a form of ritual, with the artist serving as a type of celebrant. Hillman has described creative individuals as vital, yet highly sensitive and vulnerable emissaries (*angelos*) of soul – as craftspeople,

12 Introduction

bricoleurs, and not as specialists. In addition, Hillman's notion of an "artist's fantasy," a way of crafting a soulful life that can be enacted by all, will be considered alongside his thoughts on human destiny and purpose which he called the "acorn theory." This theory points toward a unique inner personal image, or calling, that yearns for fulfillment. Taken together, these propositions open up a host of new questions that will be addressed, such as: If soul is an artist, then is the artist the human exemplar of the work of the soul? What exactly makes someone an artist, and are artists somehow different than everybody else? Are artists born or are they made?

Building upon the foundation of the previous five chapters, Chapter 6 highlights the value of myth for contemporary creators through an exploration of four key groups of mythic creators seen in various traditions: the tricksters and magicians; the creators and destroyers; the wounded healers; and the lovers and hermaphrodites. Each of the archetypal figures featured within these groupings represents a type of consciousness; they are personifications of the creative in its many manifestations. Today's creators may recognize themselves in more than one figure as the creative has many faces, many styles of operating in the world. To understand oneself as an artist is to understand that the archetypal dynamisms that power one's call to create are the same archetypal dynamisms powering the tales of mythic creators the world over. This chapter moreover emphasizes the responsibilities of mythopoesis: the making and remaking of the stories that guide human interactions in every age – for better and for worse. Scholars of myth and ancient culture such as Joseph Campbell, Mircea Eliade, Thomas McEvilley, Michael Tucker, Lewis Hyde, and Karen Armstrong will be called upon in this chapter to demonstrate the value of mythological insights to creative practice and to living a creative life.

Chapter 7 brings this book to a close by offering both new and integrated insights into the key areas of inquiry that have woven their way through the previous chapters, beginning with the idea that the soul, the creative, and the artist are each a crossroads where transformation and manifestation occur. The crossroads offer the possibility of movement and intercommunication between worlds, which is also the task of the shaman, the archetypal ancestor of the contemporary creator. This chapter returns as well to Hillman's revivification of the notion of the *anima mundi*, or ensouled world, with the implication that artworks and experiences are themselves ensouled, alive, and autonomous – they are talismans of transformation. These creations emerge at the crossroads of desire and dissatisfaction, longing and love – the place where soul is made and where we ourselves are being created. In addition, Hillman's notion of an "artist's fantasy" is taken up once again to confirm a primary and vital type of creativity available to all in the crafting of the opus of one's life. Finally, we arrive at the destiny of the archetypal artist; whether shaman, *sourcier*, *artifex*, *bricoleur*, trickster, wounded healer, good host, or any combination of terms both mythic and ordinary – terms which ultimately *mean nothing* in and of themselves. What matters is what artists

Introduction 13

can do, what they can bring forth and bestow from the place that Kafka called the "dark rainbow."

Notes

1 Jung, "Psychological Factors Determining Human Behavior," in *The Structure and Dynamics of the Psyche* (*CW8*), pp. 325–326, para. 618.
2 Hillman, *Suicide and the Soul*, p. 46.
3 Hillman, *Re-Visioning Psychology*, p. xvi.
4 Hillman, *The Myth of Analysis*, p. 5.
5 Read, *The Origins of Form in Art*, p. 138. See Chapter 3 for a dedicated section on Read.
6 Oliver, *Upstream: Selected Essays*, p. 30.
7 De Mille, *Martha: The Life and Work of Martha Graham*, p. 264.
8 Campbell, *The Hero's Journey: Joseph Campbell on His Life and Work*, p. 139.
9 See Chapter 1 for historic evidence of the creative individual's shamanic lineage, as well as Chapter 6 for the diverse and multicultural mythic lineage.
10 Dissanayake, *What Is Art?*, p. 92.
11 Jung, "Psychological Factors Determining Human Behavior," in *The Structure and Dynamics of the Psyche* (*CW8*), p. 118, paras. 245–246.
12 Hillman, *The Myth of Analysis*, pp. 35–36.
13 Hillman, "Pothos: Nostalgia of the Puer Eternus," in *Loose Ends*, p. 54.
14 Lears, *Something for Nothing: Luck in America*, p. 7.
15 Kunitz and Lentine, *The Wild Braid: A Poet Reflects on a Century in the Garden*, p. 133.
16 Ibid., p. 101.
17 Samuels, Shorter and Plaut, *A Critical Dictionary of Jungian Analysis*, pp. 43–44.
18 Hillman, *Re-Visioning Psychology*, p. xvii.
19 Read, *Icon and Idea: The Function of Art in the Development of Human Consciousness*, p. 117.
20 McEvilley, *The Shape of Ancient Thought: Comparative Studies in Greek and Indian Philosophies*, p. 15.
21 Noë, *Strange Tools: Art and Human Nature*, p. 140.
22 Jung, "The Problem of Types in the History of Classical and Medieval Thought," in *Psychological Types* (*CW6*), p. 52, para. 78.
23 Neumann, "Art and Time," in *Art and the Creative Unconscious*, p. 83.
24 Jung, "On the Relationship of Analytical Psychology to Poetry," in *The Spirit in Man, Art and Literature* (*CW15*), pp. 71–72, paras. 108–110.
25 Jung, "The Transcendent Function," in *Structure and Dynamics of the Psyche (CW8)*, pp. 86–87, para. 180.
26 Ibid., pp. 39–40.
27 Hillman, *Archetypal Psychology*, pp. 13–17.
28 See Chapter 2 for Hillman's articulation of the "artifex" in relation to Jung's life and work.
29 See Cambray's *Synchronicity: Nature and Psyche in an Interconnected Universe*. See Chapter 3 for an extended discussion of Susan Rowland's contributions to contemporary Jungian thought on a number of topics.
30 Rowland, *Remembering Dionysus: Revisioning Psychology and Literature in C.G. Jung and James Hillman*, p. 35.
31 For example, see Kim Krans's *Wild Unknown Archetype Deck and Guidebook*.

14 Introduction

32 Jung, "Psychology of the Child Archetype," in *The Archetypes and the Collective Unconscious (CW9i)*, pp. 156–157, para. 266.
33 Hillman, *Re-Visioning Psychology*, p. xix.
34 Hillman, *Archetypal Psychology*, p. 25.
35 Jung, "Background to the Psychology of Christian Alchemical Symbolism," in *CW9ii*, p. 180, para. 280. See also Chapter 3 for Rosemary Gordon's insights into "symbolizing."
36 See Chapter 6 for an extended discussion on the mythic ancestors of today's artists.
37 Jung, *The Red Book/Liber Novus: A Reader's Edition*, p. 394.
38 Nin, *The Diary of Anaïs Nin*, Vol. 4. 1944–1947, p. 150.
39 Berry, *Dream of the Earth*, p. 211.
40 Ibid., p. 212. In addition, see Chapter 2 for an assessment of Jung's own shamanic sensibility.
41 See Chapters 2 and 7 for connections between the historic and mythic shamanic personality and the contemporary creator, as well as the connections to the various branches of depth psychology.
42 Harari, *Sapiens: A Brief History of Humankind*, p. 105.
43 Paglia, "Introduction," in *Glittering Images: A Journey Through Art from Egypt to Star Wars*, p. xviii.
44 Hollis, *Tracking the Gods: The Place of Myth in Modern Life*, p. 30.
45 See Chapter 7.

References

Berry, Thomas. *The Dream of the Earth*. 1988. Berkeley, CA: Counterpoint. 2015.
Campbell, Joseph. *The Hero's Journey: Joseph Campbell on His Life and Work*. 1990. Edited by Phil Cosineau. Novato, CA: New World Books. 2003.
De Mille, Agnes. *Martha: The Life and Work of Martha Graham*. New York, NY: Vintage. 1992.
Dissanayake, Ellen. *What Is Art for?* Seattle, WA: University of Washington Press. 1988.
Harari, Yuval Noah. *Sapiens: A Brief History of Humankind*. New York, NY: Harper Perennial. 2015.
Hillman, James. *The Myth of Analysis: Three Essays in Archetypal Psychology*. 1972. New York, NY: Harper Colophon. 1978.
Hillman, James. "Pothos: The Nostalgia of the Puer Eternus." In *Loose Ends*. 1975. Dallas, TX: Spring Publications. 1986.
Hillman, James. *Re-Visioning Psychology*. 1975. New York, NY: Harper Perennial. 1992.
Hillman, James. *Archetypal Psychology*. 1983. The Uniform Edition of the Writings of James Hillman. Vol. 1. Putnam, CT: Spring Publications. 2004.
Hillman, James. *Suicide and the Soul*. 1965. Putnam, CT: Spring Publications. 2011.
Hillman, James and Margot McLean. "Permeability." In *ARAS: Art & Psyche Online Journal*. Vol. 4. 2009.
Hollis, James. *Tracking the Gods: The Place of Myth in Modern Life*. Toronto, Canada: Inner City Books. 1995.
Jung, Carl Gustav. "On the Relationship of Analytical Psychology to Poetry." 1922. In *The Spirit in Man, Art and Literature: CW15*. Edited by Herbert Read, Michael Fordham, Gerhard Adler and William McGuire. Translated by R.F.C. Hull. Reprint. Princeton, NJ: Princeton University Press. 1966/1978.
Jung, Carl Gustav. "Background to the Psychology of Christian Alchemy." 1950. In *Aion: Researches into the Phenomenology of the Self: CW9ii*. Edited by Herbert Read, Michael

Fordham, Gerhard Adler and William McGuire. Translated by R.F.C. Hull. Princeton, NJ: Princeton University Press. 1968.

Jung, Carl Gustav. "The Psychology of the Child Archetype." 1951. In *The Archetypes and the Collective Unconscious: CW9i*. Edited by Herbert Read, Michael Fordham, Gerhard Adler and William McGuire. Translated by R.F.C. Hull. Princeton, NJ: Princeton University Press. 1968.

Jung, Carl Gustav. "Psychological Factors Determining Human Behavior." 1937. In *The Structure and Dynamics of the Psyche: CW8*. Edited by Herbert Read, Michael Fordham, Gerhard Adler and William McGuire. Translated by R.F.C. Hull. Princeton, NJ: Princeton University Press. 1969.

Jung, Carl Gustav. "The Transcendent Function." 1958. In *The Structure and Dynamics of the Psyche: CW8*. Edited by Herbert Read, Michael Fordham, Gerhard Adler and William McGuire. Translated by R.F.C. Hull. Princeton, NJ: Princeton University Press. 1969.

Jung, Carl Gustav. "The Problem of Types in the History of Classical and Medieval Thought." 1921. In *Psychological Types: CW6*. Edited by Herbert Read, Michael Fordham, Gerhard Adler and William McGuire. Translated by R.F.C. Hull. Princeton, NJ: Princeton University Press. 1971.

Jung, Carl Gustav. *The Red Book/ Liber Novus: A Reader's Edition*. Edited by Sonu Shamdasani. Translated by Mark Kyburz, John Peck and Sonu Shamdasani. New York and London: W.W. Norton and Co. 2009.

Kunitz, Stanley and Genine Lentine. *The Wild Braid: A Poet Reflects on a Century in the Garden*. New York, NY: W.W. Norton and Company. 2005.

Lears, Jackson. *Something for Nothing: Luck in America*. New York, NY: Penguin. 2003.

McEvilley, Thomas. *The Shape of Ancient Thought: Comparative Studies in Greek and Indian Philosophies*. New York, NY: Allworth Press. 2002.

Nin, Anaïs. *The Diaries of Anaïs Nin: Volume Four, 1944–1947*. Edited by Gunther Sthulmann. New York, NY: Harvest Books. 1971.

Noë, Alva. *Strange Tools: Art and Human Nature*. New York, NY: Hill and Wang. 2015.

Oliver, Mary. *Upstream: Selected Essays*. New York, NY: Penguin. 2016.

Paglia, Camille. *Glittering Images: A Journey Through Art from Egypt to Star Wars*. New York, NY: Pantheon. 2012.

Read, Sir Herbert. *The Origins of Form in Art*. London: Thames and Hudson. 1965.

Read, Sir Herbert. *Icon and Idea: The Function of Art in the Development of Human Consciousness*. 1965. New York, NY: Shocken. 1967.

Rowland, Susan. *Remembering Dionysus: Re-Visioning Psychology and Literature in C.G. Jung and James Hillman*. London and New York, NY: Routledge. 2017.

Samuels, Andrew, Bani Shorter and Fred Plaut. *A Critical Dictionary of Jungian Analysis*. 1986. Hove and New York, NY: Routledge. 2013.

Chapter 1

An Archaeology of Soul, Creativity, and Transformation

The soul before psychology

"What is soul, and does it truly exist?" "How is soul revealed?" "Who can best understand and care for the soul?" For millennia, these have been essential questions in humanity's search for meaning and truth. For answers to these questions, Western cultures have long looked to specialists – even when these specialists argue against the very idea of a "soul." Nevertheless, the notion of a soul persists across numerous disciplines, including psychology, medicine, philosophy, spirituality, and creative expression. Today's practitioners of soul have long been separated into distinct disciplines, yet modern-day artists, philosophers, spiritual teachers, and healers share a significant bond as the inheritors of the traditions and practices of a single unified figure – the ancient shaman.

The terms "shaman" and "shamanism" have been utilized to describe a type of medicine person appearing throughout history in a variety of traditions, cultures, and regions. The terms come to us from the Russian translation of the Tungusic *saman*, and in their strictest sense, they refer to a religious phenomenon which emerged in Siberia and Central Asia. Mircea Eliade described the shaman as a *psychopomp*, or guide of souls, who may also be a priest, mystic, poet, magician, or sorcerer. While a shaman may combine a variety of these roles, shamanism's complexity led Eliade to underscore the element of ecstatic trance, during which the shaman's soul is believed to leave the physical body and journey into other realms of reality. Shamanism was, and still is, a technique of ecstasy utilizing artistic means to address various types of suffering or imbalances; the shaman is a practitioner devoted to the human soul.[1] In addition to the evidence of early shamanism in Central Asia and Siberia, traces of this type of practitioner can also be found at the roots of Western civilization.

In his brilliant study of the cross-cultural religious and philosophical influences of ancient Greek thought, Thomas McEvilley explained that a figure very much like the multidimensional shaman was still evident in Plato's third century BCE contrary to the common notion that the Greeks had by that time supplanted older mystical, healing, and religious traditions with philosophies of rationality:

> The specialized profession of "physician" had not yet separated itself out from the larger profession of shaman or "medicine man," which included

DOI: 10.4324/9780429057724-2

functions of magic, mythmaking, protophilosophy, and song or poetry; along with the healing. Some of those whom we now regard as Greek philosophers would have appeared to the Persian kings as "physicians."[2]

For centuries prior to Plato's era, Persia had been a meeting ground, an "intermediate culture" where Greeks and Indians made contact with each other, sharing their myths, art forms, and healing practices. Gathered in the Persian courts were "craftsmen of the sacred" from both Greece and India. These craftsmen could be described as philosophers, seers, physicians, and magicians, although their skills were not totally distinct.[3] McEvilly noted that both Greek and Indian philosophical traditions of this era included mystical and transcendentalist schools, alongside those focused on empiricism and protoscientific rationalism.[4] Both cultures had long been concerned with the most fundamental mysteries of existence, including the origin and nature of "soul."

The soul, according to the early Greek philosopher Heraclitus (544–484 BCE) remains undiscovered, "though explored forever, to a depth beyond report."[5] Even with this recognition of the unknowable depths of the soul, Heraclitus urged his fellow Greeks to "inquire within" and seek wisdom in those depths. Taken as a whole, his aphorisms describe a cosmos in constant creative flux, where one thing necessitates its opposite, where opposites play and wrestle with each other, and where opposites ultimately exist as a unity that is beyond moral judgment: "The cosmos works by harmony of tensions, like the lyre and bow," "therefore good and ill are one."[6]

While Heraclitus has long been described as a philosopher, his writings also resemble poetry and prophecy. Indeed, as Brooks Haxton has pointed out, during Heraclitus's lifetime the word "philosopher" or "lover of wisdom" had yet to be invented. However, even without a designated name for such activity, the human pursuit of wisdom, or *sophos*, predates even Heraclitus and stretches back into antiquity.[7] The unified figure of the shaman comes to mind as *sophos* was – and still is – the province of the artist, healer, and seer, as well as that of the philosopher.

Heraclitus's visionary insights regarding soul, human nature, and the nature of existence itself exhibit striking parallels to earlier Indian and Orphic thought; particularly his enigmatic shaping of the idea of "soul," or "the soul," an entity or essence which undergoes a type of constant transformation or reincarnation[8] These ideas were inspirational to early Christian thought, to later philosophers and artists, and to depth psychologists including both C.G. Jung and James Hillman. Philosopher Philip Wheelwright offered a sketch of the Heraclitean soul that prefigured Hillman's bold assertion that soul is not so much a "thing" as it is a "perspective":

> "Soul" for Heraclitus is almost a noun; it is more of a noun that it is anything else. Yet by employing it without the article he avoids a full grammatical commitment, and the noun . . . hovers on the brink of being an adjective, perhaps also a verb. The phrase, "the soul," is likely to carry, for a modern

reader . . . a suggestion of permanence – which, of course, is absent from Heraclitus's conception. Soul, to Heraclitus, is quality, substance, and activity in one.[9]

Hillman counted Heraclitus among the primary ancestors of archetypal psychology and depth psychology as a whole. He traced this lineage back in time from Jung – Hillman's most recent ancestor – to Freud, Dilthey, Coleridge, Schelling, Vico, Ficino, Plotinus, and finally from Plato to Heraclitus:

> Heraclitus lies near the roots of this ancestral tree of thought, since he was the earliest to take psyche as his archetypal first principle, to imagine soul in terms of flux and to speak of its depth without measure. 'Depth psychology,' the modern field whose interest is in the unconscious levels of the psyche – that is, the deeper meanings of the soul – is itself no modern term. . . . Ever since Heraclitus brought soul and depth together in one formulation, the dimension of soul is depth (not breadth or height) and the dimension of our soul travel is downward.[10]

In Heraclitus, Hillman found an elder brother and fellow "archetypal thinker." According to Hillman, "archetypal thought transcends time and place." This type of thought includes what he described as the "postmodern" and "deconstructive" Heraclitean aphorisms where whatever is stated brings out an equally valid opposing statement, such as "The way up is the way back," and "The beginning is the end."[11] The emphasis on change, transformation, and the absence of stability as signified by "fire" points to what Hillman calls a "poetic dissonance," or "tension in the heart of the mind," which he witnessed in the work and lives of writers and artists, as well as psychologists.[12]

The earliest beginnings

Following Heraclitus's lead, a move back in time is a way to move forward. We return then to the shaman and to the world's first artists: the archaic cave painters. In the remote past, possibly as early as 30,000 to 50,000 years ago, our human ancestors created stunning and enigmatic images deep within the earth on the walls and ceilings of caves that began to be discovered only in the nineteenth century. Bison, horses, birds, and mammoths were etched and painted into the rock at sites like Altamira in Spain and Lascaux, Les Trois-Frères and Chauvet in France. Among the glorious images of beasts at rest and in motion are human handprints and at least two puzzling human or human/animal hybrid images which have become known at Lascaux as "The Shaman," and at Les Trois-Frères as "The Sorcerer."

These human-like figures, according to Michael Tucker, are two of the earliest images known to us of the shaman or seer – a figure who was charged with the responsibility of maintaining the health of the tribe. Tucker argued that the prehistoric shaman remains the archetype of all artists:

> Image maker, dancer and drummer; actor and singer, healer and holy one, the shaman epitomizes the human need to bridge worlds – to fly beyond the everyday realm of the visual in order to conjure worlds of visionary presence and power.[13]

In a similar fashion, Germain Bazin described the Paleolithic artists as magicians, "whose drawing had all the virtue of a magic spell, an incantation." Their underground creations were not meant to be "art" as we know it today; rather they were aimed at skillfully intervening in the play of natural forces in which the tribe was embedded.[14]

The first painters, according to John Berger, were also hunters, yet the "act of painting was not the same as the act of hunting," the relationship between painter and animal was magical:

> Painting was used to confirm a magical "companionship" between prey and hunter, or to put it more abstractly, between the existent and human ingenuity. Painting was a means of making this companionship explicit and therefore (hopefully) permanent. This may be worth thinking about, long after painting has lost its herds of animals and its ritual function. I believe it tells us something about the nature of the act.[15]

The strands of magic that Berger identified as a kinship between the ancient cave painter and the contemporary artist could also be described as strands of prayer – a yearning for blessing and a desire to bless in turn.

Of course, we cannot know with certainty whether any of these interpretations are correct. Interpretation has been troublesome for various scholars of prehistoric art, including for Jean Clottes and David Lewis-Williams who proposed that many cave paintings – particularly those found in the smaller, more remote portions of cave complexes – were made by tribal shamans who were reproducing visions experienced while in a state of magic trance, possibly enhanced by hallucinogens or plant medicines.[16]

In *Shamanism: The Beginnings of Art*, Andreas Lommel argued that,

> [S]hamanism came into being at a time when man could not help feeling inferior in relation to his environment. He began to carry on the struggle for existence by spiritual means and come to attach special important to the state of his soul as a condition of survival.

In addition to states of ecstasy and trance, Lommel cites the "dreamtime" of Australian aboriginal peoples as another description of the "creative condition";

a "psychic state" wherein certain specially prepared individuals may come into relationship with the "soul force" of the images being created, such as those painted on the walls of caves or on rock outcroppings. Paralleling depth psychology's insistence upon "psychic reality," Lommel went on to suggest that the "spirits" (usually of helpful animals), images, and symbols experienced in this type of psychic state are no less "real" than objects in the material world – the realities are simply different. However, these psychic realities still require shaping in the material world, and "without artistic creation of some form or other there is no shaman."[17]

The shaman's path mirrors that of the artist in that there is oftentimes an early wounding, tragic loss, illness, or a combination of other challenging events that act as an initiatory threshold into one's calling. While this initiatory experience may come later in life, the destinies of the artist and the shaman are intertwined as they are called to *both* revelation and *poesis* or making. We will continue to return to the multidimensional shaman, seer, artist, magician, and healer in later chapters, particularly as reflected in the life of C.G. Jung, along with examples of a "shamanic sensibility," a type of archetypal patterning that continues to guide the lives of many contemporary creators. For now, this figure is the ideal guide into the origins of depth psychology, with its deep roots in creative practices and a shamanic sensibility attuned to hidden realities.

The roots of depth psychology

Depth psychology takes soul as its first principle and care of the soul as its chief responsibility. The variety of schools and practices that carry the name "depth psychology" developed over many decades with contributions not only from science and medicine but from myth, religion, the arts, and the humanities as well. Depth psychology is more a collection of psychologies, philosophies, and practices rather than one monolithic discipline. It was not, as is commonly thought, simply invented by European physicians and thinkers such as Sigmund Freud and C.G. Jung.

As we have seen, early practitioners of "soul work" blended the roles of healer/ physician, philosopher, seer, artist, and even magician. In his expansive study on the origins of dynamic psychiatry, Henri F. Ellenberger began with this very same multidimensional shamanic figure. He explained that while the shaman or medicine man was for many years mostly thought of as a primitive curiosity or imposter, recent historical and anthropological research has revealed evidence that ancient peoples utilized many of the same healing techniques used in modern psychotherapy.[18] "Could not the therapist," questioned Ellenberger, "be considered the modern successor of those shamans who set out to follow the tracks of a lost soul . . . and bring it back to the world of the living?"[19]

In addition to the therapist, the creative individual is also a successor to the shaman as ancient healing practices included what we would label today as art or creative practice. The use of drama, ritual, costumes, song, music, dance,

An Archaeology of Soul, Creativity, and Transformation   21

drawing, painting, and installations may be considered a type of transformational "beauty therapy." Ellenberger cited the healing practices of the Navajo people as an enduring example of the undifferentiated powers of ancient artistic expression and therapeutic intervention.[20] Additional techniques of archaic healing that combine aspects of creative practice are still valued today; these include hypnosis, movement, guided imagery, and dreamwork; the latter of which was practiced as temple incubation in ancient Greece and associated with the mythic figures of Asclepius and Telesphoros.

The complex, imaginative, and imperfect era of the ancient Greeks has been considered by many to be the most fertile and enduring soil of Western culture. It is in this soil where the roots of depth psychology are most firmly planted and where we now concentrate our attention.

Greek myth, philosophy, and soul

The world of the ancient Greeks was not so dissimilar from our own: profound inequality combined with an elite patriarchal grip on power coexisted alongside brilliant creative achievements and deep inquiry into the nature of consciousness, soul, the human condition, and reality itself. The period between the sixth and third centuries BCE is typically thought of as the era when rationality triumphed over earlier mythic ways of knowing – but the actual situation was much more nuanced – and much more interesting. While the early Greek philosophers were indeed challenging the knowledge-seeking techniques of prophets, sages, and poets, they did not totally abandon a mythic sensibility in their own attempts to know the world – and to know what might lie behind and beyond it.

Prior to the first philosophers, the archaic Greeks inhabited a world which Lawrence Hatab has described as one of "mythic disclosure." Human beings were embedded into, rather than subjective observers of, a single two-dimensional world where the sacred and extraordinary lies dormant in the profane and ordinary. In this type of mythic dwelling, the sacred could disclose itself at any time, or be invoked through ritual, while the profane acted as something of an intermission between irruptions of the sacred.[21] The sacred was a mystery beyond human comprehension but nonetheless a power that shaped human lives. Hatab stressed that the mythical mind was not ignorant of empirical or natural causes of events, it simply prioritized the sacred and yielded to forces beyond immediate (profane) control. In addition, Hatab's arguments mirror depth psychological perspectives that liken mythic experience to our modern moods: We do not project our moods – they come over us. Likewise, primitive experience did not *project* the sacred but *found* the world infused with a sacred existential mystery.[22]

Hatab described early Greek philosophy (such as in Heraclitus, Parmenides, Pythagoras, and Empedocles) as not an outright denial of a mythic or lived world but rather a reflective account of the background of myth, a hiddenness presented as an all-embracing origin.[23] While the myths themselves became less important, early Greek philosophy still exhibited a mythical sense of the world. Like the archaic prophet–sage–poets, these early philosophers acknowledged a sacred background to existence, although they formulated their ideas through conceptual thought and not through story. Hatab concluded that they maintained the traditional mythic notion of the world as "yielding to" an unknown "other" as they "gathered the general meaning of mytho-poetic disclosure *without myths*."[24]

These pre-Socratic philosophers exhibited traits of the undifferentiated shaman, who was at once physician, poet, magician, and prophet. F.M. Cornford described the thought of Empedocles (who was a physician) as blending religion, poetry, and philosophy with healing practices. Cornford went so far as to call Empedocles a "physician of the soul" who possessed a "poetic imagination" that could "see into the life of thing."[25] C.G. Jung was oftentimes described in strikingly similar terms. In addition, the poetic imagination and a "poetic basis of mind" were foundational to James Hillman's archetypal psychology, as we will discover.

Regarding the nature of soul, E.R. Dodds argued that early encounters with shamanic practices (such as soul journeying and soul retrieval) from regions beyond Greece began to shift long-held notions of the soul as the "life or spirit of the body." Instead, the soul began to be imagined as distinct from the body, introducing into European culture "a new interpretation of human existence."[26] Pythagoras, Empedocles, and other early philosophers introduced the idea of a detachable soul into Greek culture; a soul that might live any number of lives within any number of different mortal forms, including human, animal, and plant. Both Pythagoras and Empedocles recounted personal past incarnations as part of their embrace of the soul as immortal, ever transforming, and distinct from the human body.

In conjunction with the assertions that the soul was distinct from the body and could travel beyond it, the concept of *anamnesis*, or recollection, added weight to arguments for the immortal nature of the soul and for the special abilities of poets, prophets, and sages. *Anamnesis* proposes that the soul, through endless rounds of transformation, already possesses knowledge of all things. Through opportunities for reflection in each life, the soul remembers what it had forgotten; some souls remember more and some less. The "theory of recollection" does not refer to "personal memory" but rather to an impersonal memory, a type of unconscious knowledge available to all that is superior to sense perception as a means to gain (or recollect) knowledge.[27]

As we will explore in the following chapters, the "impersonal memory" of *anamnesis* is not so distinct from Jung's concept of the collective unconscious. In addition, Plato's eternal forms or *eidos* are quite similar to, although not totally synonymous with, Jung's archetypes of the collective unconscious.

Plato and (the) soul

It is in Plato's work where Greek ideas of soul, inspiration, human agency, consciousness, and creativity were modified and shaped into forms that became foundational aspects of Western thought and continue to influence our thinking on the same topics.[28]

A growing sense of self-consciousness, or the notion of a separate self, marked the overlap of early philosophies with Platonic thought. While the rationality associated with Plato (429–347 BCE) did not entirely abandon a mythic past, in his philosophy we find a "clear distinction between mind and world [and] the crystallization of self-consciousness with decisive psychological, moral, and intellectual consequences."[29] We also find a "surprising combination of rationalism and mysticism, logic and myth, conscious and unconscious forces" and a new view of the soul.[30]

The Platonic soul reinforced the psyche–soma split begun within Greek shamanic traditions: Psyche was not a life force but a type of self-consciousness that came to be seen as divine and in opposition to the worldly "other" of the body.[31] The earlier Greek duality between god and human became a duality between soul and body. Dodds used the term "puritan" to describe the Greek shamanic conception of the soul that was so influential for Plato. In this construct, the soul is our true nature, while the body and the physical world comprise an alien territory into which the soul has descended or fallen. Not unlike Indian notions of reincarnation, the soul passes through numerous embodiments in these alien settings until it can eventually gain a fully disembodied immortal existence.

Plato concluded the *Republic* with "The Myth of Er," a tale of reincarnation where souls make both wise and foolish selections for their next incarnations based on the lots cast before them. Once the lots are selected, the souls go before the Moirai, or Fates, and along with a daimon, or soul companion, the two descend to earth. Along the way the souls drink from the River of Lethe or forgetfulness; some souls do not drink as much as others, thus allowing them greater powers of *anamnesis* or recollection. It is unknown whether Plato truly accepted ideas of reincarnation or not, but his convictions that the soul was real and immortal, that it was exemplified by movement, and that it possessed powers of recollection are emphasized not only in the *Republic* but in the *Meno, Phaedo,* and *Pheadrus* as well. Without advocating for literal reincarnation, Hillman constructed his most widely read work, *The Soul's Code: In Search of Character and Calling* upon the foundations of a recollecting soul found in Plato's dialogues.[32]

It is in the *Phaedrus* where the bonds between the Platonic soul and creative inspiration become clearest. In this dialogue, Socrates engages the young Phaedrus in a discussion about speechmaking, which evolves into a dialogue on love, beauty, and inspiration. In addition, Socrates instructs the young pupil on the nature of the soul utilizing an image of a chariot pulled by two opposing horses, which is driven with near constant difficulty, by a charioteer. This tripartite soul made up of reason (the charioteer), a noble spiritedness (the white horse), and an ignoble, desirous beast (the black horse) is strikingly similar to Freud's tripartite conception of the psyche comprising the ego, superego, and id.

In regard to inspiration, Socrates tells Phaedrus that "the greatest of goods come to us from madness, provided that it is bestowed by divine gift" and goes

24 An Archaeology of Soul, Creativity, and Transformation

on to describe four types of *theia mania* or divine madness.[33] The first type of madness is bestowed upon those who practice divination. Socrates recognizes the worth of inspired prophecy that issues from the mouths of priestesses and prophets while explaining how "manic" oracular techniques became known as "mantic" techniques – a name still applied today to all types of divinatory practices such as Tarot consultations and casting the *I Ching*. The second kind of madness provides the inspiration for effective prayer and service to the gods as a means of seeking release from multigenerational "divine anger." The third type of madness comes from the Muses, the daughters of Mnemosyne or Memory, and is directed toward poets and creators:

> The man that arrives at the doors of poetry without madness from the Muses, convinced that after all expertise will make him a good poet, both he and his poetry – the poetry of the sane are eclipsed by that of the mad, remaining imperfect and unfulfilled.[34]

Here, Plato recognized a certain necessary madness, or loss of self, inherent in the creative process while establishing one of the most enduring links in the Western mind regarding creative expression: that creativity and something akin to "madness" are intertwined. Plato's fourth, and highest type of divine madness, is witnessed in those whose souls are stimulated as if falling in love. In this state they can recollect glimpses of the transcendent forms underlying all reality, notably beauty in the context of *Phaedrus*. Philosophers, for Plato, are in the best position to experience this advanced form of *anemnesis* due to their noble, moderate character and their sincere love of wisdom.

While acknowledging the value of the wisdom brought forth through the divine possessions of oracles and poets, Plato found them unreliable and capable of misleading the public. In keeping with the Greek concept of *pharmakon* (healing poison) the inspired words of poets and oracles could indeed act as medicines, although in the wrong hands the same words could become poisons. In Plato's ideal state, both rulers and the public at large would turn to the philosopher as the most reliable source of wisdom. Ironically, his preferred technique for expressing these views utilizes storytelling techniques that are closer at times to poetic expression than they are to reasoned discourse. Moreover, Plato admitted that the way in which philosophers receive flashes of insight is ultimately the same as the divine inspiration of poets – both behold, receive, and subsequently collaborate with something that feels like a gift; a gift given from a realm outside of ordinary consciousness.

Also within *Phaedrus* is the idea of soul as a process of dynamic and immortal movement:

> All soul is immortal. For that which is always in movement is immortal; that which moves something else, and is move by something else, in ceasing from movement ceases from living. So only that which moves itself, because it

does not abandon itself, never stops moving. But it is also source and first principle of movement for the other things which move.[35]

Plato's ideas surrounding the autonomous and immortal nature of the soul, along with his likening of the inspiration as a type of possession beyond full conscious control found fresh expression in Jung's articulation of the creative process, as will be evident in the next chapter. Many of Jung's associates, such as Erich Neumann, would continue to develop these compelling ideas as outlined in Chapter 3. Contemporary creators have also given renewed life to the idea of *theia mania*. For example, singer and songwriter Brittany Howard has likened her intense and distinctively unselfconscious live performances to an immersion into another world:

> I call it "the spirit world." . . . Latching on to a feeling, riding it, trying not to come out of it. You stop thinking you're performing – that's the spirit world. . . . Sometimes between songs I have nothing to say. It's not because I'm not appreciative of the applause, the love. I'm just still *on* it and I'm trying to keep on it.[36]

Howard's assessment illustrates that ancient ideas about inspiration and creativity are as valid today as they ever were. Like Jung's image of the underground rhizome that continually brings forth seasonal expressions, depth psychology's ever-evolving perspectives are also anchored in an ancient past. While its visible branches offer renewed and rearticulated perspectives for our modern era, its roots are firmly planted in devotion to soul and to inspired creativity. Entangled within these same roots, modern creators, philosophers, psychologists, seers, and healers find the origins of their ancestral tree.

Care of the soul: from Plato to Freud

Over two thousand years would pass between the founding of Plato's Academy and the beginnings of modern depth psychology. Like the ever-changing Heraclitean fire, the classical world of the Greeks was absorbed into the Roman era, which itself reached a peak of influence and power only to eventually decay. This set the stage for the rise of Christianity, which continued the reshaping of the ancient world. The soul and its concerns came to be dominated by the Catholic Church, which retained some Greek conceptions of soul and selfhood while diminishing or reshaping others. The immortality of the soul and the psyche–soma split were maintained and expanded, although the soul was now envisioned as attached to a singular individual rather than possessing the ability to reincarnate indefinitely into various forms. The archaic cyclical view of time was overtaken by a linear view of time where both soul and individual moved toward a judgment that acted as a threshold to an eternal time to follow.

While aspects of pagan ritual were transformed into new rituals such as the Catholic mass and pilgrimage to sacred sites, the care and perfecting of the soul through philosophical inquiry was seen as irrelevant in the face of a system where freedom and salvation were found through the embrace of Christian truths and the grace of Christ.[37] The hierarchical power structure of the Catholic Church and the elevation of ordained priests above the philosopher, poet, and healer/physician served to further separate these roles into specializations. Plato's description of the poet and prophet as faulty guides to truth and his calls to monitor their power were renewed and amplified in the Church's efforts to maintain dominance in all matters of essential truth – a dominance that would last for centuries and one that was oftentimes maintained through the most brutal of means. The Church was the primary patron of knowledge and the arts and its clergy the sole literate class.[38] Of course, Christianity itself was not immune from transformation in the centuries from its inception through the Reformation and into the modern secular era.

Beyond, yet including its Judeo-Christian roots, the larger history of the West reads like a palimpsest; complex eras emerged over time, only to be partially erased or remade by subsequent eras, which either overlapped or overtook them. Poets, prophets, sages, philosophers, and healers continued to answer their callings, with their fates – for better or worse – embedded into their particular eras and geographic regions. Looking back over the last two millennia from classical Greece to the transitional years which bridged the late nineteenth and twentieth centuries, particular individuals and movements stand out as highly influential in regard to the nature of the soul and to the nature of soul work.[39]

While differentiated for many centuries in the West, the philosopher and the artist have always shared concerns with the ultimate mysteries of existence, including the idea of soul. These early depth psychologists joined generations of philosophers and artists as they focused on the same mysteries. A *philosophical* continuum of soul leading to the advent of depth psychology can be traced from Heraclitus and Plato through the early Neoplatonists such as Plotinus; to Christian saints and mystics (Saint Augustine, Meister Eckhart, and Saint Teresa of Avila); to Petrarch, to the revival of Platonism during the Renaissance (Ficino); then to Descartes, Vico, Kant, Schopenhauer, Nietzsche, and James; and on to Freud and Jung.[40]

An *artistic* continuum of soul may be traced from the Greek poets and tragedians (such as Homer, Sappho, Sophocles, and Aeschylus) to Dante, Michelangelo, da Vinci, Shakespeare, Goethe, and Carus; from the Romantic poets (Coleridge, Keats, Shelley, Blake, and de Nerval); to Kandinsky, Joyce, and Picasso; and on to Freud and Jung. Of course, this continuum begins even earlier in the archaic era of the early cave painter, with the pre-differentiated figure of the shaman – at once philosopher and artist, healer, and prophet.

At the turn of the last century, the founding figures of depth psychology, along with their avant-garde artistic counterparts, were the inheritors of well over two thousand years of rich philosophical, creative, and scientific history, yet as Richard Tarnas has reminded us, this history was overwhelmingly masculine. The "masculinity of the Western mind has been pervasive and fundamental, in both men and women, affecting every aspect of Western thought, determining its most basic conception of the human being and the human role in the world."[41] Tarnas argued that the evolution of the Western mind has been founded on the repression of those aspects of life that have been identified with "the feminine." This repression includes a progressive denial of,

> an undifferentiated unitary consciousness, of the *participation mystique* with nature, of the *anima mundi*, of the soul of the world, of the community of being, of the all-pervading, of mystery and ambiguity, of imagination, emotion, instinct, body, nature, woman – of all that which the masculine has projectively identified as "other."[42]

Although founded by men who were inheritors of this limited and unbalanced evolution, depth psychology recognized that the sufferings of the modern soul called for a critical exploration and reappraisal of the historic, cultural, and psychic forces that had contributed to a growing sense of alienation and meaninglessness in the world around them.

Soul and a new science

Along with the profound inheritance of centuries of Western philosophy, art, mythology, and religion, depth psychology inherited centuries of Western scientific thought also. Challenges to the Church's conceptions of the cosmos and domination of knowledge from Copernicus, Galileo, Newton, Kepler, and Darwin, along with the esoteric experimentation of the European alchemists paved the way for even further challenges to humankind's supposedly exalted and central place in the universe. Building upon earlier theories of self and other, the human psyche itself was now envisioned as being comprising two realms: consciousness, and what was to become known as "the unconscious," a more mysterious realm consisting of hidden drives and potentialities that could exert considerable influence over any human life.

Early depth psychologists were eager to establish a distinct discipline concerned with the totality of psychic life; one not aligned with religion or spiritualism and one that would be accepted as empirically rigorous by the scientific community. In his comprehensive history of psychologies of the unconscious, Ellenberger explained that the precursors to Freud and Jung, such as Mesmer (1734–1815) and Puységur (1751–1825) both associated with "animal magnetism," and Charcot (1825–1893), who was associated with hypnosis, reflected the prevailing cultural trends of their time. These trends were reflections of both declines and renewals of the major cultural movements of the West after the Renaissance: the Baroque, Enlightenment, Romanticism, and Positivism. A resurgence of Romanticism at the turn of the twentieth century influenced the way that both Freud and Jung approached their professions: Like the artist and writer, both drew upon their own life experiences, a deep interest in the lives of others, and their formidable individual creative skills.[43]

28 An Archaeology of Soul, Creativity, and Transformation

Biographers and historians have demonstrated the affinities of the two men to artists and mystics alike in the manner in which they incorporated their charismatic personalities and private "creative illnesses" into the development of their theories and their work with patients. Ellenberger defined "creative illness" as a prolonged period of suffering prior to a creative breakthrough; the breakthrough may yield revelations with the power to transform and redirect the course of one's life.[44] Enduring a "creative illness" is a form of personal soul work and is akin to the self-sacrifice and oftentimes risky initiatory experiences of the shaman. The benefits derived from these types of ordeals are not only received by the sufferer but also are subsequently offered as gifts to the community. This was true for Freud and Jung and has been true as well for legions of artists, philosophers, and mystics – both known and unknown.

Depth psychology has continued to evolve since the early days of Freud and Jung; however, their pioneering work on the nature of the soul and the nature of the creative calling continues to be influential – even against the backdrop of the West's general dismissal of "the soul." This brief account of the foundations of depth psychology – which rests equally upon thousands of years of healing, wisdom, and creative practices – will assist in solidifying its position as a crossroads of insight for the multidimensional contemporary creator.[45] A closer look at both Freud and Jung as healer/creators will assist in doing the same.

Art and soul in Freud

Unlike C.G. Jung and James Hillman, Sigmund Freud (1856–1939) is not necessarily remembered as a sensitive champion of the artist. Freud's most well-known descriptions of creative individuals include the assessment that they are frustrated, dissatisfied, and "not far removed from neurosis." Freud described the artist as one who is "oppressed by excessively powerful instinctual needs" for honor, power, wealth, fame, and "love of women," which lead the artist to transfer "all his interest, and his libido too, to the wishful constructions of his life of phantasy, whence the path might lead to neurosis."[46] These views, however, represent only part of Freud's complex relationship to art, creativity, and artists. He recognized the "transforming power of art" and concluded that the artist possesses a gift that is ultimately "unanalysable."[47] Freud could be quite generous in describing these gifts, particularly regarding writers and poets:

> But creative writers are valuable allies and their evidence is to be praised highly, for they are apt to know a whole host of things between heaven and earth of which our philosophy has not yet let us dream. In their knowledge of the mind they are far in advance of us everyday people, for they draw upon sources which we have not yet opened up for science.[48]

These thoughts echo Freud's often-quoted aphorism: "Everywhere I go, I find that a poet has been there before me."[49] Contrasted against the descriptions of creative expression as compensation, infantile wish fulfillment, or sublimation in many of Freud's writing are his personal lifelong passions for history, mythology, literature, and archaic art. According to Benjamin Nelson, "to know Freud only in the guise as a psychiatrist is to know hardly half the man."[50]

From his boyhood, Freud was "haunted by the riddles and triumphs of culture and "hoped to wrest from them basic clues to the understanding of man and his works."[51] Over the course of his lifetime, Freud built up a personal library of over 2,500 volumes with subjects ranging from ancient art to world history, mythology, religion, language, and anthropology. Beginning in the mid-1890s, Freud began to compare the work of psychoanalysis to that of archaeology; both deal with layers of history that require careful excavation. In a letter dated January 30, 1899, to his close colleague and collaborator, Wilhelm Fliess, Freud shared his enthusiasm for how his investigations into ancient cultures often mirrored his theories about the contemporary psyche: "I am reading Burckhardt's *History of Greek Civilization*, which is providing me with unexpected parallels. My predilection for the prehistoric in all its human forms remains the same."[52] The arc of the Freud–Fliess friendship has been well-documented, including their shared passion for Goethe, Shakespeare, and the classics of Greece and Rome.[53]

Freud's "predilection for the prehistoric," combined with his comfort in ancient languages, prepared him to become an astute collector of art and antiquities. First in his Vienna study – and later in London, where his study was recreated due to Austria's Nazi occupation – Freud surrounded himself with a massive collection of rare objects from Egypt, Greece, Rome, and China. Lynn Gamwell described Freud's collection as an "attentive audience," particularly those very special figures that Freud arranged upon his desk to face him as he worked. These included an "Egyptian scribe, a Greek goddess of wisdom, and a Chinese sage."[54] An ancient bronze figure of Imhotep, the Egyptian architect revered as a healer, shared Freud's desktop with Athena, the Greek goddess of wisdom, war, and the arts. The bronze figurine (first or second century CE) of Athena was the sole piece that Freud selected to be smuggled out of Austria in 1938, when the fate of his entire collection was threatened.[55] Gamwell proposed that the figures that Freud collected provided him with a sense of *Erquickung*, or "life and power," while serving as embodiments of "his excavated truths of psychoanalysis."[56] It is also important to consider the fact that the ancient objects that Freud collected with such passion were not considered "art" in their own time; most were considered offerings to, or embodiments of, specific gods, goddesses, or cosmic forces.

Freud's passion for myth and literature is reflected in his frequent references to Goethe's *Faust* and to Shakespeare's *Hamlet*. In *Hamlet on the Couch: What Shakespeare Taught Freud*, James Grove turned to legendary art critic Harold Bloom to assert that the character of Hamlet was Freud's mentor, and that contrary to traditional explanations, psychoanalysis is not the "subtext of literature" – "literature is the unconscious of psychoanalysis."[57] It is significant to note that Freud's highest honor was not the Nobel Prize, which always alluded him, but the Goethe Prize for literature which he received in 1930.

30 An Archaeology of Soul, Creativity, and Transformation

Beyond the characters of Hamlet and Faust, Freud has primarily been associated with the character of Oepidus from Sophocles's trilogy of Greek tragedies. A pivotal dream during a time of deep suffering impressed itself upon Freud with a force that impelled him to write, "I am Oepidus" in his private journals. In her sensitive appraisals of Freud and the relevance of his work for our era, myth and religious studies scholar, Christine Downing has made clear that for Freud, "Oedipus was not an illustration or clever designation for an insight which might have been articulated otherwise, but the medium of discovery."[58] Moreover, Freud's understanding "of the oedipal continued to unfold for decades" as he searched for ways to communicate what he had discovered within himself, and what he felt existed in all people: "a profound inextinguishable longing for the unconditional love we know at the breast, in the womb."[59]

Freud's fascination with this myth spurred the development of his theories on sexual desire, frustration, and fulfillment as the sources of human behavior. At the same time, however, his attachment to this single myth may have occluded his vision into the powerful and valuable themes to be found in other enduring myths. Downing has suggested otherwise: that behind the myth of Oedipus, Freud discovered the myth of Narcissus and "behind that, the myth of the eternal struggle between Death and Love [Eros]."[60] In working with these myths, with dreams, and with the unconscious, Freud leaned toward personal interpretations, an approach which was at odds with the more universal interpretations developed by his most prominent associate, C.G. Jung. This was one key area of disagreement that led to the dramatic and well-documented split between the two men.[61]

Prior to the dissolution of the Freud–Jung relationship, Freud endured a personal "creative illness" that was pivotal to his life and career. Comprising several losses, failures, and insecurities – especially the death of his father – this period of isolation and frequent despair lasted for six years, from 1894 to 1900.[62] In keeping with cyclical pattern of shamanic creative illness proposed by Ellenberger, Freud withstood the depths of his suffering aided by his colleague and friend Fleiss, who acted as something akin to an elder or shaman master. Freud's practice of self-analysis allowed him to gradually emerge with a sense that he had discovered great truths, including his psychoanalytic method of inner soul work with its new model of the psyche.

Freud's familiarity with Platonic philosophy may have influenced the development of his theory of a tripartite soul made up of the ego, superego, and id. As previously noted, these distinctions are quite close to Plato's imaginative rendition of a tripartite soul in *Phaedrus* consisting of a charioteer and two competing horses. However, contrary to Plato's conception of soul as separate from the human body, Downing has emphasized that Freud viewed the body as "the dwelling place of the soul":

> To speak of the soul, of its deepest longings and most profound terror, is to speak of the body, of sexuality and death. . . . [Freud] sought a language for the self that takes seriously that we are embodied souls, ensouled bodies.[63]

An understanding of Freud's model of the soul must also include an understanding of how the German words he employed for soul, "*die Seele*" and "*seelisch*," had been mistranslated into English in his time and thus misinterpreted for decades. According to Bruno Bettelheim, Freud's translators relegated what Freud meant as "the essence of man" entirely to "the I, the thinking and reasoning part of man," that is, the mind.[64] Freud's conception of *Seele* "has nothing to do with immortality," but as Downing has also pointed out, it has everything to do with "what is most valuable" during one's lifetime as an embodied being. Freud's *Seele*, "psyche or soul," is "comprehensively human and unscientific" and the "seat of both the mind and of the passions" of the body.[65]

Creators approaching Freud today, especially after encountering Jung's writings on the creative individual, will find a similar sensitivity to the play of polarities that animate life. As with Jung, there are essential elements in Freud's philosophies that echo those of ancient wisdom traditions such as the dynamic relationship of yin and yang in Taoism and the eternal (and necessary) battle of the gods of light and darkness in Egyptian mythology:

> There can be no question of the antithesis between an optimistic and a pessimistic theory of life; only the simultaneous working together and against each other of both primordial drives, of Eros and the death drive, can explain the colorfulness of life, never the one of the other all by itself.[66]

Freud's ideas regarding the artist as one who is driven by the conflict of powerful internal forces and "not far removed from neurosis" were not new; they reinforced much older notions linking creativity with longing, melancholy, or illness and with Plato's *theia mania*, a divine madness which can – and must, at least to some degree – overtake the will of the artist, prophet, and philosopher alike.

Poet Hilda Doolittle (known as H.D.) knew Freud as both analyst and friend during the last tumultuous years of his life. In her *Tribute to Freud*, she affectionately referred to Freud as "The Professor," describing him as an elegant, father-like but ultimately enigmatic figure who shared her passions for ancient history, language, and art – especially the world of ancient Greece. Her account of their warm relationship, and of her own analysis, offers an artist's firsthand perspective into Freud's deep humanity and reverence for the creative spirit alive in all people, especially as witnessed through dreams:

> He had dared to say that the dream came from an unexplored depth in man's consciousness and that this unexplored depth ran like a great stream or ocean underground, and the vast depth of the ocean was the same vast depth today as in Joseph's day. . . . He had dared to imply that this [same] consciousness proclaimed all men one. . . . The picture-writing, the hieroglyph of dream, was the common property of the whole race; in the dream, man, as at the beginning of time, spoke a universal language, and man, meeting in the universal

> understanding of the unconscious . . . would forgo barriers of time and space, and man, understanding man, would save mankind.[67]

It is both ironic and poignant to note that Freud's words on universal understanding were spoken to H.D. just as Nazism was ascendant in Austria, and that the two friends would not see each other again after Freud's last-minute exodus to London in advance of the Nazi occupation of Vienna. Given Freud's own circumstances, one could doubt his belief (as understood by H.D.) that humankind could save itself by means of the universal meeting ground of the unconscious where every soul speaks a common language. Artists may see past the doubt to something else: a call toward a destiny to re-create and refashion the old "picture-writing" or hieroglyphs of the soul into living images for the present age in need of saving. This is part of depth psychology's legacy of gifts for the contemporary creator, which, as we have seen, did not begin with Freud or his contemporaries but were nevertheless shaped in important ways over a century ago by these modern pioneers of "soul work."

A science of soul or a soulful art?

It is clear that creative expressions such as myth, ritual, visual art, literature, song, dance, and theatrical performance, along with interrelated philosophical, shamanic, and divinatory practices, illuminated the human condition for millennia prior to the emergence of modern sciences, psychologies, and more recently, neuroscience.

Depth psychology, so indebted to the arts, humanities, and to ancient healing and wisdom traditions, faces new challenges in the twenty-first century as neuroscience seeks to explain – and so often explain away – the mysteries of soul, creativity, and the creative calling. Ginette Paris has suggested that the time has come for depth psychology to bid farewell to its tenuous relationship with the sciences and align itself more closely with its true relatives: the arts and humanities.[68] Practitioners of depth psychology, particularly analysts, may disagree with Paris. However, the shift that she proposed could serve to reinvigorate a psychology that is more often than not at odds with other therapeutic methods including behavioral and cognitive psychologies. With an embrace of its ancestral rhizomic heritage in the arts, the humanities, the indigenous, and the occult, depth psychology may more fully serve as a crossroads where the artist, philosopher, healer, and mystic may come together in a new synthesis – a dynamic center of transdisciplinary creativity and renewal.

Notes

1 Eliade, *Shamanism: Archaic Techniques of Ecstasy*, pp. 4–8.
2 McEvilley, *The Shape of Ancient Thought: Comparative Studies in Greek and Indian Philosophies*, p. 15.
3 Ibid., p. 16.

An Archaeology of Soul, Creativity, and Transformation 33

4 Ibid., p. 300.
5 Heraclitus, "Fragment 71," in *Fragments: The Collected Wisdom of Heraclitus*, p. 45.
6 Ibid., "Fragments 56 and 57," p. 37.
7 Haxton, "Introduction." In *Fragments: The Collected Wisdom of Heraclitus*, p. xx.
8 McEvilley, *The Shape of Ancient Thought: Comparative Studies in Greek and Indian Philosophies*, pp. 39–41.
9 Wheelwright, *Heraclitus*, p. 61.
10 Hillman, *Re-Visioning Psychology*, p. xvii.
11 Ibid., "Foreword." In *Fragments: The Collected Wisdom of Heraclitus*, p. xi.
12 Ibid., p. xvi.
13 Tucker, *Dreaming with Eyes Open: The Shamanic Spirit in Twentieth Century Art and Culture*, p. xxii.
14 Bazin, *A Concise History of Art*, p. 11.
15 Berger, *The Shape of a Pocket*, p. 15.
16 Curtis, *The Cave Painters: Probing the Mysteries of the World's First Artists*, p. 217.
17 Lommel, *Shamanism: The Beginnings of Art*, pp. 145–149.
18 Ellenberger, *The Discovery of the Unconscious: The History and Evolution of Dynamic Psychiatry*, p. 3.
19 Ibid., p. 9.
20 Ibid., p. 30.
21 Ibid., p. 22.
22 Ibid., p. 26.
23 Hatab, *Myth and Philosophy: A Contest of Truths*, p. 201.
24 Ibid., p. 199.
25 Cornford, *Principium Sapientiae*, pp. 122–123.
26 Dodds, *The Greeks and the Irrational*, pp. 139–140.
27 Cornford, *Principium Sapientiae*, p. 53.
28 Conceptions of the soul from non-Western cultures are equally valid to those that developed in ancient Greece, however, this study will focus primarily on those strands that found their way into the Western imagination rather than offering a global survey of the nature and meaning of soul.
29 Hatab, *Myth and Philosophy: A Contest of Truths*, p. 207.
30 Ibid., p. 208.
31 In addition to pre-Socratic Greek and Indian philosophies of the soul, earlier Egyptian ideas about the soul were very likely to have contributed to the conception of the Platonic soul. These include the Egyptian Ba (the part of a person that would live on after death and was oftentimes symbolized as a bird with a human head) and the Ka (a type of non-immortal body-double or twin personality that could unite or separate with the human body at will.)
32 See Chapter 5 for an expanded exploration of Hillman's "acorn theory" and its relationship to creative individuals.
33 Plato, *Phaedrus*, (244a5–250c5), pp. 23–31.
34 Ibid., (245a–b1), pp. 24–25.
35 Ibid., (245c5–d1), p. 25.
36 Lamont, "Alabama Shakes: From Small Town Bar Band to Titans of Rock," in *The Guardian*.
37 Tarnas, *The Passion of the Western Mind*, p. 117.
38 Ibid., p. 160.
39 See Tarnas's *The Passion of the Western Mind* for a masterful and illuminating history of Western thought and culture.
40 See Stewart Goetz and Charles Taliaferro's *A Brief History of the Soul* for concise historical and contemporary philosophical arguments for and against the existence of a soul from ancient Greece through the twenty-first century.

34 An Archaeology of Soul, Creativity, and Transformation

41 Ibid., p. 441.
42 Ibid., p. 442.
43 Ellenberger, *The Discovery of the Unconscious: The History and Evolution of Dynamic Psychiatry*, p. 888.
44 Ibid., pp. 447–448.
45 In addition to Ellenberger, see Sonu Shamdasani's *Jung and the Making of Modern Psychology* and Jung's lectures on the origins of depth psychology in *C.G. Jung: History of Modern Psychology* edited by Ernst Falzeder.
46 Qtd. in Storr, *The Dynamics of Creation*, p. 2.
47 Spitz, *Art and Psyche*, p. 40.
48 Ibid., p. 5.
49 Qtd. in Nin, "The New Woman," p. 14.
50 Nelson, "Introduction," in *On Creativity and the Unconscious: The Psychology of Art, Literature, Love and Religion*, p. ix.
51 Ibid.
52 Qtd. in Botting and Davies, "Freud's Library and an Appendix of Texts Related to Antiquities," in *Sigmund Freud and Art: His Personal Collection of Antiquities*, p. 185.
53 Farrell, *Collaborative Circles: Friendships Dynamics and Creative Work*, p. 170.
54 Gamwell, "The Origins of Freud's Antiquities Collection," in *Sigmund Freud and Art: His Personal Collection of Antiquities*, p. 21.
55 Botting and Davies, "Athena," in *Sigmund Freud and Art: His Personal Collection of Antiquities*, p. 110.
56 Gamwell, "The Origins of Freud's Antiquities Collection," in *Sigmund Freud and Art: His Personal Collection of Antiquities*, p. 29.
57 Grove, *Hamlet on the Couch: What Shakespeare Taught Freud*.
58 Downing, "Freud's Mythology of Soul," in *The Luxury of Afterwards: The Christine Downing Lectures at San Diego State University, 1995–2004*, p. 61.
59 Ibid., p. 61.
60 Ibid., p. 57.
61 For more on the Frued–Jung split, see Sonu Shamdasani's introduction to Jung's *Liber Novus/The Red Book*, Shamdasani's *Jung and the Making of Modern Psychology: The Dream of a Science*, along with Deirdre Bair's *Jung: A Biography*, and Andrew Samuels's *Jung and the Post-Jungians* among other sources.
62 Freud's pivotal "Opedipus dream" occurred during this time period, almost exactly a year after the death of his father. See Downing's "Freud's Mythology of Soul" in *The Luxury of Afterwards: The Christine Downing Lectures at San Diego State University, 1995–2004*, p. 61 for more.
63 Ibid., pp. 57–58.
64 Bettelheim, *Freud and Man's Soul*, p. 76.
65 Ibid., pp. 12, 77.
66 Ibid., p. 111.
67 H.D., *Tribute to Freud*, p. 71.
68 Paris, *Wisdom of the Psyche: Depth Psychology After Neuroscience*, pp. 85–86.

References

Bair, Dierdre. *Jung: A Biography*. Boston, New York, NY and London: Little, Brown and Co. 2003.

Bazin, Germain. *A Concise History of Art*. Part I. 1958. London: Thames & Hudson. 1962.

Berger, John. *The Shape of a Pocket*. New York, NY: Vintage Books.

Bettleheim, Bruno. *Freud and Man's Soul*. New York, NY: Alfred A. Knopf. 1983.

An Archaeology of Soul, Creativity, and Transformation   35

Botting, Wendy and J. Keith Davies. "Freud's Library and an Appendix of Texts Related to Antiquities." In *Sigmund Freud and Art: His Personal Collection of Antiquities*, 184–192. Edited by Lynn Gamwell and Richard Wells. New York, NY and London: Harry N. Abrams, State University of New York and the Freud Museum. 1989.

Cornford, F.M. *Principium Sapientiae: The Study of the Origins of Greek Philosophical Thought*. 1952. Edited by W.K.C. Guthrie. New York, NY: Harper and Row. 1965.

Curtis, Gregory. *The Cave Painters: Probing the Mysteries of the World's First Artists*. New York, NY: Alfred P. Knopf. 2006.

Dodds, E.R. *The Greeks and the Irrational*. 1951. Berkeley, CA: University of California Press. 1977.

Doolittle, Hilda (H.D.). *Tribute to Freud*. 1956. New York, NY: New Directions. 2012.

Downing, Christine. "Freud's Mythology of Soul." In *The Luxury of Afterwards: The Christine Downing Lectures at San Diego State University 1995–2004*. New York, NY: iUniverse. 2004.

Eliade, Mircea. *Shamanism: Archaic Techniques of Ecstasy*. 1964. Princeton, NJ: Princeton University Press. 2004.

Ellenberger, Henri F. *The Discovery of the Unconscious: The History and Evolution of Dynamic Psychiatry*. New York, NY: Basic Books. 1970.

Farrell, Michael P. *Collaborative Circles: Friendship Dynamics and Creative Work*. Chicago and London: University of Chicago Press. 2001.

Fischer, Thomas and Bettina Kaufmann. "C.G. Jung and Modern Art." In *The Art of C.G. Jung*. Edited by Ulrich Hoerni, Thomas Fischer and Bettina Kaufman. Translated by Paul David Young and Christopher John Murray. New York and London: W.W. Norton and Co. 2019.

Gamwell, Lynn. "The Origins of Freud's Antiquities Collection." In *Sigmund Freud and Art: His Personal Collection of Antiquities*, 21–32. Edited by Lynn Gamwell and Richard Wells. New York, NY and London: Harry N. Abrams, State University of New York and the Freud Museum. 1989.

Hatab, Lawrence. *Myth and Philosophy: A Contest of Truths*. 1990. Chicago and La Salle: Open Court. 1992.

Heraclitus. *Fragments: The Collected Wisdom of Heraclitus*. Translated by Brooks Haxton. New York, NY: Viking. 2001.

Hillman, James. *Re-Visioning Psychology*. 1976. New York, NY: Harper Perennial. 1992.

Hillman, James. "Foreword." In *Fragments: The Collected Wisdom of Heraclitus*. Edited by Heraclitus. Translated by Brooks Haxton. New York, NY: Viking. 2001.

Hillman, James. *Archetypal Psychology*. 1983. The Uniform Edition of the Writings of James Hillman. Vol. 1. 1983. Putnam, CT: Spring. 2004.

Hillman, James and Sonu Shamdasani. *Lament of the Dead: Psychology After Jung's Red Book*. New York and London: W.W. Norton and Co. 2013.

Hoerni, Ulrich. "Images from the Unconscious: An Introduction to the Visual Works of C.G. Jung." In *The Art of C.G. Jung*. Edited by Ulrich Hoerni, Thomas Fischer and Bettina Kaufman. Translated by Paul David Young and Christopher John Murray. New York and London: W.W. Norton and Co. 2019.

Jung, Carl Gustav. *Memories, Dreams, Reflections*. 1963. Edited by Aniela Jaffé. Translated by Richard and Clara Winston. New York, NY: Vintage Books. 1989.

Lamont, Tom. "Alabama Shakes: From Small Town Bar Band to Titans of Rock." In *The Guardian*. 25 Mar. 2015.

Lommel, Andreas. *Shamanism: The Beginnings of Art*. New York, NY: McGraw-Hill. 1967.

McEvilley, Thomas. *The Shape of Ancient Thought: Comparative Studies in Greek and Indian Philosophies*. New York, NY: Allworth Press. 2002.

Nelson, Benjamin. "Introduction." In *On Creativity and the Unconscious: The Psychology of Art, Literature, and Religion*, ix–xiii. Edited by Sigmund Freud and Benjamin Nelson. New York and London: Harper Perennial. 1958.

Nin, Anaïs. "The New Woman." 1966. In *In Favor of the Sensitive Man and Other Essays*, 12–19. New York and London: Harcourt Brace & Co. 1994.

Paris, Ginette. *Wisdom of the Psyche: Depth Psychology After Neuroscience*. Hove and New York, NY: Routledge. 2007.

Plato. *Phaedrus*. Translated by Christopher Rowe. London and New York, NY: Penguin Books. 2005.

Spitz, Ellen Handler. *Art and Psyche: A Study in Psychoanalysis and Aesthetics*. New Haven and London: Yale University Press. 1985.

Storr, Anthony. *The Dynamics of Creation*. 1972. New York, NY: Ballantine Books. 1993.

Tarnas, Richard. *The Passion of the Western Mind: Understanding the Ideas That Have Shaped Our World View*. New York, NY: Ballantine Books. 1991.

Tucker, Michael. *Dreaming with Eyes Open: The Shamanic Spirit in Twentieth Century Art and Culture*. San Francisco, CA: Aquarian, Harper. 1992.

Wheelwright, Philip. *Heraclitus*. Princeton, NJ: Princeton University Press. 1959.

Chapter 2

C.G. Jung
Reluctant Artist, Servant of the Creative Spirit

Artist and daimon

Was C.G. Jung an artist? It would be difficult to think otherwise judging by the newly available materials documenting a lifetime of drawing, painting, writing, sculpting, and building – yet Jung insisted that he was not an artist.[1] The 2009 publication of the *Red Book/Liber Novus* (Jung's private illuminated manuscript documenting fantastic encounters with the imaginal figures of his unconscious) elicited a new wave of interest surrounding Jung as a psychological pioneer, a complex and imperfect man, a possible mystic, and a prolific creator. Fascination with Jung has kept his autobiographical memoir *Memories, Dreams, Reflections* in print since its initial publication in 1963.[2] It is in this volume, where he describes himself as a "creative person" but not as an artist. He recounts an episode that occurred during the years in which he experienced profound encounters with the unconscious; the encounters that would later be articulated into the *Red Book*:

> When I was writing down these fantasies, I once asked myself, What am I really doing? Certainly this has nothing to do with science. But then what is it? Whereupon a voice within me said, "It is art." I was astonished. It had never entered my head that what I was writing had any connection with art. . . . I said very emphatically to this voice that my fantasies had nothing to do with art, and I felt a great inner resistance. . . . "No, it is not art! On the contrary, it is nature" and prepared myself for an argument.[3]

"Anima" was the name that Jung gave the feminine voice that spoke to him and through him. In this same passage he indicates that he shared his own "speech centers" with the voice, so that she might explain to him why she considered his writing and painting to be "art." Unfortunately, neither Jung nor his editor and secretary Aniela Jaffé included the Anima's "lengthy" reply in the final version of the memoir.

What did Jung mean by making a distinction between art and nature, and what were his conceptions of art, nature, and anima? What can these conceptions, along with his insights into creativity itself, contribute to the contemporary creator? One

DOI: 10.4324/9780429057724-3

38 C.G. Jung

way to approach these questions is to consider Jung's lifetime of personal creative expression; he never claimed the title of "artist" but had no hesitation referring to himself as creative. He spoke about his personal creative struggles just as an artist would:

> I have had much trouble getting along with my ideas. There was a daimon in me and in the end its presence proved decisive. It overpowered me. . . . I could never stop at anything once attained. I had to hasten on, to catch up with my vision. . . . A creative person has little power over his own life. He is not free. He is captive and driven by his daimon. . . . The daimon of creativity has ruthlessly had its way with me.[4]

Creative individuals will surely recognize and relate to Jung's feelings of captivity to a power greater than himself. Poet Stanley Kunitz referred to this power as a "dark angel," while dancer Martha Graham called it a "quickening" that propels the creator into a state of "blessed unrest and divine dissatisfaction."[5] The idea of a daimon, a personal guiding spirit companion, has a long and complicated history in Western culture. The souls who chose their lots at the end of Plato's *Republic* in the Myth of Er undertook their journeys into human life with the companionship of a daimon, a personal guide who would remember their destinies. Socrates's *daimonion*, as featured in Plato's *Phaedrus* and *Apology*, offered critical direction and admonitions that Socrates always obeyed. While most contemporary scholars are quick to diminish or dismiss Socrates's relationship with his *daimonion*, Plato's dialogues themselves reveal Socrates's devotion to a force, or an entity, that spoke to him personally.[6] Like Socrates, Jung's legacy is also complicated by his insistence on the reality of unconscious forces, or psychic entities, that he did not create but which communicated personally with him.

Jung's close associate, Marie-Louise von Franz described Jung's daimon as "the god of creative Eros" who drove him relentlessly toward deeper and deeper inquiry into the human psyche. Von Franz surmised that the Eros principle – already visible in Jung's early childhood dreams and fantasies – combined with the *compassio* of the medical healer, along with Jung's creative "genius," were "*the* decisive components of Jung's fate."[7] Here, the term "genius" may be understood in two ways: as the Roman counterpart to the Greek daimon or guiding spirit and as the manifestation of exceptional abilities in a given individual.

These reflections on Jung's relationship with his creative daimon offer an entry into his thinking about creativity, art, nature, anima, and soul. A more comprehensive exploration begins with Jung's creative boyhood complete with castles, mythic battles, secret dreams, séances, and *Faust*.

From young creator to scholar and physician

As a boy, Jung was oftentimes lonely and insecure, but he was already creating. His primary biographer Deirdre Bair has documented how he found escape from his rigid family life through fantasy and the making of tiny kingdoms made of sand and stones.[8] Jung's creative play was mostly kept secret from others. One particular carving, a wooden manikin of a man about two inches tall, became the focus of much reflection later in Jung's life, even though the actual carved figure had long since been lost:

> Years after Jung created the little man and his world . . . he read about the totems of native peoples, among them the soul-stones of Arlesheim, Australian churingas, and the Telesphoros of Asklepios. He did not remember his father's library containing books on any of these subjects, nor to the best of his recollection, had his father ever spoken of any of them. He credits his association of these entities with his little man as the first time he thought "archaic psychic components" might have entered "the individual psyche without any direct line of tradition." . . . It was one of his first attempts to define what he later called the collective unconscious.[9]

Around this same time, Jung was receiving private classes in Latin, and excelling at most subjects in his small rural school. He struggled however, with mathematics, and as analyst Barbara Hannah recounted, Jung was actually removed from his drawing class for "utter incapacity." As these drawing classes consisted of "soulless copying," Jung was not engaged and could only draw when something stirred his imagination.[10]

Many things did stir Jung's early imagination including visions of castles, stately villages, and battle scenes, which he rendered in graphite or pen and ink. Jung began to explore the contents of his father's modest library and his mother suggested that her son read Goethe's *Faust*. Jung recalled: "it poured into my soul like a miraculous balm."[11] Reading *Faust* sparked Jung's passion for philosophy, literature, and religious studies, including the works of Pythagoras, Heraclitus, Empedocles, Plato, Schopenhauer, Kant, and Meister Eckhart. The sciences also began to attract Jung's attention, especially zoology, paleontology, archaeology, and geology.[12]

In his memoir, he described his younger self as being composed of two personalities: No. 1 and No. 2. He noticed that personality No. 2 was intensely interested in the humanities, especially ancient archaeology and comparative religion. Science, with its emphasis on empiricism, appealed to personality No. 1:

> What appealed to me in science were the concrete facts and their historical background, and in comparative religion the spiritual problems, into which philosophy also entered. In science I missed the factor of meaning; and in religion, that of empiricism. Science met, to a very large extent, the needs of No. 1 personality, whereas the humane or historical studies provided beneficial instruction for No. 2.[13]

By the time Jung became a young man, he was steeped in both the humanities and science and was torn between the two as the time came to decide upon his future

40 C.G. Jung

course of studies and ultimately on a profession. Many factors would play into his decision, including the modest nature of his family's finances and his determination not to follow his father's path into theology. Ultimately, he chose a scientific path:

> I came to see that a new idea, or even just an unusual aspect of an old one, can be communicated only by facts. . . . More than ever I found myself driven toward empiricism. I began to blame the philosophers for rattling away when experience was lacking, and holding their tongues when they ought to have been answering with facts. . . . This was in 1898, when I began to think more seriously about my career as a medical man. I soon came to the conclusion that I would have to specialize.[14]

The *compassio* of the medical healer that von Franz attributed to Jung, along with his desire to be considered an empiricist, did not outweigh Jung's passion for the arts and humanities; his deep knowledge of mythology, religion, literature, history, and philosophy was essential in developing his theories regarding the objective and universal nature of psychic phenomena. Later in his life, he would recall his desires to have been a historian, philologist, or an archaeologist, and his move toward a medical career as a young man might have been more practical and self-serving than he generally let on. In an interview conducted·late in his life, he described his motives for becoming a doctor in one word: "opportunism."[15]

Jung did find his specialization in psychiatry; a field that at the time was generally "held in contempt" by the rest of the medical establishment. While Jung's university lectures in psychiatry left him bored, a textbook by Richard von Krafft-Ebing (*Lehrbuch der Psychiatrie*) opened a path toward merging his passions for both "biological" and "spiritual" facts:

> I had to stand up and draw a deep breath. My excitement was intense, for it had become clear to me, in a flash of illumination, that for me the only possible goal was psychiatry. Here alone the two currents of my interest could flow together and in a united stream dig their own bed. Here was the empirical field common to biological and spiritual facts, which I had everywhere sought and nowhere found. Here at last was the place where the collision of nature and spirit was a reality.[16]

Jung brought biological and spiritual inquiry together in his dissertation titled *On the Psychology and Pathology of So-called Occult Phenomena*. Spiritualism was at its peak at the turn of the last century, and Jung had read a great many books on the subject and had attended many séances and related events featuring psychic mediums. The writings of the spiritualists and the tales told by the mediums echoed the stories that Jung had heard as a child in the countryside, as well as the stories that he was hearing from his patients at the Burghölzli Psychiatric Clinic in Zürich. Moreover, Jung began to realize that the themes within these stories were objective psychic phenomena and that they were common to all people the world over. von Franz noted that Jung was now in a position to bring both of his self-described personalities together for an even deeper and more personal inquiry: Personality No. 1 could now approach the utterances of personality No. 2 as objective statements.[17]

Jung's creative illness

Much has been written about Jung's relationship with Sigmund Freud; it was the rupture of their relationship that thrust Jung into a period of doubt and disequilibrium while providing the opportunity for deep personal inquiry regarding his theories on the objective nature of the psyche.[18] For six years between 1913 and 1919, Jung struggled with what he termed his "confrontation with the unconscious." Troubled by both vivid dreams and his own uncertainties regarding the value of his theories, Jung surrendered himself to the "impulses of the unconscious."[19] This surrender demanded that Jung devote much of his time to creative activities that at first seemed childish and without purpose; later he was to state that practices became a turning point in his life. With much reluctance, and even embarrassment, he returned to his boyhood practice of building miniature cities of stone by the lakeside near his home. This "building game" released a stream of fantasies that he recorded in his private notebooks known as the *Black Books*. While clinging to the stability of his family life and his profession, Jung descended ever more deeply into the unconscious.

In the depths of his creative illness, Jung feared that he was suffering from a psychosis. Nevertheless, he carried on with his personal psychological experimentations, which he frequently began by imagining a steep descent.[20] Oftentimes fighting off a sense of panic, he experienced wildly creative fantasies, wherein he encountered figures whose autonomy and wisdom convinced Jung of the objective nature of the psyche. Philemon was the name that Jung gave to the primary psychic figure, among a small pantheon of figures, who was to become his *psychagogue* or soul guide.

von Franz described this experience as following a shamanic pattern of disorientation, descent, death, and rebirth as Jung undertook a "journey to the beyond," an initiatory ordeal that eventually culminated with a period of relief and exhilaration.[21] Having survived this ordeal, Jung would base the remainder of his life's work on his passionate conviction that the psychic phenomena and structures that he encountered were real. For Jung, structures such as a collective unconscious populated by archetypal potentials were psychological realities "that existed as certainly as did the material world around him."[22]

In addition, Jung emerged with a magnificent trove of dreams and fantasies that would fuel decades of creative practice including painting, sculpting, stone masonry, and the creation of his iconic *Red Book*. Jung had been making art since he was a child, and his artmaking did not cease during the difficult years of his descent, particularly his creation of mandalas, which for a time became a

42 C.G. Jung

daily drawing practice and would later become the launching point for his forays into alchemy.[23] Jung emerged as well with a transformed appraisal of himself as a creator. Over the ensuing years of work on the *Red Book*, he came to new understandings of the role of the artist in society and of the nature of creativity itself.

Not art, but nature

One of the most puzzling episodes during Jung's years of confrontation with the unconscious concerns his refusal to accept the anima figure's proclamation that his creative work was art. This episode becomes all the more relevant in light of the fact that Jung was not a novice to the arts; he was quite familiar with the history of Western art, traditional European art forms, and the avant-garde creations of a new generation of artists, performers, and writers, such as those associated with the Symbolist, Dadaist, and later Surrealist movements. While Jung's personal collection of visual art was weighted toward the traditional, including reproductions of historic works that he had commissioned from artists associated with the Louvre in Paris, his collection later came to include a sampling of contemporary works including an enigmatic abstract painting titled *Noyer Indifférent* by Yves Tanguy.[24]

Prior to the descent into his years of creative illness Jung had been exposed to some of the most groundbreaking work of his era in London, Paris, Basel, Zürich, and in New York, where he toured the iconic Armory Show in the spring of 1913. In addition, Jung had been painting with oils and watercolors for over a decade utilizing the versatile skills that he had honed since childhood. So why was he so adamant that his own creative work was not art?

The answer is multifaceted and begins with the lifelong tension between what he labeled his personality No. 1 and personality No. 2. His growing private practice and stature as an original scientific thinker, writer, and lecturer required a public persona focused on rationality and empiricism. This suited personality No. 1, but personality No. 2 maintained a passionate, although more private, devotion to the arts and humanities. Practical self-interest that Jung went so far as to describe as "opportunism" drove his career choice of science over the humanities along with his reflections upon two pivotal dreams. Once the decision was made, Jung did not want to look back.[25]

Among Jung's colleagues during this time was Franz Riklin, who historian Sonu Shamdasani has described as something of a doppelganger to Jung.[26] Riklin worked alongside Jung at the Burghölzli Clinic and shared Jung's passions for the arts and humanities. Riklin, however, eventually moved away from analysis as he devoted more and more of his time to painting and to apprenticing himself to other artists, including to Augusto Giacometti, uncle to Alberto Giacometti.[27] Riklin was far from a dilettante and exhibited his work alongside well-known creators such as Hans Arp, Sophie Taeuber Arp, Francis Picabia, and others associated with the Dada movement in Zürich. Riklin was also a member of the

Psychology Club that formed around Jung, although he eventually parted ways with both the organization and with Jung. The deterioration of their relationship may have contributed to Jung's critical view of Riklin as one who "vanished" into his art.[28] Jung may have secretly envied his colleague, but Riklin's surrender to a creative calling was more than Jung was willing to risk. Beyond risking his reputation, perhaps Jung's greatest concern was the possibility of losing his sanity itself if he gave himself over completely to the creative daimon. He looked to Nietzsche in particular as a cautionary tale of one who did not return from the dangers of the creative descent.

Jung's relationship to the anima figure who suggested that his work in the *Black Books* was art is another key part of the puzzle. In *Lament for the Dead: Psychology After Jung's Red Book*, Shamdasani and James Hillman considered whether Jung may have merged his imaginal conversations with the anima with actual conversations with one of his colleagues, Maria Moltzer.[29] Jung and Moltzer had worked together at the Burghölzi Clinic and may have been involved in an affair sometime prior to the period of Jung's confrontation with the unconscious and creative experimentation first undertaken in his private *Black Books*.[30]

Moltzer later set up her own analytical practice in Zürich, occasionally taking over some of Jung's client load and correspondence during his travels.[31] According to the detailed notes of one of her longtime analysands, Moltzer created her own illustrated volume of visionary experiences and reflections, which she called her "bible," although it is not clear whether Jung had knowledge of this creative project which was so similar to his own.[32] The conflation of the anima figure with Moltzer is further confirmed by Jung himself who described Moltzer as the first inspiration for his formulation of the anima.[33]

On a professional level, Moltzer made significant contributions to the development of Jung's theories of typology. Jung himself gave her credit for the discovery of the "intuitive" type, although she is mentioned only once in his entire *Collected Works*.[34] Owing to the lack of acknowledgment for her original ideas and critiques, Moltzer, along with Riklin who had become her ally, eventually split with Jung and the Zürich analytic community. The dissolution of Jung's relationships with Moltzer and Riklin – whether driven by personal animosities, professional disagreements, or both – provides additional insight into Jung's seeming elevation of science over art and his refusal to call himself an artist – at least directly. Moltzer and Riklin may have been among the first in Jung's circle to recognize the sacred, ritualistic aspects in his secretive writings and visual art. Moltzer believed that art was akin to religious experience; a position that Jung would take up in his own way.[35] Jung's negativity toward her suggestions may have simply stemmed from the fact that she beheld an aspect of Jung's destiny that he could not come to grips with at the time.

Ultimately, how Jung described himself publicly and how he privately devoted himself to his creative callings appear to be two different things. When he proclaimed that his creative work was not art, but rather nature, he grouped himself within the ranks of visionary artists whose work he considered vital revelations

44 C.G. Jung

of psyche or nature itself. "The psychic depths," according to Jung, "are nature, and nature is creative life."[36] From the perspective of psyche as nature, we gain further insight into Jung's assertion that his creative accomplishments were not "art" per se but emanations of nature. Yet for Jung, the articulation of these emanations in paint, words, or stone was only one part of his mission: He needed to also understand what the images could mean – not only to him personally but also as evidence of a transpersonal and autonomous psyche shared by all people. Jung was a scientist, but he was undeniably an artist as well. Much like his concept of the transcendent function, which bridges and partakes of each side of a set of psychic polarities, Jung held the tension between art and science as he served the creative spirit that enlivens both disciplines.

Archetype and the artist

Paradoxically, Jung's ambivalence about identifying himself as an artist is one of the key reasons why his insights are still so valuable to contemporary creators. Jung knew *exactly* what a creative life entailed; he understood the sacrifices and rewards, along with the suffering and exhilaration felt by anyone called to create. Jung admitted that his personal experimentations with the unconscious were risky, as he encountered the very same psychic material that his patients had encountered in the psychiatric hospital: The "fund of unconscious images" can fatally confuse the mental patient. But it is also the "matrix of a mythopoetic imagination."[37] His period of creative illness and his lifelong personal struggles with what he called "the daimon of creativity" deeply influenced his thinking about art, artmaking, and artists themselves.

For Jung, artmaking as a means of self-expression was insufficient; rather, the creative individual acted as a servant to the artwork: "The special significance in a true work of art resides in the fact that it has escaped the limitations of the personal and has soared beyond the personal concerns of its creator."[38] Jung went so far as to describe the artwork itself as a "living being that uses man only as a nutrient medium, employing his capacities according to its own laws and shaping itself to the fulfillment of its own creative purpose."[39]

In regard to the creative process itself, Jung likened it to "a living thing implanted in the human psyche."[40] Utilizing the terminology of analytical psychology, the "living thing" may be described as an "autonomous complex." The Jungian or analytical conception of a complex is that of a constellation or grouping of images and ideas gathered around a center composed of one or more archetypes carrying a particular emotional or feeling tone. Complexes can propel and direct behavior whether or not an individual is conscious of them or not; they can be so powerful as to act as splinter or split-off personalities. Jung considered the complex to be the *via regia* to the unconscious.

In addition to this definition of the word "complex," Jung, along with colleagues such as Toni Wolff, also employed the word "complex" to indicate that the psyche was inherently complicated, thus complex, and that it required complex methods of interaction. Both conceptions of the word "complex" were behind Jung's use of the term "Complex Psychology" as the overarching name for his ideas about the psyche.[41]

The autonomous power of a complex is evident when Jung describes artists as individuals who must obey an "alien impulse" within – even to the point of sacrificing health and "ordinary human happiness."[42] This is a sobering realization but one that sincere creators have always recognized and have articulated in ways that mirror Jung's assertions.[43] For his own part, Jung mirrored Plato's conception of *theia mania*, or the divine madness, that can – and must to some degree – overtake the human creator, when he compared the "divine frenzy" of artists to the autonomous complex.[44]

The complex is linked to Jung's conception of archetypes and archetypal images. Archetypes populate the dimension of the unconscious that is collective – in fact they are more properly referred to as "archetypes of the collective unconscious." Archetypes are not static and may be envisioned as thematic energies or dynamic potentials for expression. In the Jungian model, archetypes cannot be known per se but can be experienced through archetypal images that continually repeat motifs or themes common to all people and all times – even when these motifs or themes take on new appearances to match a given era or location. As we have seen, Jung had a strong philosophical background, and his articulation of the idea of the archetype exhibits similarities to Platonic Forms or Ideas with some important differences. Plato's ideal and original forms are transcendent, eternal, and unchanging; their representations in the world are only copies of the originals. Plato believed that these primal forms could however be experienced and known but only through philosophical inquiry. Unlike Platonic Forms, Jung's archetypes are not transcendent and unchanging; they are dynamic patterned potentials that become fleshed out and expressed through participation with conscious material as they manifest as archetypal images or symbols. Unlike Platonic Forms they cannot be known directly.

Beyond their role as primordial and patterned potentials for expression and behavior, Jung's model of the archetype includes the idea that archetypes are also perspectives – they not only shape the stories of our lives but also *the way we see* those stories:

> Archetypes are typical modes of apprehension, and whenever we meet with uniform and regularly occurring modes of apprehension, we are dealing with an archetype, no matter whether its mythological character is recognized or not.[45]

Jung believed that creative individuals possess enhanced abilities to recognize, withstand, and shape archetypal images into forms and experiences that convey eternal and necessary themes. While exhibiting eternal and recurring patterns, these themes are continually revitalized and made fresh by artists in every age and in every culture. The image impresses itself upon the creator who feels the urgent

46 C.G. Jung

call to shape it into a form that not only honors its primordial roots but also speaks to the needs of the current moment. As Jung professed:

> The impact of an archetype, whether it takes the form of immediate experience or is expressed through the spoken word, stirs us because it summons up a voice that is stronger than our own. Whoever speaks in primordial images speaks with a thousand voices. . . . He transmutes our personal destiny into the destiny of mankind. . . . By giving [the archetypal image] shape, the artist translates it into the language of the present, and so makes it possible for us to find our way back to the deepest springs of life.[46]

Jung's observations on the creative individual return us to the notion of the artist as a shaman-like figure; one charged with putting aside personal concerns in order to fulfill crucial, and even sacred, duties to the collective. The artist resides in an arguably special, but equally perilous, position as the conduit or vessel for archetypal expression. Jung described the creative individual as a synthesis of contradictory qualities:

> On the one side he is a human being with a personal life, while on the other he is an impersonal creative process. . . . The artist is not a person endowed with free will who seeks his own ends, but one who allows art to realize its purpose through him. As a human being he may have moods and a will and personal aims, but as an artist . . . he is a vehicle and moulder of the unconscious psychic life of mankind.[47]

The artist, as both human and "creative process" is torn between the longings of "ordinary man" for happiness, satisfaction, and security and "a ruthless passion for creation" with the power to override personal concerns. In Jung's estimation, art itself is a kind of "innate drive that seizes a human being and makes him its instrument." As if considering his own fate as an artist against the archetypal pattern of the artist/shaman, Jung concluded that one "must pay dearly for the gift of creative fire."[48]

Jung personally understood both the risks and rewards of surrendering personal will to the archetypal will: the descent was difficult, but the return was even harder. von Franz, remembered Jung as being "extremely sensitive to beauty," with a deep caring for art and artists. Among the creators he valued the most were Johann Sebastian Bach and William Shakespeare, whose work appeared to Jung to be "unclouded by ego elements."[49] Jung could also be quite critical of artists, especially the modern luminaries Pablo Picasso and James Joyce. Jung felt that both these creators possessed the ability to descend into the collective unconscious and return almost at will; yet they did not return with gifts, or necessary wisdom, for the collective. For Jung, this was akin to a desertion or perversion of their creative calling.[50]

Jung's critiques of modern art can seem judgmental and extreme when read today. Indeed, they were not well received at the time of their publication, although Jung maintained that he was misunderstood. He turned down invitations to lecture and write on the contemporary art of his day after the chilly reception of his writings on Picasso and Joyce.[51] However, these uncomfortable episodes did not prevent Jung from immersing himself in the artistic expression of creators whose work moved him. His discomfort with modern art did not prevent him from following a strikingly similar path of non-conformance in his own art – much of which was made in secret and shown only to those in his closest orbit – or to no one at all, such as the wall paintings in his private tower at Bollingen.

Jung's portrait of the artist as servant to a greater will is incompatible with today's Western insistence on individualism and personal will, within what Jackson Lears has described as a "culture of control."[52] Still, Jung's insights continue to ring true for sensitive creators in numerous fields. Many have articulated Jung's findings in their own words or have come to the same conclusions about the creative life in ways that reinforce Jung's models of a collective unconscious, archetypes, and complexes. For example, Stanley Kunitz described the abstract notion of an "unconscious" as "very much like the wilderness in that its beasts are not within our control. It resists the forms, the limits, the restraints, that civilization imposes."[53] Kunitz's evocative personification of the unconscious as wilderness is not far from some of Jung's more poetic suggestions that are scattered throughout his voluminous writings. Jung's model of archetypes of the collective unconscious comes alive in Mary Oliver's beautifully rendered notions of universal images:

> We all share a universal fund of perceptions. Within this fund are perceptions so ancient, dramatic, and constant that they have been, over the centuries, mythologized. They have been inexorably bound up in each of us with certain reliable responses. I am speaking of such archetypal concepts as the ocean as mother, the sun as a symbol of health and hope, and return of spring as resurrection, the bird as a symbol of the spirit, the lion as an emblem of courage, the rose as an example of ephemeral beauty – concepts that link some object of action of the natural world on the one hand, and our all but preordained response to it on the other.[54]

Like Kunitz, Oliver was not a "Jungian," yet her articulation of concepts associated with Jung, along with her assessments of the creative life can sometimes parallel Jung's in stunning ways. As we have seen, Jung believed that creative individuals have always been compelled to serve a type of innate drive, which at various times he called the "creative spirit" or the "daimon." Oliver simply called this entity "the miraculous": "So quickly, without a moment's warning, does the miraculous swerve and point to us, demanding that we be its willing servant."[55] Jung knew that for himself, and for all creators, this call to service could not be ignored without consequences. Oliver put it this way:

> My loyalty is to the inner vision, whenever and howsoever it may arrive. . . . There is no other way work of artistic worth can be done. . . . The most

regretful people on earth are those who felt the call to creative work, who felt their own creative power restive and uprising, and gave to it neither power nor time.[56]

Ultimately, most creators arrive at a crossroads comprising devotion, exhilaration, fear, and regret where they must ask themselves, "What price am I willing to pay for the gift of creative fire?" For Jung, there was no turning back once the decisive vow was made, even as he guarded against the dangerous excesses of his psychiatric patients and creators such as Nietzsche, who gave themselves over completely.

Archetype and art

Jung insisted upon the living reality of the images, themes, and figures of humanity's collective psychic depths. While autonomous agents of the collective unconscious, theses archetypal energies required forming and shaping by the creative individual to be made manifest in the world. Working as servants to psyche, artists create forms that either speak within the known parameters of human experience or, on rare occasions, forms that seem to speak from beyond the limits of the known. Jung divided these distinct modes of artistic creation into two categories: psychological and visionary.

The psychological mode is derived from "the contents of man's consciousness, from eternally repeated joys and sorrows, but clarified and transfigured by the poet."[57] This type of creative expression focuses on themes and happenings that have been repeated millions of times. Psychological art is valuable in that the efforts of the artist provide us with "a greater depth of human insight by making us vividly aware of those everyday happenings, which we tend to evade or overlook."[58] The themes may be archetypal – such as passion, suffering, beauty, and horror – but they are generally psychologically intelligible with no obscurity surrounding them. For the viewer, there is less work to be done as part of coming into relationship with this type of creative expression, thus Jung employed the term "psychological" for this broad category of creative expression that can feel both familiar and profound.

The visionary mode is the reverse of the psychological. In Jung's words, it is something strange that

> derives its existence from the hinterland of man's mind, as if it had emerged from the abyss of pre-human ages, of from a superhuman world of light and darkness. It is a primordial experience which surpasses man's understanding and to which in his weakness he may easily succumb.[59]

The visionary experience may terrify as it "bursts asunder our human standards of value and aesthetic form," but it can also feel like a revelation or a vision of profound beauty beyond words. Faced with a work of visionary depth, we may find ourselves "astonished, confused, bewildered, or even repelled."[60]

Jung identified the visionary mode in certain works of Dante, Goethe, Wagner, Blake, Nietzsche, and Joyce among others, while acknowledging that the list could be much longer.[61] In considering the visionary work of these creators, Jung surmised that that visionary mode of expression makes demands upon the artist that the psychological mode does not: there is a heightened sense of danger in losing oneself in the depths of the unconscious. Jung's fascination for visionary creators who tumbled into the abyss extended to the nineteenth-century French poet Gérard de Nerval, who committed suicide not long after completing his novel *Aurélia*; the manuscript for the work was found on his body. Jung lectured on de Nerval in 1945, with an emphasis on the visionary experiences illuminated within *Aurélia*. de Nerval's experiences with archetypal figures mirrored Jung's own experiences during his years of confrontation with the unconscious, which became the content of the *Red Book*.[62]

From a Jungian perspective, dreams, visions, and the raw material of visionary art all draw their power from a primordial and shared level of the psyche referred to as the collective unconscious, a deep archetypal well common to all humankind. Once these emissaries of the creative depths erupt onto the surface, they have the potential for rebalancing or compensating for one-sided, unbalanced, stagnant, and dangerous states of consciousness. Psyche is not static, but instead seeks a fluid type of equilibrium – one that paradoxically is also always in flux. Along with the artist, Jung included the prophet and the seer among those who psyche presses into service in order to undertake a continual process of rebalancing and renewal. This service oftentimes requires selfless sacrifice to properly receive what yearns to be made known. What is received must then be shaped into an artwork or experience that may offer benefits for both the artist and the collective. Put poetically by Jung, "psyche carries the creative individual on the wings of night to a more than personal destiny."[63]

In his conception of both psychological and visionary art, Jung emphasizes the need for the creative individual to transcend the personal to allow something transpersonal to be revealed. This diminishment of the strictly personal carries the same seriousness and devotion as exhibited by those who take vows before entering a religious order, or those, like the shaman, who submit themselves to apprenticeships within wisdom and spiritual traditions.

Jung clearly elevated visionary art and the artists capable of creating this type of work while not dismissing the value of psychological art. Moreover, he was careful to highlight specific artworks, such as Goethe's *Faust*, while not implying that the works of some creators are *always* visionary. Contemporary creators new to these distinctions may feel discouraged if their creative expression does not seem to fit Jung's idea of "visionary." These distinctions form part of Jung's theories on the exceptional gifts and exceptional duties of artists, which are quite valuable but not beyond question. Indeed, as we will see, they have been challenged and refined for our age by Hillman and many others.[64]

50 C.G. Jung

It is important to note that visionary art as delineated by Jung is not a genre of art nor does it refer to a particular type of subject matter. Jung was not referring to the type of creative expression that is commonly labeled today as "visionary": primarily visual art or writing featuring depictions of chakras, alien beings, spirit guides, and out-of-body experiences or art that is created with the assistance of hallucinogens or plant medicines such as ayahuasca. While this type of work can oftentimes seem formulaic, a Jungian notion of visionary art could indeed accommodate individual works of this nature but only if they reveal something truly new and truly necessary for the collective. Like the archetype that shapes itself into an image or symbol suited to a particular time and place, visionary contents will take on different appearances in order to make themselves known in a particular age and culture, although the revelations may at times only become clear in hindsight.

Creativity as instinct, creativity as nature

Jung so often set creative individuals apart from others; both in regard to their possession of the gifts of "creative fire" *and* the heavy burden of service that these gifts require. One senses something profound, even a type of sacredness, in the artistic calling as described by Jung. Yet there are other instances in Jung's vast body of work where he proposed that creativity was akin to an instinct and *not* the exclusive province of a select few. While seeming to contradict himself, a close reading of Jung's insights into creativity demonstrates that these propositions are not mutually exclusive; they are more like two sides of the same coin. When considered in combination they can enlarge and enhance our approaches to creativity without attempting to explain away its inherent mystery.

In a paper that Jung delivered at Harvard in 1936 titled, "Psychological Factors Determining Human Behavior," Jung positioned creativity as one of five basic human instincts. Along with commonly understood instincts such as hunger and sexuality, Jung added the drive to activity, the need for reflection, and finally, the urgings of creativity.[65] He justified using "creative instinct" as the best way to describe this particular psychic factor since instinct and creativity are both compulsive and behave dynamically. He did, however, set the "creative instinct" somewhat apart from the other instincts, which he described as more or less fixed and inherited organizations of impulses. The "creative instinct" is not fixed and possesses a certain dynamism that allows it to come into relationship with the other instincts such as sexuality, the drive to activity, and the need for reflection.

Jung went even further and proposed that the creative instinct has the power to direct, or even overrule, the other instincts in its own autonomous drive for expression. In his amplification of Jung's theory of creativity as instinct, James Hillman proposed that "the creative is able to produce images of its goal" and "orient behavior toward its satiation." Like other instincts, the creative is a "necessity of life," and "requires fulfillment."[66] Jung may have had Nietzsche and de Nerval in mind when he argued that the creative instinct is so powerful that it may overwhelm, or even destroy, the human creator, for "creation is as much destruction as construction."[67] The repetition of cycles of breaking down and building up leads to yet another one of Jung's insights into creativity: that of nature as creative life:

> The psychic depths are nature, and nature is creative life. It is true that nature tears down what she herself built up – yet she builds it once again. . . . Light is always born of darkness, and the sun never yet stood still in heaven to satisfy man's longing or to still his fears.[68]

Jung's reflections upon nature and its eternal oscillations between light and dark, construction and destruction, dismembering and re-membering echo much earlier philosophies, such as those of Heraclitus and the Chinese sages associated with Taoist traditions, including Lao Tzu/Laozi and Chuang Tzu/Zhuangzi. Jung was a scholar of both Western and Eastern wisdom traditions and found resonance and support for his theories within these ancient ways of knowing, particularly in regard to the fundamental tension between opposites or polarities, and their indivisible union. von Franz described Jung as having "lived the Taoist philosophy," while analyst C.A. Meier recalled that Jung "was tied to nature and its contradictions" and was "more Taoist than anything."[69]

One of Jung's more esoteric statements about creativity involves his comparison between his concepts of anima and animus and the Chinese concepts of *p'o*, related to the feminine yin principle, and *hun*, related to the masculine yang principle:

> For the Chinese consciousness, they are distinguishable psychic factors which have markedly different effects, and, despite the fact that originally they are united "in the one effective, true human nature," in the "house of the Creative" they are two.[70]

Jung's description of the dynamism inherent in the Taoist "house of the Creative" is reflected in his articulation of the archetypes that he called anima and animus. Beyond the common understanding of these archetypes as contrasexual forces or energies within men and women is a more subtle understanding of these forces as playful siblings or even lovers – their eternal games generating life itself: "In all chaos there is a cosmos, in all disorder a secret order, in all caprice a fixed law, for everything that works in grounded in its opposite."[71]

Jung might well have said, "everything that moves," in place of "everything that works," since every creative act is one of movement and change – precisely the unrelenting work of nature. In addition to his fascination with Taoist notions of change and movement as found in texts such as the *I Ching*, Jung was greatly influenced by the physician, early psychologist, and painter, Carl Gustav Carus (1789–1869), who proposed that the unconscious, like nature, comprised inexhaustible, active, and continuous energies. In Carus's model of psyche as creative, the unconscious is another name for nature, and "every creation is Nature's work."[72] While Carus diminished the role of ordinary consciousness in the creative

52 C.G. Jung

work of the unconscious, Jung emphasized the mingling of the conscious and the unconscious within a generative middle realm of ceaseless creativity.

Between creativity and artistry

So far, we are still spiraling around the paradox of Jung's insistence on the one hand that artists obey a special calling, and, on the other that creativity is a human instinct and even synonymous with nature itself. We find an illuminating bridge between these two positions through James Hillman's assertion that before we can seriously consider the topic of creativity, it must be unlinked from artistic ability. Hillman felt that Jung turned too frequently to the figure of the artist when discussing human creativity. As an instinct, creativity acts as a *dynamis* that energizes and propels each and every life toward realization. It is not only the artist who is driven by this sui generis force, we are each "driven to be ourselves."[73]

Even with his frequent positioning of the artist as exceptional, Jung maintained that each individual is called *by* creativity and *into* creativity, with or without any type of recognizable artistic practice or ability: "But what can a man 'create' if he doesn't happen to be a poet? . . . If you have nothing at all to create, then perhaps you create yourself."[74]

What Jung was referring to is a drive toward wholeness that he described as the development of personality or individuation; it is our deepest human calling and our greatest creative achievement regardless of our vocational callings.

The artist shares in the human drive toward creation of the self – that animating calling into life that is common to all. Yet the artist also hears a deeper calling: one oriented toward devoted service to "the creative" itself – the autonomous dynamic depths which seek expression through objects, experiences, and ideas such as visual art, song, dance, ritual, film, theatre, literature, and philosophy. Much like the urge toward individuation, the creative calling may be intermittent and may show up only later in life. The mercurial nature of the call defies consistency; it may feel at times like a whisper but can just as easily arrive as an urgent and overwhelming command – as Oliver stated, "the miraculous swerves at us" and presses us into service. Jung's personal example demonstrates how one is beaconed – and oftentimes compelled – again and again into service of the creative spirit:

> [My] work is the expression of my inner development; for commitment to the contents of the unconscious forms the man and his transformations. My works can be regarded as stations along my life's way. All my writings may be considered tasks imposed from within; their source was a fateful compulsion. [They were] things that assailed me from within myself. I permitted the spirit that moved me to speak out.[75]

Anima, psyche, and soul

It is no wonder that artists, philosophers, and those captivated by the arts and humanities have been drawn to Jung's perspectives on creativity and to living a deeply creative life. One area of difficulty, however, is the fact that he purposely refrained from any firm and final definitions of his major conceptions or hypotheses of psychic life – including the word "psyche" itself.

Psyche may be imagined as a totality consisting of consciousness combined with both the personal and collective levels of the unconscious. Within this definition, psyche is separate from, yet in relationship with, matter. To stop here would be quite limiting however, as Jung's theories on the nature of psyche evolved alongside his thinking around synchronicity as an acausal connecting principle capable of revealing an underlying unity of psyche and matter. Jung proposed that the borders between psyche and matter were permeable, going so far as to suggest that they were very likely one and the same:

> Since psyche and matter are contained in one and the same world. And moreover are in continuous contact with one another and ultimately rest on irrepresentable transcendental factors, it is not only possible but fairly probable, even, that psyche and matter are two different aspects of one and the same thing.[76]

Much like the Tao, psyche as a true totality implies that one can never ever get *out of* psyche to look back upon it. Rather than the psyche existing within us, it is we who exist within psyche:

> The uniqueness of the psyche can never enter wholly into reality, it can only be realized approximately. . . . The deeper "layers" of the psyche lose their individual uniqueness as they retreat farther and farther into darkness. . . . they become increasingly collective until they are universalized and extinguished in the body's materiality, i.e., in chemical substances. The body's carbon is simply carbon. Hence "at bottom" the psyche is simply "world."[77]

The "world" that Jung described, could also be thought of as imagination itself or as an "imagining." Inspired by his reading of Eastern philosophies, Jung proposed that "psyche consists essentially of images" and that "image *is* psyche," meaning a creator or "imaginer" of reality via fantasy – positions that would later be taken up and furthered by Hillman and other thinkers associated with archetypal psychology:

> The autonomous activity of the psyche . . . is, like every vital process, a continually creative act. Psyche creates reality every day. The only expression I can use for this activity is fantasy. . . . Fantasy it was, and ever is which fashions the bridge between the irreconcilable claims of subject and object, introversion and extroversion. In fantasy alone, both mechanisms are united.[78]

Jung used the words "psyche" and "soul" somewhat interchangeably, relying most often on the more abstract "psyche." While evocative and mysterious, the

Greek word "psyche" exhibits a certain neutrality and flexibility. The totality of psyche is reflected in Jung's assertion that "psyche is set up in accord with the structure of the universe, and what happens in the macrocosm likewise happens in the infinitesimal and most subjective reaches of the psyche."[79]

"Soul," while also evocative and mysterious, carries more of a religious charge. Jung described the soul as having a correspondence with God – or in "psychological terms, the archetype of the God-image."[80] As with Freud's model of the soul as *Seele* – which has long been mistakenly equated to "mind" – equating Jung's conception of soul to "mind" would be just as much of an error. Also as with Freud, Jung's use of the word "soul" exhibits Platonic influences.

Like Plato, Jung's hypotheses of the soul included the possibility that the soul was something distinct and autonomous, akin to "an invisible personal entity that apparently lives in a world very different from ours . . . perhaps in a world of invisible things."[81] Jung's model of the soul, like Plato's, allowed for the possibility a personal soul connected, at least temporarily, to a particular human being. For both Plato and Jung, the soul was not dependent upon a human companion for its existence.

An echo of the Platonic tripartite soul is evident in Jung's *Black Books*, which include a mysterious dialogue, or active imagination, between Jung and his soul. Jung calls out to his soul and his soul responds:

> I bind the Above with the Below. I bind God and animal. Something in me is part animal, something part God, and a third part human. . . . If I am not conjoined through the uniting of the Below and the Above, I break down into three parts.[82]

Later in this dialogue, Jung's soul reveals its multiple roles as protector, maternal nourisher, and corruptor: "I, your soul, am your mother, who tenderly and frightfully surrounds you, your nourisher and corrupter; I prepare good things and poison for you."[83]

Here, the soul seems particularly autonomous with aims of its own – aims for experiences that the human host may provide, regardless of whether the host agrees with, or is aware of, this arrangement. In his autobiography written many decades after his encounter with his soul featured in the *Liber Novus*, Jung continued to attempt to articulate the soul's desires. These, he proposed, stemmed in large part from the soul's connection to history, to ancestry, and to biological processes. Bringing both "soul" and "psyche" together he wrote: "Our souls as well as our bodies are composed of individual elements which were all already present in the ranks of our ancestors. The 'newness' of the individual psyche is an endlessly varied combination of age-old components."[84] Jung's statement is equally suited for describing the nature of all art: anything "original" is actually a re-creation or a recombination of age-old components.

Much like descriptions of artists and healers, perhaps Jung's most useful and enduring conception of the soul is that of a guide; an intermediary and mediator between worlds, who "binds the Above and the Below." The idea of a "soul guide" is reflected in Jung's writings on the anima and animus:

> As archetypes, the anima and the animus act as personified guides between the known and the unknown. "Their natural function," . . . is to remain in [their] place between individual consciousness and the collective unconscious. . . . The animus and the anima should function as a bridge, or a door, leading to the images of the collective unconscious."[85]

Whether articulated as anima, soul, or psyche, Jung positioned the soul as a creative middle realm – a two-way threshold, or portal, that is also a process linking the world of the senses (*esse in re*) and the world of spirit of pure intellect (*esse in intellectu*):

> What indeed is reality if not a reality in ourselves, an *esse in anima*? Living reality is a product neither of the actual objective behaviour of things, nor the formulated idea exclusively, but rather the combination of both in the living psychological process, *esse in anima*. . . . The autonomous activity of the psyche . . . is, like every vital process, a continuously creative act.[86]

Esse in anima, or "being in soul," describes a type of living in, and living from, the "creative imagination," the real "Ground of the psyche," and the "only form of being that we can experience directly."[87] All other realities, according to Jung, are derived from psychic reality. We will continue to amplify Jung's conceptions of archetype, anima and animus, psyche and soul in the following chapter through the eyes of contemporary Jungians and post-Jungians who closely examined these concepts in regard to their relationship to creativity and the call to create. James Hillman's reflections on these concepts, with their archetypal inflections celebrating psyche as image, will be surveyed in Chapters 4 and 5.

Jung as artist and shaman, alchemist and *artifex*

Jung's life, albeit a very human and imperfect life, was filled with a wondrous and diverse body of creative work that illustrated his assertion that the devoted scientist, healer, scholar, and philosopher serve the same creative spirit as the artist. Rigid boundaries and hierarchies between disciplines, and between artists and non-artists, begin to fall away as a kinship of devotion tempered with self-sacrifice is revealed. For Jung, "art and science were no more than the servants of the creative spirit, which is what must be served."[88] Thus there is no real conflict with Jung having considered his psychology a "science," while also likening it to art, as they both possess the power to compensate for one-sidedness while influencing the spirit of the age. His psychology was, and still is, inherently creative and transformative – it is *both* science and art.

56 C.G. Jung

Jung himself is an enduring example of a type of modern Renaissance man. He challenged the Western bias toward specialization – something that creative individuals must still do. As Jung's life and work demonstrate, the seemingly disparate callings of scientist, healer, scholar, philosopher, and artist can coexist *within a single human figure*. Looking back upon Jung's life and his enduring legacy, Hillman turned to the rich language of alchemy to describe this versatile figure as an *artifex*:

> The task of working the *materia prima* of the actual unconscious was always that of the artist who did not express merely his personal suffering but reflected the torment of the *anima mundi*, the suffering in the roots. By artist I mean *artifex*, whether artist, alchemist, or analyst – the one who takes in hand the driftwood, the cacophonic sounds, the scarps of *bricolage* and returns this unconsciousness to its roots. . . . If Jung's vision is similar to that of the *artifex* and his life conforms to the duty and destiny of the artist – despite Jung's protests . . . nonetheless this is the legacy he leaves culture and is also his therapy. If his vision compares with the artists, then the work of therapy is also to be conceived or imagined as an artistic endeavor.[89]

The "duty and destiny" of the *artifex* is the same as that of the magus, alchemist, artist, healer, therapist, and shaman – all are *psychopomps* or guides of souls. Their business is revelation and transformation. While Jung bristled at the suggestion that he was a type of mystic, magus, or shaman, he was fascinated with alchemists/healers such as Asclepius and Paracelsus; Jung's own dialogues within his *Liber Novus* recognized the sacrifices necessary for the "gift of magic."[90] Despite his protests, Jung embodied what ecotheologian, Thomas Berry called "the shamanic spirit":

> More than any other of the human types concerned with the sacred, the shamanic personality journeys into the far regions of the cosmic mystery and brings back the vision and the power needed by the community at the most elementary level.[91]

This is precisely how Jung described the most profound and necessary work of *both* the arts and depth psychology – each is capable of rebalancing deadening one-sidedness while educating and reinvigorating both the individual and the spirit of the age.[92] von Franz reflected back upon Jung's life as one lived as a *hermeneut* or interpreter who was able to decipher the "dream letters" arising from the unconscious of his patients in much the same way as shamans are able to decipher messages from the spirit world. While focusing on Jung as one who embodied the shamanic spirit, she concurred with the findings of Eliade to stress that "the shaman himself does not heal; he mediates the healing confrontation of the patient with the divine powers."[93]

Jung's multidimensional life as artist and shaman, alchemist and *artifex* can be a source of profound inspiration for today's creators, as their own "duties and destinies" emerge from the same archetypal roots. As our world faces multiple grave and even existential crises, we need the world-bridging creator more than ever. As Berry's insights continue to remind us:

> In moments of confusion such as the present, we are not left simply to our own rational contrivances. We are supported by the ultimate powers of the universe as they make themselves present to us through the spontaneities within our own beings. . . . The shamanic insight is especially important just now when history is being made not primarily within nations or between nations but between humans and the earth, with all its living creatures.[94]

Jung was dedicated to what Berry called the "spontaneities within our own being" those eternal and autonomous forces that seek to be made manifest through individual human lives. Like so many creators, Jung oftentimes doubted whether his work would be understood or whether it truly mattered. Nevertheless, he obeyed his daimon, the daimon of creativity.

Writing to his friend, Sir Herbert Read just one year before his own death, Jung likened his work to the "ancient functional relationship between the medicineman and his tribe." He could see "the suffering of mankind in the individual's predicament and vice versa." This reinforced his belief that psyche must be taken seriously and listened to and that it was, as it has always been, the role of the artist to act as the soul's mouthpiece: "All his love and passion (his 'values') flow towards the coming guest to proclaim his arrival."[95]

In describing the artist as a type of soul worker, Jung was also describing himself – his soul work was an art and his art a reflection of soul.

Notes

1 See *The Art of C.G. Jung*, edited by Ulrich Hoerni, Thomas Fischer, and Bettina Kaufman. Norton, 2019.
2 Bair, *Jung: A Biography*, p. 639.
3 Jung, *Memories, Dreams, Reflections*, pp. 186–186.
4 Ibid., pp. 356–358.
5 See Chapter 5 for more on Kunitz and Graham's comments as contrasted with James Hillman's signature idea of soul-making with its emphasis on the desires of the daimon, alternatively named the angel, image, character, or soul.
6 See Daniel B. Smith's chapter on Socrates and his *daimonion* in *Muses, Madmen and Prophets*, Penguin Books, 2007.
7 Von Franz, *C.G. Jung: His Myth in Our Time*, pp. 22–24.
8 Bair, *Jung: A Biography*, p. 22.
9 Ibid., p. 29.
10 Ibid., pp. 30, 161.
11 Jung, *MDR*, p. 60.
12 Ibid., p. 72.

58 C.G. Jung

13 Ibid.
14 Ibid., p. 104.
15 Bair, *Jung: A Biography*, p. 37.
16 Ibid., pp. 108–109.
17 Von Franz, pp. 55–56.
18 Jung's break with Freud is well-documented. See especially Bair's *Jung: A Biography*; Shamdasani's *Jung and the Making of Modern Psychology: The Dream of a Science*.
19 Jung, *MDR*, p. 173.
20 Ibid., p. 181.
21 von Franz, *C.G. Jung: His Myth in Our Time*, p. 105.
22 Ellenberger, *The Discovery of the Unconscious: The History and Evolution of Dynamic Psychiatry*, p. 673.
23 Zervas, "Intimations of the Self: Jung's Mandala Sketches for *The Red Book*," in *The Art of C.G. Jung*, pp. 179–215.
24 Fischer and Kaufmann, "C.G. Jung and Modern Art," in *The Art of C.G. Jung*, pp. 19–29.
25 See Bair, *Jung: A Biography*, p. 37; Shamdasani's *Introduction to the Red Book*, p. 6.
26 Shamdasani, *Introduction to the Red Book/Liber Novus: A Reader's Edition*, p. 37.
27 Ibid., p. 21.
28 Ibid., p. 36.
29 Hillman and Shamdasani, *Lament of the Dead: Psychology After Jung's Red Book*, pp. 44–56.
30 Shamdasani, *Jung and the Making of Modern Psychology: The Dream of a Science*, pp. 51–52.
31 Bair, *Jung: A Biography*, p. 259.
32 Shamdasani, *Introduction to the Red Book*, p. 36.
33 Bair, *Jung: A Biography*, p. 192.
34 Shamdasani, *Jung and the Making of Modern Psychology: The Dream of a Science*, pp. 70–72.
35 See Shamdasani's *Introduction to the Red Book*, p. 36; Hillman and Shamdasani, *Lament of the Dead: Psychology After Jung's Red Book*, pp. 44–45.
36 Jung, *Modern Man in Search of a Soul*, p. 215.
37 Jung, *MDR*, p. 189.
38 Jung, "On the Relation of Analytical Psychology to Poetry," in *CW15*, p. 71, para. 107.
39 Ibid., para. 108.
40 Ibid., para. 115.
41 Hillman, "Why 'Archetypal Psychology'," in *Loose Ends*, p. 144.
42 Jung, "On the Relation of Analytical Psychology to Poetry," in *CW15*, pp. 75–77, paras. 110–115.
43 See the following chapter for perspectives on this phenomenon from a variety of creators.
44 Jung, "On the Relation of Analytical Psychology to Poetry," in *CW15*, pp. 78–79, para. 122.
45 Jung, "Instinct and the Unconscious," in *CW8*, p. 137, para. 280.
46 Jung, "On the Relation of Analytical Psychology to Poetry," in *CW15*, p. 82, para. 129–130.
47 Jung, "Psychology and Literature," in *CW15*, p. 101, para. 157.
48 Ibid., p. 102, para. 158.
49 von Franz, *C.G. Jung: His Myth in Our Time*, p. 284.
50 Hillman and Shamdasani, *Lament of the Dead*, p. 51.
51 See Jung, "'Ulysses': A Monologue" and "Picasso," in *CW15*, along with Hillman and Shamdasani in *Lament of the Dead*, pp. 50–56.

52 See Lears, *Something for Nothing: Luck in America*.
53 Kunitz and Lentine, *The Wild Braid: A Poet Reflects on a Century in the Garden*, p. 87.
54 Oliver, *A Poetry Handbook*, pp. 105–106.
55 Oliver, *Upstream: Selected Essays*, p. 40.
56 Ibid., p. 30.
57 Jung, "Psychology and Literature," in *CW15*, pp. 89–90, paras. 139–140.
58 Ibid., p. 89, para. 139.
59 Ibid., p. 90, para. 141.
60 Ibid., p. 91, para. 143.
61 Ibid., p. 91, para. 142.
62 See *On Psychological and Visionary Art: Notes from C.G. Jung's Lecture on Gérard de Nerval's Aurélia*, edited by Craig E. Stephenson.
63 Jung, "Psychology and Literature," in *CW15*, p. 95, paras. 148, 152.
64 See Chapters 4 and 5.
65 Jung, "Psychological Factors Determining Human Behavior," in *CW8*, pp. 114–125, paras. 232–262.
66 Hillman, *The Myth of Analysis*, p. 33.
67 Ibid., in *CW8*, paras. 245–246.
68 Jung, *Modern Man in Search of a Soul*, p. 215.
69 Qtd. in Rosen, *The Tao of Jung: The Way of Integrity*, p. xxi.
70 Jung, Commentary to *Secret of the Golden Flower: A Chinese Book of Life*, p. 115.
71 Jung, "Archetypes of the Collective Unconscious," in *CW9i*, p. 32, para. 66.
72 Hillman, "Carus and Jung," in *Philosophical Intimations*, p. 204.
73 Hillman, "On Psychological Creativity," in *The Myth of Analysis*, p. 34.
74 Jung, "Foreword to Suzuki's 'Introduction to Zen Buddhism'," in *CW11*, p. 557, para. 906.
75 Jung, *MDR*, p. 222.
76 Jung, "On the Nature of the Psyche," in *CW8*, para. 418.
77 Jung, "The Psychology of the Child Archetype," in *CW9i*, p. 173, para. 291.
78 Jung, "The Type Problem in Classical and Medieval Thought," in *CW6*, p. 52, para. 78. See also *CW11* and *CW13*, along with Jung's commentary to Richard Wilhelm's translation of *The Secret of the Golden Flower: A Chinese Book of Life*. See also Chapters 4 and 5 on Hillman's expansion on the notion of image as psyche.
79 Jung, *MDR*, p. 355.
80 Jung, "Introduction to the Religious and Psychological Problems of Alchemy," in *CW12*, p. 11, para. 11.
81 Jung, "The Relations Between the Ego and the Unconscious," in *CW7*, p. 191, paras. 302–303.
82 Jung, "Appendix C," in the *Red Book*, p. 577.
83 Ibid., p. 582.
84 Jung, *MDR*, p. 235.
85 Jung, *Visions: Notes of the Seminar Given 1930–1934, Vol. 1*, p. 116.
86 Jung, "The Type Problem in Classical and Medieval Thought," in *CW6*, pp. 51–52, paras. 77–78.
87 Jung, "Letter to Kurt Plachte," in *Letters: Vol. 1*, pp. 59–62.
88 Shamdasani, *Introduction to the Red Book*, p. 37.
89 Hillman, "Jung's Daimonic Inheritance," in *Philosophical Intimations*, p. 211.
90 See "Paracelsus," and "Paracelsus the Physician," in *CW15*, and "The Gift of Magic," in the *Red Book*.
91 Berry, *The Dream of the Earth*, p. 211.
92 Shamdasani, *Introduction to the Red Book*, p. 63.
93 Von Franz, *C.G. Jung: His Myth in Our Time*, p. 65.

60 C.G. Jung

94 Berry, *The Dream of the Earth*, p. 212.
95 Jung, "Letter to Sir Herbert Read," in *Letters: Vol. 2*, pp. 586–592.

References

Bair, Dierdre. *Jung: A Biography*. Boston, New York and London: Little, Brown and Co. 2003.

Berry, Thomas. *The Dream of the Earth*. 1988. Berkeley, CA: Counterpoint. 2015.

Ellenberger, Henri F. *The Discovery of the Unconscious: The History and Evolution of Dynamic Psychiatry*. New York, NY: Basic Books. 1970.

Fischer, Thomas and Bettina Kaufmann. "C.G. Jung and Modern Art." In *The Art of C.G. Jung*. Edited by Ulrich Hoerni, Thomas Fischer and Bettina Kaufman. Translated by Paul David Young and Christopher John Murray. New York and London: W.W. Norton and Co. 2019.

Hillman, James. "Why 'Archteypal' Psychology?" In *Loose Ends: Primary Papers in Archetypal Psychology*. Dallas, TX: Spring Publications. 1975.

Hillman, James. *The Myth of Analysis: Three Essays in Archetypal Psychology*. 1972. New York, NY: Harper & Row. 1978.

Hillman, James. *Philosophical Intimations: Uniform Edition of the Writings of James Hillman*. Vol. 8. Edited by Edward S. Casey. Thompson, CT: Spring Publications. 2016.

Hillman, James and Sonu Shamdasani. *Lament of the Dead: Psychology After Jung's Red Book*. New York and London: W.W. Norton and Co. 2013.

Jung, Carl Gustav. *Modern Man in Search of a Soul*. 1933. Translated by W.S. Dell and Cary F. Baynes. New York, NY: Harcourt Inc. 1955.

Jung, Carl Gustav. "Commentary." 1931. In *The Secret of the Golden Flower: A Chinese Book of Life*. Edited by Richard Wilhelm. New York, NY: Harvest Books. 1962.

Jung, Carl Gustav. "The Relations Between the Ego and the Unconscious." 1928. In *Two Essays on Analytical Psychology: CW7*. Edited by Herbert Read, Michael Fordham, Gerhard Adler and William McGuire. Translated by R.F.C. Hull. Princeton, NJ: Princeton University Press. 1966.

Jung, Carl Gustav. "Introduction to the Religious and Psychological Problems of Alchemy." 1943. In *Psychology and Alchemy: CW12*. Edited by Herbert Read, Michael Fordham, Gerhard Adler and William McGuire. Translated by R.F.C. Hull. Princeton, NJ: Princeton University Press. 1968.

Jung, Carl Gustav. "Foreword to Suzuki's *Introduction to Zen Buddhism*." 1939. In *Psychology and Religion: CW11*. Edited by Herbert Read, Michael Fordham, Gerhard Adler and William McGuire. Translated by R.F.C. Hull. Princeton, NJ: Princeton University Press. 1969.

Jung, Carl Gustav. "Instinct and the Unconscious." 1948. In *The Structure and Dynamics of the Psyche: CW8*. Edited by Herbert Read, Michael Fordham, Gerhard Adler and William McGuire. Translated by R.F.C. Hull. Princeton, NJ: Princeton University Press. 1969.

Jung, Carl Gustav. "On the Nature of the Psyche." 1954. In *The Structure and Dynamics of the Psyche: CW8*. Edited by Herbert Read, Michael Fordham, Gerhard Adler and William McGuire. Translated by R.F.C. Hull. Princeton, NJ: Princeton University Press. 1969.

Jung, Carl Gustav. "Psychological Factors Determining Human Behavior." 1937. In *The Structure and Dynamics of the Psyche: CW8*. Edited by Herbert Read, Michael Fordham, Gerhard Adler and William McGuire. Translated by R.F.C. Hull. Princeton, NJ: Princeton University Press. 1969.

Jung, Carl Gustav. "The Type Problem in Classical and Medieval Thought." 1921. In *Psychological Types: CW6*. Edited by Herbert Read, Michael Fordham, Gerhard Adler and William McGuire. Translated by R.F.C. Hull. Princeton, NJ: Princeton University Press. 1971.

Jung, Carl Gustav. *Letters*. Vol. 1, 1905–1950. Edited by Gerhard Adler and Aniela Jaffé. Translated by R.F.C. Hull. Princeton, NJ: Princeton University Press. 1973.

Jung, Carl Gustav. *Letters*. Vol. 2, 1951–1961. Edited by Gerhard Adler and Aniela Jaffé. Translated by R.F.C. Hull. Princeton, NJ: Princeton University Press. 1975.

Jung, Carl Gustav. "On the Relation of Analytical Psychology to Poetry." 1931. In *The Spirit in Man, Art, and Literature: CW15*. Edited by Herbert Read, Michael Fordham, Gerhard Adler and William McGuire. Translated by R.F.C. Hull. Princeton, NJ: Princeton University Press. 1978.

Jung, Carl Gustav. "Psychology and Literature." 1930/1950. In *The Spirit in Man, Art, and Literature: CW15*. Edited by Herbert Read, Michael Fordham, Gerhard Adler and William McGuire. Translated by R.F.C. Hull. Princeton, NJ: Princeton University Press. 1978.

Jung, Carl Gustav. *Memories, Dreams, Reflections*. 1963. Edited by Aniela Jaffé. Translated by Richard and Clara Winston. New York, NY: Vintage Books. 1989.

Jung, Carl Gustav. "The Archetypes and the Collective Unconscious." 1959. In *The Archetypes and the Collective Unconscious: CW9i*. Edited by Herbert Read, Michael Fordham, Gerhard Adler and William McGuire. Translated by R.F.C. Hull. Princeton, NJ: Princeton University Press. 1990.

Jung, Carl Gustav. "The Psychology of the Child Archetype." 1951. In *The Archetypes and the Collective Unconscious: CW9i*. Edited by Herbert Read, Michael Fordham, Gerhard Adler and William McGuire. Translated by R.F.C. Hull. Princeton, NJ: Princeton University Press. 1990.

Jung, Carl Gustav. *Visions: Notes on the Seminar Given 1930–1934*. Vol. 1. Edited by Claire Douglas. Princeton, NJ: Princeton University Press. 1997.

Jung. Carl Gustav. *The Red Book/ Liber Novus: A Reader's Edition*. Edited by Sonu Shamdasani. Translated by Mark Kyburz, John Peck and Sonu Shamdasani. New York and London: W.W. Norton and Co. 2009.

Kunitz, Stanley and Genine Lentine. *The Wild Braid: A Poet Reflects on a Century in the Garden*. New York, NY: W.W. Norton and Co. 2005.

Oliver, Mary. *A Poetry Handbook: A Prose Guide to Understanding and Writing Poetry*. Boston, MA: Houghton, Mifflin Harcourt Publishers. 1994.

Oliver, Mary. *Upstream: Selected Essays*. New York, NY: Penguin Press. 2016.

Rosen, David. *The Tao of Jung: The Way of Integrity*. New York, NY: Viking Arkana. 1996.

Shamdasani, Sonu. *Jung and the Making of Modern Psychology: A Dream of a Science*. Cambridge: Cambridge University Press. 2003.

von Franz, Marie-Louise. *C.G. Jung: His Myth in Our Time*. 1975. Translated by William Kennedy. Toronto, CA: Inner City Books. 1998.

Zervas, Diane Finiello. "Intimations of the Self: Jung's Mandala Sketches for *The Red Book*." In *The Art of C.G. Jung*. Edited by Ulrich Hoerni, Thomas Fischer and Bettina Kaufman. Translated by Paul David Young and Christopher John Murray. New York and London: W.W. Norton and Co. 2019.

Chapter 3

A Thousand Voices

Inflections and Interpretations of Jung's Creative Vision

Jung as performer of imagination

Getting to know Jung is an ouroboric enterprise – a sense of mastery regarding his signature concepts and ideas on creativity and imagination – inevitably circles back around to a sense of beginning again as an initiate to his work. Confronted with Jung's inconsistencies and clever skirting of fixed meanings and definitions, one is left to ask, "What did Jung really mean by this?" Susan Rowland has argued that to approach Jung through the lens of "author intention" is neither very creative nor very effective. Rather, she suggested that Jung wrote as an expression of the soul and not as an outside observer of the soul – he was a thinker, writer, and crafter not so much *about* imagination but *of* imagination. His writing could be viewed as a type of extended and complex performance; Jung performed his ideas through a multitude of voices over a great number of years. Jung aimed not so much at consistency but toward a "liberation of psyche"; through his multivocal – and sometimes inconsistent writing – he revealed himself to be as much trickster as sage. Rowland surmised that Jung did not write to inform but to transform.[1]

Perhaps anticipating the type of writing that would occupy him for decades, Jung recounted a visionary conversation with "the spirit of the depths" within the pages of the *Red Book*. As part of his vision, Jung receives a type of gift or mercy, which grants him the courage to speak from the depths: "My speech is imperfect. Not because I want to shine with words, but out of the impossibility of finding those words, I speak in images. With nothing else can I express the words from the depths."[2]

Contemporary creators encountering Jung's *Red Book* and his *Collected Works* will find a kindred spirit, a fellow devotee of soul and imagination, although not one inclined, nor perhaps able, to perfectly spell things out. James Hillman was well aware of this and advised that Jung cannot be read with the intellect alone: "Conscious comprehension in Jungian psychology means as well feeling comprehension. All the principle conceptual symbols (e.g., introversion, shadow, archetype, self, synchronicity) are as well experiences of feeling."[3] The journey to and within Jung becomes richer and more nuanced with experienced guides – the

DOI: 10.4324/9780429057724-4

kind of explorers who have approached his work with imagination, feeling, and intellect. Their personal explorations maintain the mystery in Jung's ideas while demonstrating their value for modern creative lives.

This chapter will highlight the contributions of two of Jung's contemporaries, Erich Neumann and Sir Herbert Read, along with the post-Jungian scholars Rosemary Gordon and Susan Rowland. While a "thousand voices" have indeed provided fine commentary and re-visioning of Jung's core ideas over many decades, the voices featured here have all significantly amplified, questioned, and advanced Jung's ideas on creativity and the creative calling through their sustained engagement with his work enriched by their own unique insights and personal creative practices.

Neumann on creativity, the artist, and the numinous

The contemporary creator cannot truly know Jung without knowing Neumann. The analyst, philosopher, poet, and literary critic, Erich Neumann (1905–1960) was one of Jung's closest friends and associates; although thirty years younger than Jung, he shared Jung's Renaissance spirit of curiosity – a spirit of inquiry and wonder which could not be contained in any single discipline. Even after Neumann relocated to Israel, the two men would meet frequently in Europe, including at the famed conferences held at Eranos, Switzerland. Considered to have been one of Jung's most gifted students, Neumann wrote numerous now classic books on the nature and origins of consciousness, the archetype of the Great Mother, and the marginalization of the feminine in Western cultures.

Before his untimely death at age fifty-five, Neumann had turned his attention to exploring the creative process, the nature of the artist, and the meaning of the art object or art experience to the human community. He melded Jung's insights regarding the critical value of creative expression with his own discoveries, eventually creating into a body of writing on creativity that is arguably more focused and comprehensive than Jung's. Like Jung with his painting, drawing, carving, and building, Neumann was not a stranger to personal creative expression. Although Neumann did not possess the artistic skills apparent in Jung, he nonetheless worked for years creating paintings and dialogues based on his imaginal encounters with the figures encountered in his dreams and during sessions of active imagination.

Building upon Jung, Neumann positioned psychic creativity as parallel to – and ultimately not separate from – nature's visibly abundant and never-ending creativity:

> The creative function of the unconscious . . . produces its forms spontaneously, in a manner analogous to nature, which – from atom and crystal through organic life to the world of the stars and planet – spontaneously

creates forms susceptible of impressing man as beautiful. Because this substratum and background of the psychophysical world is forever bringing forth forms, we call it creative. And to the unknown in nature which engenders its forms of the external world there corresponds another unknown, the collective unconscious, which is the source of all psychic creation: religion and rite, social organization, consciousness, and finally art.[4]

Even with his emphasis upon the collective unconscious, Neumann didn't dismiss the role of conscious participation in creative expression. Like Jung, Neumann's writings on the creative process reveal the influences of Plato's *theia mania*/divine mania as the artist is described as one who is seized by the autonomous force of the unconscious, becoming an instrument of the transpersonal. For Neumann, this type of creative possession ranged from the "lowest unconscious stages of ecstatic frenzy and somnambulism to the highest level of conscious acceptance, in which the artist takes full responsibility and a formative, interpreting consciousness plays an essential part."[5]

Neumann observed that the interplay of consciousness with the creative depths of the collective unconscious holds the potential for generating sensations of timelessness, interconnection, and awe. Indeed, creators across the centuries have described their work, and their lives, as frequently enveloped by a type of spiritual or religious feeling that is difficult to articulate in words. One term that comes close, and one that is closely associated with Neumann, is "the numinous." As utilized by Neumann, "numinous," "the numinous," and "numinosity" refer to a feeling of humility and awe before the splendor that is revealed once the hypothetical boundaries between the physical and the psychical fall away. Numinosity is closely aligned with the mysterious, formless, generative, and overwhelming power of the archetype. A sense of being arrested by wonder – if only for moments at a time – is "characteristic of the archetypal field underlying all reality which appears in both psychic and physical form."[6]

As with Jung, Neumann held that creativity was akin to an instinct, an influential force available to all in varying degrees. At the same time, he followed Jung in setting the artist apart as one who risks more frequent, sustained, and profound encounters with the transpersonal archetypal depths, with the numinosum. Balancing these two positions, Neumann argued that while the roots of *every* human personality "extend beyond the historical area of . . . factual existence into the world of the numinosum,"[7] it is the creative individual who, through conscious devotion and surrender, draws the formless energies up from the dark roots and transforms them into images, words, and experiences charged with their own autonomous power.

The "creative principle" as described by Neumann manifests itself though the artist and encompasses both construction and destruction. Artists work at a type of crossroads between the "too rigid" and the "too chaotic" as they participate in the endless transformation associated with existence itself: "Across the diabolical axis of rigidity and chaos cuts the transformative axis of life and death."[8]

Magic and revelation

Neumann's essays on creativity included meditations on well-known creators such as Leonardo da Vinci, Chagall, Picasso, and Kafka, as well as Freud and Jung. Without making the connection explicit, Neumann's many descriptions of the artist across his body of work are descriptions of the multifaceted shaman whose characteristic archetypal patterning transcends time and place:

> The need of his times works inside the artist without him wanting it, seeing it, or understanding its true significance. In this sense he is close to the seer, the prophet, the mystic. And it is precisely when he does not represent the existing canon but transforms and overturns it that his function rises to the level of the sacral, for he then gives utterance to the authentic and direct revelation of the numinosum.[9]

Neumann argued that the domination of specialization and differentiation over millennia had severed the closeness of the individual with the psychic substratum or original unitary reality. Culture, he argued, can begin to function as an empty shell and a protective safeguard *against* direct inner experiences with the awe-inspiring, but equally terrifying, numinosum. Jung utilized the term "apotropaic" for this type of protective device or situation, applying it not only to culture but to sterile forms of religion as well. It is the creative individual who is charged with scaling the walls of these protections to confront and renew the human relationship to the wilderness of the numinous – a task that is vital not only for the individual but also for the collective in every epoch. This is how Jung viewed the parallel aims of his psychology and of art. This is also the calling of those who embody the shamanic spirit.

As was common in his era, Neumann generally used the term "creative man" to refer to all creative individuals. Regardless of the datedness of that term, he positioned this type of individual as standing in opposition to the demands of the cultural canon, "holding fast to the archetypal world and to his original bisexuality and wholeness, or, in other words, to his self."[10] Here Neumann stresses an archaic or primal unity, *hieros gamos* or *coniunctio* of polarities, where the creator is not only a bridge between worlds but also a resident of both.

Neumann's description of the creative individual is consistent with yet another description of the shaman: a type of consciousness known as the "wounded healer":

> The suffering of the artist is not only a private and personal suffering but at the same time a largely unconscious existential suffering from the fundamental human problems that constellate themselves in every archetype. . . . He does not tend to heal the personal wounds involved in all development by an increased adaptation to the collectivity. His wounds remain open, but his suffering from them is situated in depths from which another curative power arises, and this curative power is the creative process. . . . Because in his own

suffering the creative man experiences the profound wounds of his collectivity and his time, he carries deep within him a regenerative force capable of bringing forth a cure not only for himself but also for the community.[11]

The "cure" that Neumann referred to is the same as what Jung observed as the power of both art and psychology: the rebalancing of one-sidedness, the realization that beneath any personal sufferings are transpersonal themes shared by all, along with the ongoing "education of the age" in which that artist is embedded. The wound is not so much cured, as it is honored, tended to, and transformed; it is made sacred.[12]

Wholeness and transformation

Both Jung and Neumann lamented the fact that the modern world had lost most of the efficacy of "the symbol-creating forces of myth and religion, rites and festivals." Art, however, can still fulfill this necessary function. For this reason, Neumann argued, "the creative principle in art has achieved a unique prominence." Every opus, or new creative expression, is akin to its creator's child, at once the "product of his individual psychic transformation and wholeness, and at the same time a new objective entity which opens up something to mankind . . . a creative revelation."[13]

"Great art," according to Neumann possesses the power of creative revelation, a power that reveals the unitary reality underlying all phenomena – "the 'one reality' of existence, in which no enduring thing can endure, because all is transformation."[14] By "great art" he did not mean famous art, or popular art, but rather sincere acts of creative expression that function as portals of transformation. "The great experience" is how Neumann described encounters that produce a "numinous feeling of amazement in the face of something eternally enigmatic, which accompanies and relativizes our experience, but can also transform it and render it transparent." The "great experience" transports us into a quasi-mystical "state of deep involvement as it transcends the conscious mind."[15] Mythologist Joseph Campbell spoke of these rare encounters as moments of "aesthetic arrest" – moments when we become transparent to the transcendent, when we come face to face with the *mysterium tremendum et fascinans*.[16]

Discovering, or rediscovering, Neumann is to realize that "artistic creation has magic power; it is experience and perception, insight and differentiation in one."[17] With or without Neumann's ability to articulate these feelings, most creators, at some level, have experienced this same revelation: Artistic creation is a form of magic or alchemy. This revelation brings with it stirrings of the magician, alchemist, or shaman with their ecstatic desire to create; this in turn oftentimes transforms into a deep sense of humility and even dread. The duty and destiny demonstrated by these archetypal figures – the "magic power" of artistic creation – comes with great responsibilities. Beyond Neumann's revelatory and

A Thousand Voices 67

arguably mystical writing, his personal example of service to the creative spirit is an enduring inspiration for those fortunate enough to discover this humble genius of the imagination.

Read, Jung, and the Renaissance spirit

Throughout his life, Jung attracted brilliant friends, colleagues, and correspondents from a variety of backgrounds. Jung's Renaissance spirit and restless creative multiplicity found their match in the British polymath Sir Herbert Read (1893–1968). As an art historian, critic, curator, poet, novelist, educator, and editor, Read stands out for his tenacious curiosity, versatility, prolific creativity, and influential writing. As a key member of the original transatlantic group dedicated to publishing Jung's *Collected Works*, Read developed a comprehensive understanding of Jung's work and served as the editorial director for the multi-year project of collecting, translating, and publishing all of Jung's writings.[18] In addition, the two men enjoyed a long friendship, which centered upon conversations about the nature of the creative process and the value of the creative individual to the human community.

Jung turned to Read to complain about the criticism that he received over his essays on modern art. As both a trusted friend and an expert on modern art, Read could challenge the negativity in Jung's thinking about the "fragmentation" in Picasso and Joyce, while at the same time supporting and introducing Jung's theories of the collective unconscious, archetypes, and symbols to the art world at large.[19] Read's own ideas, so influenced by Jung, were also criticized at times – mainly for their construction upon core Jungian hypotheses such as the existence of archetypes and the collective unconscious. Nevertheless, Read's prolific writings proved to be inspirational for a multitude of international creators, scholars, philosophers, educators, and lovers of the arts and humanities, particularly during the 1930s through the 1960s.

A decorated World War I veteran turned pacifist and self-proclaimed anarchist, Read was an important advocate for contemporary British artists. He wrote dozens of monographs and catalogue essays for modern artists such as Ben Nicholson, Barbara Hepworth, and Henry Moore; all of whom benefited from his enthusiasm about their work, his connections in the art world, and from their exposure to Read's philosophies of art and creative practice. Like Jung and Neumann, Read was a frequent presenter at the famed Eranos conferences. It was at Eranos – and at similar international forums devoted to the intersections of art, philosophy, psychology, and contemporary culture – where Read's insights were tested and honed.

The union of art and life

As with so many great thinkers and creators of the past, Read's work has largely faded from view. However, sixty years after his passing, Read's powerful voice continues to offer contemporary creators critical perspectives addressing the joys, duties, and challenges of a creative life, along with the anxieties and threats that have only accelerated in our time. Read argued that modern Western civilizations had separated art away from life, turning it into a type of luxury; an exclusive indulgence that severed it from its original and necessary connection to daily life. This resulted in an "artistic decadence" and "decay of sensibility" due to what he called "a corruption of consciousness." This ongoing corruption diminishes our awareness and receptivity of a "primal vitalism" that is revealed through artistic expression. There can be "no artificial separation of art and life" he proclaimed, without both suffering the consequences.[20]

Read insisted that from the earliest cave paintings, art has been the means by which humankind was able to comprehend the nature of those things significant to human experience; in other words, artmaking is an expansion of consciousness. Read was careful to differentiate between "expansion" and "evolution" when speaking of consciousness, he saw no discernable process of evolution involved in human consciousness nor hierarchy of modern consciousness over ancient or so-called primitive consciousness. Instead, he viewed the development of consciousness as an expansion in a thousand directions, like a tree. He described the artistic activity at the root of this process as "a crystallization, from the amorphous realm of feeling, of forms that are significant or symbolic." With this, he positioned art as *the primary activity* capable of establishing a "symbolic discourse," which in turn allows religion, philosophy, and science to follow as consequent modes of thought.[21] First comes the creative shaping power of art, then culture.

Creators as craftspeople and conquistadors

As with Jung and Neumann, Read described the artist as a type of shaman-like figure, who may be humble and unknown, but who is nevertheless capable of bringing moments of revelation to the collective:

> [artists] make conquests of consciousness that are afterwards occupied by the mind in the widest commonality. . . . I prefer to regard artists as great conquistadors who lead their people into new dimensions of reality, and I think the very fact that in the most significant epochs of art the artist is a craftsman, often anonymous, not isolated as a laureate, proves my point.[22]

Read insisted that sincere artists do not mirror reality, but instead they work like magicians and alchemists to transform one element with roots in the unconscious into another element made conscious in time and space. A "conquest" may occur when a new sense of reality is brought forth out of the chaos and confusion of an unintelligible world into a new ordering: "A work of art is a moment of arrest in the stream of consciousness. . . . [The challenge for the artist] is to arrest the stream at a significant moment. This 'moment' we can call an 'image'."[23]

The concept of "consciousness" is a philosophical problem that continues to perplex and enchant us. Read turned to Giambattista Vico, William James, and Jean-Paul Sartre among others to formulate his working hypothesis of consciousness, which underpinned his theories of art and the creative process:

> Consciousness is always intentional. That is to say, we become conscious of an object in the course of an action, in order to situate that object in our pursuit of Being. Consciousness is therefore a creative (or . . . "concreative") activity – without consciousness there would not be a world, mountains, rivers, tables, chairs, etc.; there would be *only* Being. In this sense *there is no thing* without consciousness, but there is not *Nothing*. Consciousness causes *there to be* things because it is itself nothing. Only through consciousness is there differentiation, meaning and plurality for "Being."[24]

Read is not so far here from Jung's well-known aphorism regarding the nature of human existence itself, with its primary purpose aimed at kindling a light in the darkness of mere being. As part of this same thought, Jung went further to suggest that "just as the unconscious affects us, so the increase in our consciousness affects the unconscious."[25] This dialectical relationship includes the composing of new orders. The first order introduced into [humankind's] conception of the world, according to Read, was an aesthetic order – the order of ritual and myth created by the multifaceted artist.[26]

Anima, *mana*, and muse

As with Jung and Neumann, the artist for Read is a channel whose function is to "transmit the forces of nature in the forms of art."[27] As an intermediary or bridge between worlds, the discoveries and conquests of the artist are not intentional or willed but come about by a combination of inner necessity and a particular readiness and receptivity – even surrender – on the part of the creator. But how does this transmission actually occur, and how does the creative individual participate in this experience without, on the one hand, becoming overwhelmed, or, on the other, exerting so much control that the transmission is blocked?

Read addressed this by considering Jung's conception of the "*mana*-personality" alongside Jung's conceptions of the "anima" and the "self." *Mana* refers to magical knowledge or power and exudes an occult and bewitching quality that Read identified in both the ancient concept of the muse and in Jung's concept of the anima. For Read, the muse/anima is "the power of inspiration in poetry and all other creative arts."[28]

As destructive as it is constructive, the muse/anima selects the time and place of its appearance – an appearance that may overwhelm with the power of a possession. What sets the artist apart in regard to encounters with *mana* energies is a type of dual ability: the ability to receive the arrival of the muse/anima and partake of

70   A Thousand Voices

its *mana* without becoming subsumed or hopelessly inflated, plus the ability to shape that encounter into forms. These dual or mediating abilities are emblematic of Jung's idea of the "self."

Within Jung's model of the psyche, the self (or Self) is the archetype of wholeness; an aspect that can unite, balance, and mediate the ever-shifting energies of the archetypal depth of the psyche. There is something both paradoxical and numinous about the self as it is not only the center of psychic life "but the circumference which embraces both conscious and unconscious."[29] The self, according to Jung,

> Is poised between two world pictures and their darkly discerned potencies. This "something" is strange to us and yet so near, wholly ourselves and yet unknowable, a virtual centre of so mysterious a constitution that it can claim anything – kinship with beasts and gods, with crystals and with stars. . . . This "something" claims all that and more . . . it is surely wiser to listen to this voice.[30]

The self as both a voice and a place of wisdom and unity poised between worlds has been imagined visually as the encircled quarternity; Jung himself painted such images in the *Red Book*. The self also exhibits teleological aims: "It is our life's goal, for it is the completest expression of that fateful combination we call individuality, the full flowering not only of the individual, but of the group, in which each adds his portion to the whole."[31]

Read's subtle and thorough understanding of Jung's psychic models combined with his decades of engagement with the arts and humanities, further combined with his own personal experiences as a poet/creator, allowed Read to formulate his own theories of poetic inspiration and the creation. The meeting of the centered and all-encompassing self with the *mana*-bearing anima/muse is, as Read proposed, a "reasonable explanation" of the creative process which had for millennia been expressed in mythological terms. Even with his affection toward Jung and his ideas, Read observed that the modern model of the unconscious had simply usurped the place formerly occupied by the muses and that in "substituting psychology for mythology we are merely substituting one kind of picture-language for another kind of picture-language."[32]

Art, archetype, and the principle of vitality

Related to Read's contributions to an understanding of the creative process are his insights into the nature and value of those objects and experiences that we call "art." Central to Read's contributions is his application of the Jungian concept of the archetype. Whether called "archetypes" or "primal images," Read stressed the connection between these "dynamos" and the hidden forces of nature. Beginning as formless potentialities, they are not unconscious, rather, they are un-activated.

Once they move toward action, they do so in a way predetermined by their inner nature; there is a patterning inherent in their expression.

Read highlighted music as an example of the dynamism of creative expression, which may appear to be totally free and original but is in fact always a variation of fixed forms – or what in depth psychological terms may be called archetypes:

> The freedom which we inevitably associate with the creative activity, can perhaps be explained as an apparently infinite series of variations on a relatively few fixed forms. There is no need to shrink from such an explanation as from an intolerable restriction of the possibilities of art, for what has the art of music, to a naïve apprehension the freest of all forms of art, every been but such a play with a determinate number of fixed forms?[33]

The "play" of making new arrangements from eternal forms is the task of the artist as channel, vessel, medium, or as Read beautifully stated, the "field of operation." In the same way as an artist's sketch is not a finished painting, nor a melody a symphony, Read argued that the archetype's activation, or intervention, has the potential to convert the personal to the supra-personal, the ordinary into the extraordinary. A certain readiness, ripeness, and maturity on the part of the creative individual is required however, the type of alertness long associated with the mystic, shaman, and the alchemist:

> The forms of art are only significant in so far as they are archetypal, and in that sense predetermined; and only vital in so far as they are transformed by the sensibility of the artists and in that sense free. . . . In this sense the artist has become the alchemist, transmuting the *material prima* of the unconscious into those "wondrous stones," the crystal forms of art.[34]

Both Read and Jung recognized that the ancient alchemists did not assert their will upon nature, rather they refined themselves to a point of patient readiness to collaborate with nature once the shapeless energies at the depths of both matter and psyche became activated. These timeless thematic energies are autonomous, and their drive toward expression parallels Jung's assertions of creativity as instinct. Read called this instinctual drive the "principle of vitality" or "vitalism":

> The only priority in human development is the vital one – the will to live. All our faculties serve this imperious need, and art, as well as magic (and later religion) [are] . . . part of a complex response to this single impulse. . . . Vitalism is not merely animalism: it is rather the Life Force itself, and as such can be manifested in the human form as well as in the animal form.[35]

Following Jung, and quoting his friend, the sculptor Henry Moore, Read went further to propose that a supposedly inanimate object, such as a painting, a

72 A Thousand Voices

song, or a sculpture, may possess its own autonomous vitality: "A work can have its own pent-up energy, an intense life of its own, independent of any object it may represent." In other words, "vitalism" is the same force that poet Dylan Thomas understood as "the force that through the green fuse drives the flower" and what Jung observed as the archetypal drive toward expression. The dynamos known as archetypes, the creative instinct, and the principle of vitality are simply different, yet related, attempts at naming something ineffable, a something that seeks to live over and over again through the artist and through the entire cosmos.

Re-membering the muses and ourselves

Read's contributions to the bridging of artistic practice with depth psychology cannot be fully appreciated without his comments upon originality and the essential responsibilities of the creative individual in every age.

In contrast to the long-held understanding of creativity as originality, Read professed that the creative individual does not actually "create" anything totally new or original. Instead, Read turned once again to Jung's conception of the archetypes of the collective unconscious and to Shakespeare who knew that the poet, painter, composer, and the like "bodies forth the forms of things unknown" – first the "things unknown," then the work of combining them into newly significant orders.[36]

Much like Plato, Read described the artist as gifted with a type of "divine faculty" similar to the Jungian conception of the "self" that is capable of bringing a new order or arrangement to chaos – or in other words, of forming a moment out of flux. This new moment, arrangement, or order is recollected or re-membered from deep, collective sources; recalling Plato, it can be seen as a type of recollection or *anamnesis* of what was already known or what already existed. Read's substitution of "re-creation" for "creation" realigns our contemporary insistence on the primacy of personal will. This realignment also reminds us that inspiration, especially when personified as a muse, is inseparable from memory – the muses were after all daughters of Mnemosyne or memory.

An important part of Read's legacy was his consistent criticism of the soul-crushing mechanization, aggression, individualism, and the blind economic allegiance emblematic of modern Western societies. He returned to the image of the muse as he cautioned against the loss of the soul in the modern world – what he called the corruption of consciousness:

> This corruption is the key, not only to the distortion and loss of inspiration in the individual artist, but also to the decline of art in a civilization – and therefore, consequently, to the decline of that civilization. And that is the point of my argument: corruption for consciousness takes place when the Poet abandons his Muse.[37]

Taking upon the mantle of the magician, alchemist and shaman is a heady, and serious, adventure – one that can easily go astray when the muse, as emissary of the unconscious, is abandoned along with the mission of art itself. Approaching artistic creation as an activity that fulfills a mission as it operates as a type of service was fundamental for both Read and Jung, although today this attitude is largely dismissed or forgotten altogether. Read described this mission as transpersonal and intertwined with the expansion of consciousness – a mission vital for the well-being of humankind and of all beings. He found a distillation of his many commentaries on this subject in the words of philosopher Max Scheler, who stated that the mission of all true art,

> is not to reproduce what is already given (which would be superfluous), nor to create something in the pure play of subjective fancy (which can only be transitory and must necessarily be a matter of complete indifference to other people), but to press forward into the whole of the external world and the soul, to see and communicate those objective realities within it which rule and convention have hitherto concealed.[38]

Read's passionate life filled with making art, thinking about art, and writing about art acts not only as an inspiration but also as a powerful reorientation to our contemporary ideas about what it means to be an artist and what it means to create. "What we call art," affirmed Read, and too often treat as "an ornament of civilization, is really a vital activity, an energy of the senses that must continually convert the dead rain of matter into the radiant images of life."[39] To know Read is to know that the best critic and philosopher of art is the devoted lover and maker of art itself.

Bridging into the present: Rosemary Gordon

Rosemary Gordon inhabited a unique position as a practitioner and researcher whose life and work formed a bridge between Jung's time and our own. Gordon (1918–2012) was a London-based Jungian analyst, clinical psychologist, lecturer, and writer. She studied at the Sorbonne and the University of London and served for a time as Chair of the Society of Analytical Psychology. She later became the editor of the Society's publication, *The Journal of Analytical Psychology*. In her most influential book, *Dying and Creating: A Search for Meaning*, she recalled how she became attracted to Jung's theories due to the seriousness with which he approached the human need to create.[40]

Gordon differentiated between "the creative" and "the artistic" in a clearer fashion than had Jung; she found the process of creativity evident in any number of human arenas and activities and not only in the work of artists. Even with a more direct distinction, Gordon, like Jung, still seemed to have found the best evidence for her theories on the creative process among "artists and mystics" as they both

74 A Thousand Voices

"share a greater than average capacity to experience wonder and awe," as well as "a passionate need to find meaning and not just facts."[41]

A concern with "meaning" held a central role in her theories, just as it had with Jung:

> Essential to and underlying the creative process is the search for meaning [which] evolves out of a synthesis of the process of differentiation and ordering on the one hand and the making and discovering of something new on the other. It is thus inseparable from the capacity for awe and wonder and from the courage to be genuinely available to any kind of experience, however unfamiliar, new, bewildering or unknowable it may be.[42]

Gordon found support for the second part of her statement in what the Romantic poet John Keats called "negative capacity," which entails the courage to remain in mystery and doubt without rushing to reason and fact, to risk a state of "not knowing" and make oneself available to the possibility of "sacred awe."[43] Interrelated to this argument was Gordon's agreement with Neumann that every artist is in essence a bisexual person capable of moving between polarities such as activity and receptivity, control and surrender.[44]

Rituals of dying and creating

One of Gordon's primary areas of research concerned the process of dying, which included the theme of death as it appeared in the dreams of her analysands and as it was expressed in rituals of death and rebirth still practiced in non-Western cultures. She observed that her own thoughts about the nature of death inevitably led to thoughts about the nature of creativity. Gordon came to understand that there was an inexorable linkage between the two: Everything existing must invariably surrender to death and transformation for something new to emerge; that new thing as well must surrender in time. Gordon likened this endless progression to rites of initiation as illuminated by Mircea Eliade: "The scenario for initiates . . . is always the same: it is suffering, torture, death – and resurrection."[45] These stages informed Gordon's theories about stages in the creative processes, which she identified as a preparation, incubation, inspiration, and verification. The progression was not necessarily fixed, but much like the stages of the alchemical process which include breaking down and dissolution, long periods of waiting and doubt, and (just maybe) sudden illumination, these stages captured Gordon's attention as she observed how often they occurred in the work of creators.

Gordon's insights on the connection between dying and creating are at odds with much contemporary advice on the creative process, which promises techniques for getting around the difficult parts of the process, with bypassing or controlling the sacrifice, suffering, and waiting. Gordon insisted that the process must be lived through and could not be cheated: While there is indeed a time for conscious productivity, there will be no product without the equally important stage of receptivity.

Symbolization, play, and meaning

Yet another area of Gordon's work that carries great significance for today's creative individual centers on what she called the "third area of the psyche." She described this space "in between" all polarities including conscious and unconscious, and ego and self, as the "wellspring of culture – that is, of play, imagination, religion and the arts."[46] Gordon considered this middle area to be consistent with Donald Winnicott's model of the "area of illusion," which he developed through observing creativity in children:

> Creativity involves paradox and play and depends on a person's capacity to tolerate contradictory – yet also complimentary – qualities or processes, such as, for instance activity and passivity; receptivity and productivity; consciousness and unconsciousness; masculinity and femininity. It might also involve the capacity to balance surrender and control, effort and passivity, waiting and forging ahead, solitude and communication.[47]

It is not difficult to see affinities between this "third area" and the Taoist concepts of the interplay of yin and yang, as well as the paradoxical *wu wei*, a type of fully aware yet relaxed acting without action. The "area of illusion" or "third area of psyche" forms a connecting bridge or territory between polarities, much like Jung's notion of the "transcendent function," which posits that a new "third" resonating with meaning may emerge if the tensions of two opposites can be endured for long enough.

According to Gordon, Jung's "transcendent function" is synonymous with the "symbolic function." This process is characterized by an "as if" attitude of play and free imagination that enables humankind to "relate to unobservable realities in terms of observable phenomena and so mediate the experience of the world as having meaning and significance."[48] Gordon is clear that she does not utilize the word "play" as a metaphor, and as we learned earlier, Jung himself returned to actual "playing" by building miniature stone castles on the lakeside in an effort to rebuild the bridge of creativity and childlike wonder between his inner and outer worlds.[49] Gordon's work is a powerful reminder that the creative individual is the quintessential world-bridger, the one whose shamanic sensibilities honed through repeated cycles of sufferings and exhilarations may result in forms and experiences (symbols) that bring meaning and enrichment not only to themselves but to the entire collective.

From transcendent function to transdisciplinarity

What we know as "Jungian" in the twenty-first century is actually a continually critiqued, re-visioned, and re-enlivened collection of core ideas about eternally interwoven concepts such as psyche and matter, consciousness and the unconscious, nature and humanity, good and evil, life and death. Contemporary thinkers – whether analysts, scholars, creators, philosophers, or a hybrid of all of these – continually reappraise, reject, and renew Jung's thinking for the new century. There is much to criticize in Jung and much to save and continue to move forward.

Some of the most exciting contemporary contributions come from Susan Rowland, a Jungian scholar, author, and professor of depth psychology, creativity, and the humanities. Rowland understands why Jung and his theories still matter for today's creators and for a world still suffering from the splitting off, and elevation of, humankind above nature, masculine above feminine, reason above the irrational. As we have seen, Jung's model of a transcendent function provides an imaginal meeting place in the middle, where a marriage of opposites may occur and a vibrant "third" may emerge. Rowland sees this same possibility in the more recent concept/method of transdisciplinarity, which is a bold and invigorating approach to dissolving barriers and challenging hierarchies, particularly between privileged disciplines and marginalized ways of knowing.

Transdisciplinarity proposes that human beings live on several levels of reality at the same time and that rational consciousness is not the only basis for the formation of knowledge. Rowland has looked to the pioneering scholar, Basarab Nicolescu, whose vision of transdisciplinarity "vitally undoes the classical subject/object division in favor of the ternary: subject, object, hidden third that is both subject and object."[50] This is of course, the "bridge" that Gordon extoled.

Rowland has extended this further to propose that a transdisciplinary approach to learning, creating, and being in the world is one of radical inclusiveness, which can be visualized as an interconnected web of knowledge. This participatory web recognizes unity in diversity and diversity in unity as it exchanges hierarchy for permeability and deep curiosity and cooperation *between*, *across*, and *beyond* disciplines/way of knowing. These ways of knowing include the indigenous; the sacred; the feminine; the irrational (such as artmaking); the somatic; and the divinatory (such as mantic techniques like astrology, tarot, and the *I Ching*) *along with* the so-called rational and objective sciences. She has argued that Jung's model of a polyvalent psyche anticipated transdiciplinarity's model of many-ness comprising equally valued parts.

Transdisciplinarity comes into relationship with Complexity Theory, or "Emergence," which replaces the evolutionary model of existence based on competition with a model that emphasizes interpenetration and cooperation between complex and adaptive life systems. Nicolescu argued that "from a transdisciplinary point of view, complexity is a modern form of the very ancient principle of universal interdependence."[51]

What all of this offers to creators, and to others on the margins of modernity, is a cutting-edge model for reclaiming their rightful roles as equal participants in what Read called "the expansion of consciousness." This expansion, or creative illumination, is accomplished in the middle, in the spaces "in-between," no matter if the space is called the "transcendent function," the "symbolic function," or "emergence." What "emerges" is meaning via the symbol.

Symbol as portal

The classical Jungian understanding of the symbol is that it is the best possible representation of something unknown, yet to be known, or not fully knowable. Unlike a "sign" which points to what is known, a symbol retains its mystery even as it communicates and resonates with meaning and even numinosity. While one can construct a sign, one cannot intentionally set out to construct a symbol – one hosts and beholds a symbol.

The etymology of the word is helpful in that "symbol" entails the contradictory actions of both "throwing" and "gripping" – a bringing together of two parts that, while distinct, are also related to a whole. For the Greeks, the *symbolon* was an actual object, such as a bone or coin, that was broken in half and distributed to individuals who may need to recognize one another or their proxies as allies at some time in the future; when the pieces matched, each side could be assured that a relationship had already been established.

Jung believed that symbols were the natural language of the unconscious due to their ability to go beyond intellectual formulations to create relationships in a dynamic space of "in-between" – relationships such as soma with psyche, reason with passion, and consciousness with the unconscious.[52] While the symbol has long been successfully imagined as a bridge, Rowland has offered us an even more potent image: symbol as portal.

In Rowland's estimation, the psyche is inherently creative and productive, as it continually "generates images of its own 'living mystery,' in the cause of psychic completion. . . . The symbol is therefore a gateway to the unconscious":

> The symbol is where matter and energy meet. It is a way of experiencing and holding the tensions between immanence and transcendence. . . . The symbol can be creative in a way that addresses one of the greatest wounds of our age: the split between human and non-human nature. . . . the symbol is a reciprocal portal to nature and a means of necessary psychic evolution.[53]

Here, Rowland is referring to the devastating rupture that came about in the transition between pre-Christian animism and monotheism. The earlier Earth Mother creation myth associated with animism, immanence, and embodiment has been almost entirely eclipsed by an aggressive form of the Sky Father creation myth with its emphasis on transcendence, disembodied rationalism, and discrimination. Rowland argues that "Jung's entire project was driven by a possibly barely conscious awareness of the desperate need to revive Earth Mother embodied 'feminine' consciousness, because the dominance of Sky Father separation had made modernity sick."[54] The symbol – especially when expressed in the arts – has the potential to become an "evolutionary portal to psyche" offering a creative rebalancing of these inseparable archetypal polarities.

When imagined as a threshold or portal, the symbol fosters dialogue and healing between the entities on either side. As to the relationship between symbols

78   A Thousand Voices

and archetypes, it is important to remember that symbols are archetypal images or manifestations of archetypes, which are thematic/patterned primal energies or shaping powers that cannot be known directly. The symbol's archetypal energy is ignited within the depths of the collective unconscious and emerges into consciousness as it comes into relationship with the world around us. Symbols affect the conscious world and are affected by it: "The Jungian symbol is both body and history; it therefore knits the individual psyche into the fabric of the world."[55]

Symbol, synchronicity, and art

Rowland has gone further to propose that the symbol – as expressed through creative expression of all types – is a "form of reciprocal unconscious, synchronous communication" with the power to join "the embodied psyche to cosmos in its linking of psyche and matter."[56] The symbol is synchronous because its emergence follows no causal path to manifestation: The symbol appears both *within and as* the meaning-filled and permeable crossroads between psyche and matter. Symbols are less "things," than they are experiences – they are how we *see and feel* our soulfulness and our ensoulment.

In his later years, Jung speculated upon the proposition that there may be no real differentiation between psyche and matter at all. He used the odd word "psychoid" to express the merging ground of the two in relation to the archetypes:

> The phenomenon of archetypal configurations – which are psychic events *par excellence* – may be founded upon a psychoid base, that is, upon an only partially psychic and possibly altogether different form of being. For lack of empirical data, I have neither knowledge nor understanding of such forms of being, which are commonly called spiritual.[57]

In other writings, Jung called this spiritual "form of being" that is at once beyond and underlying all differentiation the *unus mundus* in keeping with the European alchemists; he referred to it also as the Heraclitean "flux" and the Tao.

Jung described his model of synchronicity as an "acausal connecting principle," further clarifying that the force that does the connecting is an unmistakable sense of meaning. Chance, time, and place also play their roles in the creation of meaning in synchronous events; with these factors in mind, synchronicity may be thought of as a "falling together in time, a kind of simultaneity" or as "an act of creation in time."[58]

"Creation in time," is also a precise definition of artmaking. In *Jung on Art: The Autonomy of the Creative Drive*, author Tjeu van den Berk credits Rowland with a unique understanding of creativity as synchronicity:

> [Synchronicity] is a way of reading reality non-rationally and symbolically, in ways traditionally assigned to the making of art. So synchronicity treats time and space as aesthetic components of momentary artistic wholes. It is

possible therefore to argue that synchronicity is reality an aesthetic (non-rational) mode, or that it represents the human mind "reading," or "composing," acausal events into art without being entirely aware of doing so.[59]

In his own complimentary argument, van den Berk proposes that the sense of meaning encountered in a work of art is due to a kind of synchronistic mirroring:

> The symbol that is elicited by the work of art exists in the psyche of the artist and in the outer world. . . . There is a mirroring of similar and simultaneous processes which do not cause each other directly.[60]

Alchemy, synchronicity, and a psychology of magic

The Jungian concepts of archetype, individuation, symbol, and synchronicity are inherently creative, as are the long-marginalized practices of alchemy, magic, and witchcraft. These practices, along with astrology, tarot, the *I Ching*, and other intuitive, ritualistic, and divinatory expressions linked to the feminine, the shamanic, and the occult, are enjoying renewed interest among people who sense their potential for illuminating and rebalancing a world desperately out of balance.

Today's sincere creators can – and should – unapologetically see themselves reflected in the figures of the alchemist, the magician, the shaman, and the witch. Whether seen in myth and literature or as reflected in the ritual practices of diverse peoples over millennia, these figures dissolve the imagined barriers between subject and object and psyche and matter, as they prepare for and welcome a synchronous union in the middle where a hidden third may be invoked.

Rowland has argued that a renewal of just this sort of "witch consciousness" with its respect for multiple realities, including the sacred *and* the sciences, mythos *and* logos, is a necessity for the twenty-first century.[61] Synchronicity demonstrates this type of consciousness when viewed not as an abstract construct but as a layered intersection of matter, space, time, and psyche forming a meaningful living whole. The opus of the artist, witch, magician, and alchemist is not directed toward a personal goal nor is it an attempt to somehow transcend the world. Instead, it is aimed at fostering a mutual relationship of creativity *in and with* the world as the crossroads of multiple realities both seen and unseen. Synchronicity is thus a psychology of magic.[62]

The next bridge

Through an alchemy of his empirical and imaginal work, Jung sought to bridge ancient and modern worldviews. His work with synchronicity "articulates a psychophysical ontology. . . . implicitly aimed at reinstating the antique conception of the correspondence between the physical and the spiritual worlds."[63]

80 A Thousand Voices

Like Jung himself, Jungian-oriented practitioners and scholars such as Neumann, Read, Gordon, and Rowland have performed what James Hillman referred to as *epistrophé*, a reaching back to essentials that may resonate with renewed meaning after undergoing a process of revivification for the current era. Our focus will now shift to Hillman and to his revolutionary re-visioning of Jungian thought merged with his own eloquent and passionate understandings of creativity, the creative process, and the role of the artist in our contemporary world.

Notes

1 Rowland, "C.G. Jung's Dramatic and Imaginative Writing."
2 Jung, *The Red Book/Liber Novus: A Reader's Edition*, p. 123.
3 Hillman, in von Franz and Hillman's *Lectures on Jung's Typology*, p. 104.
4 Neumann, "Art and Time," in *Art and the Creative Unconscious*, pp. 81–82.
5 Ibid., p. 98.
6 Neumann, "The Psyche and the Transformation of the Reality Planes: A Metaphysical Essay," in *The Essays of Erich Neumann: The Place of Creation, Vol. 3*, p. 25. See also Jung's comments on the numinous in *CW11* and Rudolf Otto's *The Idea of the Holy*.
7 Neumann, "Art and Time," in *Art and the Creative Unconscious*, p. 131.
8 Neumann, "Creative Man and Transformation," in *Art and the Creative Unconscious*, p. 163.
9 Ibid., p. 97.
10 Ibid., p. 181.
11 Ibid., p. 186.
12 See Chapter 6 for extended commentary on the mythic wounded healer.
13 Neumann, "Creative Man and Transformation," in *Art and the Creative Unconscious*, p. 166.
14 Ibid., p. 202.
15 Neumann, "The 'Great Experience'," in *The Essays of Erich Neumann: The Place of Creation, Vol. 3*, pp. 138, 181.
16 Campbell, "Creativity," in *The Mythic Dimension: Selected Essays 1959–1987*, p. 187.
17 Neumann, "Art and Time," in *Art and the Creative Unconscious*, p. 86.
18 See William McGuire's *Bollingen: An Adventure in Collecting the Past* for Read's critical role in the conception of Jung's *CW* and its publication, along with Read's relationships with Jung and the Mellon family, the underwriters of the Bollingen series.
19 See Jung's letters to Read from 1960, along with portions of Read's replies in Vol. 2 of *C.G. Jung: Letters*.
20 Read, *Icon and Idea: The Function of Art in the Development of Human Consciousness*, p. 137.
21 Ibid., pp. 18–19.
22 Ibid., p. 138.
23 Ibid.
24 Ibid.
25 Jung, *Memories, Dreams, Reflections*, p. 326.
26 Read, *The Origin of Form in Art*, p. 31.
27 Ibid., p. 14.
28 Ibid., p. 135.
29 Jung, "Definitions," in *CW12*, para. 44.
30 Jung, "Essay Name Unconscious," in *CW7*, pp. 237–238, para. 398.
31 Ibid., pp. 239–240, para. 404.

32 Read, *The Origins of Form in Art*, p. 136.
33 Read, *The Forms of Things Unknown*, p. 59.
34 Ibid., p. 75.
35 Read, *Icon and Idea: The Function of Art in the Development of Human Conscious-ness*, pp. 21, 33.
36 Ibid., *The Origins of Form in Art*, p. 113.
37 Ibid., p. 138.
38 Read, *Icon and Idea: The Function of Art in the Development of Human Conscious-ness*, p. 4.
39 Ibid., p. 140.
40 Gordon, *Dying and Creating: A Search for Meaning*, p. 129.
41 Ibid., p. 144.
42 Ibid., p. 130.
43 See Chapter 5 for a more expansive treatment of Keats's "negative capability" in rela-tionship with archetypal psychology.
44 Ibid., 134.
45 Ibid., p. 159.
46 Gordon, *Bridges: Metaphor for Psychic Processes*, p. 338.
47 Ibid., p. 339.
48 Gordon, *Dying and Creating: A Search for Meaning*, p. 179.
49 See Chapter 2.
50 Rowland, *Remembering Dionysus: Revisioning Psychology and Literature in C.G. Jung and James Hillman*, p. 34.
51 Ibid., p. 35.
52 Gordon, *Dying and Creating: A Search for Meaning*, p. 107.
53 Rowland, "Jung's 'Living Mystery' of Creativity, Symbols, and the Uconscious in Writing," in *The Unconscious Roots of Creativity*, Kathryn Madden, Editor.
54 Ibid., p. 65.
55 Ibid., p. 64.
56 Ibid., p. 66.
57 Jung, *MDR*, p. 351.
58 Cambray, *Synchronicity: Nature & Psyche in an Interconnected Universe*, pp. 14–17.
59 Qtd. in van den Berk, *Jung on Art: The Autonomy of the Creative Drive*, p. 134. Also in Rowland, *Jung as a Writer*, p. 147.
60 Van den Berk, *Jung on Art*, p. 135.
61 Rowland, Conference Presentation at "Magic from the Margins: Women, Witches, and Emerging Ecologies of Psyche."
62 Rowland, *C.G. Jung in the Humanities: Taking the Soul's Path*, pp. 20–21.
63 Shamdasani, Foreword to "Synchronicity: An Acausal Connecting Principle," p. ix.

References

Campbell, Joseph. *The Mythic Dimension: Selected Essays 1959–1987*. New York, NY: Vintage. 2007.

Cambray, Joseph. *Synchronicity: Nature & Psyche in an Interconnected Universe*. College Station, TX: Texas A&M University Press. 2009.

Gordon, Rosemary. *Bridges: Metaphor for Psychic Processes*. London: Karnac Books. 1993.

Gordon, Rosemary. *Dying and Creating: A Search for Meaning*. 1978. London: Karnac Books. 2000.

82 A Thousand Voices

Jung, Carl Gustav. "The Relation Between Ego and the Unconscious." 1928. In *Two Essays on Analytical Psychology: CW7*. Edited by Herbert Read, Michael Fordham, Gerhard Adler and William McGuire. Translated by R.F.C. Hull. Princeton, NJ: Princeton University Press. 1966.

Jung. Carl Gustav. "Introduction to the Religious and Psychological Problems of Alchemy." 1948. In *Psychology and Alchemy: CW12*. Edited by Herbert Read, Michael Fordham, Gerhard Adler and William McGuire. Translated by R.F.C. Hull. Princeton, NJ: Princeton University Press. 1968.

Jung, Carl Gustav. *Memories, Dreams, Reflections*. 1963. Edited by Aniela Jaffé. Translated by Richard and Clara Winston. New York, NY: Vintage Books. 1989.

Jung. Carl Gustav. *The Red Book, Liber Novus: A Reader's Edition*. Edited by Sonu Shamdasani. Translated by Mark Kyburz, John Peck and Sonu Shamdasani. New York and London: W.W. Norton and Co. 2009.

Neumann, Eric. "Art and Time." In *Art and the Creative Unconscious: Four Essays*. 1959. Translated by Ralph Manheim. Princeton, NJ: Princeton University Press. 1974.

Neumann, Eric. "Creative Man and Transformation." In *Art and the Creative Unconscious: Four Essays*. 1959. Translated by Ralph Manheim. Princeton, NJ: Princeton University Press. 1974.

Neumann, Eric. "Creative Man and the Great Experience." In *The Essays of Erich Neumann: The Place of Creation*. Vol. 3. 1959. Translated by Hildegard Nagel. Princeton, NJ: Princeton University Press. 1989.

Neumann, Eric. "The Psyche and the Transformation of the Reality Planes: A Metaphysical Essay." In *The Essays of Erich Neumann: The Place of Creation*. Vol. 3. 1952. Translated by Hildegard Nagel. Princeton, NJ: Princeton University Press. 1989.

Read, Sir Herbert. *The Forms of Things Unknown*. New York, NY: Horizon Press. 1960.

Read, Sir Herbert. *The Origins of Form in Art*. London: Thames and Hudson. 1965.

Read, Sir Herbert. *Icon and Idea: The Function of Art in the Development of Human Consciousness*. 1965. New York, NY: Shocken. 1967.

Rowland, Susan. *C.G. Jung in the Humanities: Taking the Soul's Path*. New Orleans, LA: Spring Journal Books. 2010.

Rowland, Susan. "C.G. Jung's Dramatic and Imaginative Writing." Paper presented at Pacifica Graduate Institute, Santa Barbara, CA. June 2013.

Rowland, Susan. "Jung's 'Living Mystery' of Creativity, Symbols and the Unconscious in Writing." In *The Unconscious Roots of Creativity*. Edited by Kathryn Madden. Asheville, NC: Chiron. 2016.

Rowland, Susan. *Remembering Dionysus: Re-Visioning Psychology and Literature in C.G. Jung and James Hillman*. Abingdon and New York, NY: Routledge. 2017.

Rowland, Susan. "Magic from the Margins: Women, Witches, and Emerging Ecologies of Psyche." Conference Presentation. Pacifica Graduate Institute, Santa Barbara, CA. June 2020.

Shamdasani, Sonu. Foreword to C.G. Jung, "Synchronicity: An Acausal Connecting Principle." *CW8*. 1960. Edited by Herbert Read, Michael Fordham, Gerhard Adler and William McGuire. Translated by R.F.C. Hull. Princeton, NJ: Princeton University Press. 2011.

van den Berk, Tjeu. *Jung on Art: The Autonomy of the Creative Drive*. Hove and New York, NY: Routledge. 2009.

von Franz, Marie-Louise and James Hillman. *Lectures on Jung's Typology*. 1971. Thompson, CT: Spring Publications. 2020.

Chapter 4

Archetypal Creativity
Image, Imagination, and Instinct

Bridging across Jung to Hillman

As both an iconoclast of ideas and a devoted champion of images and imagination, archetypal psychologist James Hillman (1926–2011) challenged therapists, creators, academics, politicians, and the rest of us to recognize the soul – or lack thereof – in our work, our relationships, our religion, our cities, our countries, and our cultures. If Jung, as Hillman submitted, was less of an empiricist and more an *artifex* (a craftsman and *bricoleur* of soul), then Hillman mirrored and extended his mentor's aesthetic and imaginative approach to psyche; he grew his archetypal psychology, not from science and medicine, but from the ancient and fertile soil of the arts and humanities.

Hillman was adamant that his work was not personal and offered no more than glimpses into his personal life through his writing, teaching, and public lectures. Hillman grew up in Atlantic City and traveled widely with his parents who owned hotels on the East Coast and elsewhere. He served in the US Navy for two years before spending the next thirty years in Europe; first as a student at the Sorbonne in Paris and at Trinity College in Dublin, then onto doctoral studies and analytical training in Zürich. Upon receiving his analyst's credentials, he served as director of studies at the C.G. Jung Institute for a decade. Hillman left the Institute in 1969, amidst multiple personal and philosophical conflicts with the Institute's leadership and the extended Jungian community. This parting was a fall from grace that ended a critical chapter of Hillman's life. What followed was Hillman's own "creative illness," which eventually cleared the way for his dramatic return to the forefront of depth psychological thought and cultural criticism.[1]

Beginning in the early 1970s, he began articulating the key themes of an "archetypal psychology," which advanced many of Jung's ideas – such as the primacy of imagination and image, and the value of mythology, literature, and the arts for insights into the nature of psyche – while challenging others, such as Jung's preference for wholeness, the heroic underpinnings of individuation, and the characteristics and function of archetypes.

Hillman shared Jung's Renaissance spirit with an array of interests and endeavors spanning disciplines, cultures, and continents. Comfortable in at least four

DOI: 10.4324/9780429057724-5

languages, he displayed seemingly endless energy for writing, public speaking, teaching, travel, and advocacy, as well as for operating a publishing house dedicated to advancing the work of an international roster of thinkers from multiple fields.

Twenty-first century creators who are discovering, or rediscovering, the work of James Hillman will find a tireless and unapologetic advocate for beauty, for the soul and soulfulness, for justice and equality, for the rights of animals, and for the necessary work of artists: those crafters of experiences and objects that arrest our senses – senses that are too often numbed by the mundane, the superficial, the commercial, and by a myopic existence in the strictly personal. His work is an enlivening and challenging invitation into active participation with imagination, with each other, and with the living depths of the *anima mundi* or ensouled world.

While Hillman was a psychologist, he constantly expanded the definition of therapy to encompass a "therapy of ideas," as well as a therapy of places, institutions, governments, and above all a therapy of the animated world around us. He expanded the idea of the therapist and recovered the word's etymological roots in the Greek *therapeutes* to include individuals attending to the seen and unseen world with awareness, devotion, courage, vulnerability, and artistry – the very same poetic sensibility shared by artists and makers.

While many therapists are indeed also artists, Western societies have long forgotten that artists too are therapists in the original sense of the *therapeutes*. Hillman did not forget this as he encouraged creators to embrace their full range of powers:

> The term "therapy" does not have to designate only the contemporary practice of professional problem-solving . . . by licensed organized "care providers." Psycho (soul) therapy (service) is a broadly applicable term, descriptive of any activity by anyone or anything that attends to the needs of the soul and performs rituals (deliberate acts addressed to powers beyond the human) that minister to the soul.[2]

Hillman modeled his particular approach of "ministering to the soul" on art itself, with its ability to "blow our minds" rather than settle them. In doing so, his work continues to remind creative individual of their power and purpose.[3] And artists do need reminding as Western societies are accustomed to paying lip service to the arts and to artists while ignoring or mistrusting imagination itself. This has only intensified with the rise of brain-centric disciplines, such as neuroscience, which positions itself as the chief explainer of human experience.

This chapter will consider three main areas of Hillman's work which overflow with relevance for creators: 1) the enmeshing of archetypal psychology with the arts and humanities including the overlap into expressions of the sacred; 2) the aesthetic nature of psyche as image and "imaginer" of reality; and 3) Hillman's advancement of Jung's idea of a "creative instinct" propelling each human life,

Archetypal Creativity 85

alongside his own insights into various key "archetypal styles" of creativity and his call for a separation of creativity from artistry.

A lineage of archetypal imagination

Soon after leaving the C.G. Jung Institute, Hillman began publishing influential essays and transcripts of his talks aimed at introducing his emerging approach to psychology and differentiating it from analytical or Jungian psychology. From its inception, archetypal psychology was envisioned as more of a cultural movement than a method of psychotherapy. Hillman, along with a close group of colleagues such as Pat Berry and Raphael López Pedraza, aimed to move out of the consulting room and into culture – into life where it's lived. Archetypal psychology was, and still is, "deliberately affiliated with the arts, culture, and the history of ideas, arising as they do from the imagination."[4]

Hillman believed that one had to turn to culture – to mythology, religion, art, architecture, epic, drama, and ritual –to study human nature at its most basic level, since those practices and areas of inquiry display archetypal patterning most clearly. These primal patterns, or *archai*, appear spontaneously in all cultures and may manifest in dreams, religion, art, social customs, and in the sufferings of the soul, which are oftentimes labeled as "mental disorders." Hillman described this move toward culture and the imaginative and away from a purely scientific basis of inquiry as a "poetic basis of mind," one that also expands beyond human nature to the nature of an interconnected, living cosmos.[5]

Beginning with Jung as his most immediate philosophical forefather, Hillman constructed a "family tree" of inspirational ancestors who all shared concerns for the ceaselessly creative and fantasy-generating powers of the soul.[6] Beyond Jung, the roots of archetypal psychology are a fascinating tangle, which includes the influences of Henry Corbin (1903–1978), the French scholar, philosopher, and mystic known for his interpretations of Islamic spiritual thought. According to Corbin, reality consists of at least three interrelated worlds (the visible, the intermediate, and the spiritual) each having their own organs of perception related to the triad of body, soul, and mind. The sensible, visible world is perceived through the senses, the intermediate world of soul through the imagination, and the third world of spirit through a visionary type of intellect.[7] Corbin's conception of the *mundus imaginalis*, the intermediate imaginal world, provided archetypal psychology with a location for the essential components of imagination that exist in a reality between the spiritual world and the world of sense perception.

While the philosophical roots of both analytical and archetypal psychology emerge from Platonic sources, the roots of archetypal psychology grow closer to the regions and cultures adjacent to the Mediterranean, in contrast to Jung's more northerly and Germanic roots. In the writings of the Italian philosopher and historian, Giambattista Vico (1668–1774), Hillman saw a connection between Vico's articulation of metaphorical thinking as the primary mode of thought and Jung's

86 Archetypal Creativity

insistence on the primacy of fantasy thinking. Vico's *universali fantastici*, universal images or poetical characters such as those found the world over in myth, are strikingly prescient of Jung's archetypes. For Hillman, Vico was poised between the ancient past and the modern concerns of depth psychology:

> On the one hand his undertaking reaches back to the polytheistic imagination to be found in the Neoplatonist approach to the psyche, while on the other hand it adumbrates forward to Jung's thought in which the daemons and Gods are indeed fundamental real structures because they are psychically prior to the minds which believe they project them.[8]

Hillman followed Vico's own influences back to the early Italian Renaissance and to Marsilio Ficino (1433–1499), the Florentine philosopher, theologian, astrologer, and translator of Plato. Key to Ficino's thought was his assertion that the human soul was a multiplicity that held a central position between the divine and the earthly. "By placing soul in the center, Ficino's philosophy became a psychological philosophy" as he recognized that all philosophies are based upon primary psychological experiences. Hillman found parallels to Jung in Ficino's insistence of the importance of fantasy and in the proposition that "the mind has its home *in the soul*" and that everything known is via the soul, that is, transmitted through psychic images, which is our first reality.[9]

Ficino's writings describe a soul with a tripartite nature: The first portion is the mind or rational intellect; the second is *idolum* or imagination or fantasy, which links each of us with fate or to the stories of our lives; the third is body or instinct, through which we are all linked with nature. Paralleling Jung's idea that the fantasy-producing creative instinct can influence the basic instincts, such as hunger and sexuality, the *idolum* or fantasy images in Ficino's model of the soul enable the soul to join instinct and nature together "in service of an individual fate. Our fate is revealed in fantasy, or as Jung might put it: in the images of psyche we find our myth."[10] Ficino's influence on archetypal psychology is profound as fantasy and fate are never far from Hillman's thinking.

Hillman looked back even further to the Neoplatonist and mystic Plotinus/Plotino (205–270) as yet another forefather of archetypal psychology. The teachings of Plotinus have long been recognized in the West as having had a formative influence on Christian theology. This designation, according to Thomas McEvilley, has hindered a more comprehensive understanding of the Indian influences in Plotinus's philosophy, including remarkable synchronicities with the Upanishadic–Vedantic tradition and with Vijnanavada Buddhism.[11]

In Plotinus, Hillman recognized an archetypal perspective (which tradition has called Neoplatonic) concerned with the nature of psychic reality – in other words, with the nature of the soul. Hillman identified a number of important parallels between Plotinus's thought and the basic ideas of archetypal psychology including the observation that consciousness at one level of the soul may exist simultaneously with unconsciousness at another: "As Plotinus has been called the 'discoverer of the unconscious,' so has his universal psyche been compared with Jung's collective unconscious."[12] In Plotinus's thought, soul is certainly not ego and consciousness itself is multiple and mobile:

> Because for Plotinus, there is no "fixed fulcrum of self-consciousness as the center of our world and our activities," we become precisely the activity we enact, the memory we remember, man is many, Proteus, flowing everywhere as the universal soul and potentially all things.[13]

The Neoplatonic soul is both subject and object as it continually reflects upon itself: "Everything said is both a statement of the soul and by the soul as well as a statement on and about the soul." Like the palimpsest that displays layer after layer of earlier writing and imagery, the soul is "ever-writing on itself."[14]

Hillman was particularly struck by the importance of imagination in Plotinus's thought "as consciousness depends upon imagination and imagination holds a central place in the soul." Hillman saw this also in Jung where at "the base of consciousness there are psychic (archetypal and primordial) fantasy-images. . . . In short, the essential activity of the psyche, that which characterizes its very essence is the continued creation of fantasy-images."[15] For Plotinus, Jung, and Hillman alike, psyche is the quintessential artist. While our vision may be dulled to psyche's boundless creativity expressing itself through our daily lives, we meet psychic images most clearly in dreams when we ourselves are images among images. If we are attentive enough, we encounter them also through the work of artists in songs, films, poems, dances, novels, paintings, rituals, and more.

Archetypal poetics

As noted earlier, Hillman identified Heraclitus as archetypal psychology's eldest ancestor. Hillman viewed the writings of Heraclitus not as fragments but as aphorisms, where the style is part of the message: brief snapshots of a moment – that like the flux of the Heraclitan fire or the stream that never ceases to flow – will surely transform into the next moment and then into the next.[16] The world is revealed in quick glances and through the well-shaped and disorienting paradox that prods us into awakening, even as we realize that ultimately "things keep their secrets." This too is the promise of art at its most prophetic and enduring: "The prophet's voice possessed of god requires no ornament, no sweetening of tone, but carries over a thousand years."[17]

Hillman wrote about the value of developing an "archetypal eye" as a means of remembering that "the archetypal" precedes and transcends the human psyche and that psyche's archetypal fantasies underlie all theories and methods meant to understand it. Further linking archetypal psychology to the arts and humanities, Hillman stated that the "archetypal eye" is a mythical perspective and is developed through "profound appreciation of history and biography, of the arts, of ideas and culture" with a particular attunement to myth.[18] Whether articulated

88   Archetypal Creativity

as "archetypal" or "mythical," what Hillman described is the eye of the artist and seer – an eye that can "see through" while realizing that it itself is being "seen through."

In addition to the masters highlighted here, the ancestors of archetypal psychology include many others who concerned themselves with the soul, with image, imagination, and the nature of creativity. William Blake, Gaston Bachelard, Owen Barfield, and the Romantic poets, such as John Keats and Samuel Taylor Coleridge figure prominently in archetypal psychology's abiding concerns for the primacy of the imagination and the life of the image. It was Blake who, in his early nineteenth-century poem "Milton," declared that "imagination is not a state, it is the human existence itself."[19]

Building upon Blake's declaration, Bachelard argued that the "imaginary" is the "very experience of openness and newness," which more than any other power, "determines the human psyche."[20] Hillman allied himself with Bachelard, who believed, like Corbin, that the "imaginary" or "imaginal" was a psychic reality not to be explained away as "make believe." Hillman's devotion to the living image was nourished by Bachelard's belief that "images are psychic realities" and that, "in experience itself, everything begins with images."[21] For both Bachelard and Hillman, images possess the power to occupy the "heart of our imagining being." An image may seize us and hold us, as it "infuses us with being."[22] In Barfield, Hillman found support for some of the root affirmations of archetypal psychology: that imagination is creative and aesthetic and that only by imagination can the world be known.[23] It is to image and imagination where we now turn our attention.

Image as psyche, psyche as imagination

Jung made one of his most enigmatic statements about the nature of the soul – "image *is* psyche" – within his commentary to *The Secret of the Golden Flower: A Chinese Book of Life*, a Taoist text translated into German by Jung's friend Richard Wilhelm in the late 1920s. Jung's statement acted as a motivating spark for the development of archetypal psychology and as a touchstone for Hillman for decades to come as he returned to it on multiple occasions across his body of work.

The receipt of the translation of this ancient text was a life-changing event for Jung as he found confirmation for many of his own developing theories in the archaic philosophies of the East. The phrase, "image *is* psyche" [Jung's italics] occurs in the context of Jung's complaint that Western minds dismiss the psyche or try to explain it away with abstract concepts:

> The depreciation of psychic things is still a typical Western prejudice. If I make use of the concept "autonomous psychic complex," my reader immediately comes up with the prejudice, "nothing but a psychic complex." How can we be so sure that the soul is "nothing but"? It is as if we did not know,

or else continually forgot, that everything of which we are conscious is an image, and that image *is* psyche.[24]

As outlined in Chapter 2, Jung considered psyche to be a continually creative process of imagination, an "image and an imagining."[25] Hillman picked up where Jung had left off and began to shape a psychology that would begin with the image and stay true to the actual image as it presented itself. To start with, Hillman eschewed the term "the unconscious," suggesting that "imagination" was a superior term for the enigma that depth psychology had named "the unconscious":

> I tend to use "imagination" instead of that word "unconscious" . . . not that there isn't unconsciousness in us all the time. . . . The word "unconscious" is loaded with subjectivity and has become a psychologism. "Imagination" connects you at once with a tradition and with aesthetic activity. With language. It refers directly to images which Jung himself says are the main content of the unconscious.[26]

It is important to note that Jung declined to fully commit himself to the word "the unconscious," although it suited the aims of positioning depth psychology among the so-called dispassionate sciences. He considered equally enigmatic terms such as *mana*, daimon, and God alongside the unconscious as they too are earnest but never totally satisfactory attempts to apply language to mystery.[27]

For both Jung and Hillman, the "place" of imagination is not in the mind, rather the mind is in the imagination. Like psyche, imagination cannot be stepped out of in order to formulate definitions and theories. Instead, all statements about psyche involve psyche imagining itself. Following Blake, Hillman professed that imagination is not "merely a human faculty." He went further to declare that imagination is an "activity of soul to which the human imagination bears witness. It is not we who imagine but we who are imagined."[28] However, far from being an activity that predetermines life, imagination *plays* as it "images." Jung declared that,

> not the artist alone, but every creative individual owes all that is greatest in his life to fantasy. . . . without the play of fantasy, no creative work has ever yet come to birth. The debt we owe to the play of imagination is incalculable.[29]

Another angle into this play of imagination is reflected in poet William Carlos Williams's suggestion that "there is neither beginning nor end to imagination, but it delights in its own seasons, reversing the usual order at will."[30] We become aware of the playfulness of imagination through its self-revelation in images – images that can arrest our forward motion, stop us in our tracks, and reverse our usual order.

When we consider the word "image," what generally comes to mind is a picture; something visual, such as a photograph, a painting, or the images that we see on film with their close affinity to those we see in our dreams. As we have seen in

90 Archetypal Creativity

an earlier chapter, human beings created images long before there was anything called "art." Certain images associated with the sacred, such as icons, statuary, and *ex votos*, have been thought to possess a *dynamis*, a type of autonomous aliveness and/or supernatural power.[31] The West's history of iconoclasm attests to the continued contentiousness around the idea of images as living and autonomous and contributes to depth psychology's difficulties in advocating for the primacy of imagination and for psyche itself, which is not something "supernatural."[32]

The depth psychological "image" includes all manner of human-created things from the sacred to the profane, along with those things created by nature and psyche (or psyche-nature) such as dreams, emotions, mountains, oceans, plants, and animals. As Glen Slater has explained, "raw emotion or bodily sensations become images as soon as any significant awareness of them occurs." Feelings too become images once "recognition and reflection" begin. An image, is, essentially, "a piece of imagination."[33]

These pieces of imagination, when noticed with care, might be thought of as revealing their souls to the attentive and patient observer. Images then can be seen as having multiple meanings: They are the thing crafted or made manifest *and* the deep interiority or essence that is synonymous with soul. Like souls, images are both complete and complex. Hillman proposed that, much like the hexagrams associated with the *I Ching*, entire dreams may be approached as a single image with all parts being "co-relative and co-contemporaneous."[34] Instead of the Jungian emphasis on amplifying images via symbolic correspondence, Hillman and Berry recommended sticking with an image, "restating" it until one merges into or gets "lost in the labyrinth" of meaning already present in the image. In this way the image grows in worth, thus "image making = meaning."[35] This work of curiously and patiently spiraling around an image and gazing upon it from every angle within the container of therapy or personal reflection parallels the movements made by the artist in the container of the studio, workshop, or writing room.

Artists are known for noticing things deeply and for working, reworking, and living with those things for weeks or even years. A thing closely considered – including bodily sensations and emotions – may become an image or a piece of imagination. An image, no matter how common, becomes "archetypal" when its inherent value is recognized; that value consists of a wealth of insight and meaning. An archetypal image is not so different from the Jungian conception of a symbol, as both captivate and never seem to exhaust their sense of meaningfulness. The emergence of an archetypal image, like a symbol, has the power to halt the flow of time with a sense of the timeless. However, in contrast to the notion of the Jungian symbol, which resonates with history, myth, and mystery, archetypal psychology privileges each unique image just as it presents itself. Thus *any* image may be considered archetypal without the need of an archetype or historic and/or mythic cross-cultural correlates supporting it in the background. This inflection is particularly illuminating for those who are considered "commercial" creators (the architect, interior designer, graphic designer, videographer, etc.), as the things that

Archetypal Creativity 91

they create are also capable of exhibiting the type of value and depth associated with the word "archetypal."

It is not unusual for creators to develop relationships with images, to speak to them, and most importantly, to listen to them. Contemporary scholars who deal with images as part of visual culture, media studies, and art history also "listen" to images in their own way; some have gone so far as to suggest that visual images (including advertisements and other commercial examples) are not only mediums of transmission but instead possess a type of vitality and have desires of their own.[36] Ian Heywood and Barry Sandywell have described images, along with art objects and artifacts, as being "grenades of meaning, often with their own lives and fortunes."[37] While Hillman might have loved the description of images as "grenades of meaning," scholars of contemporary visual culture (while edging close to Hillman's ideas) do not extend the category of image beyond the visual and human-made nor do they seriously consider the nature and role of psyche in image making. In short, they flirt with the idea of images as beings but ultimately view them through a scientific eye and not an "archetypal eye."

Hillman's description of the "archetypal eye" is no different than the artist's eye that notices images and befriends them:

If, as Jung says, "image is psyche," then why not go on to say, "images are souls," and our job with them is to meet them on that soul level. . . . We might equally call the unfathomable depth in the image, love, or at least say we cannot get to the soul of the image without love for the image.[38]

The sensuous image

To love an image is to break free of the Cartesian subject–object paradigm, where the knowing and ensouled human subject moves through a world of lesser or inanimate matter. Hillman observed that Western culture, along with the various psychologies that grew within it, had long diminished the sensuous, separating aesthetic experience from life as it's actually lived. Yet we ourselves are "sensuously imagining animals," capable of cultivating an aesthetic appreciation of how things, when beheld as images, present themselves to us. This is the artist's way of looking at, and living with, images:

They are in some way formed, ensouled, and are speaking to imagination. This way of looking is a combination of the Neoplatonic *anima mundi* and pop art; that even a beer can or a freight care or a street sigh has an image and speaks of itself beyond being a dead throwaway object.[39]

Hillman described images as animals and animals themselves as images. He was inspired by the Swiss zoologist, Adolf Portmann, whose research included the study of "unaddressed appearances," meaning the way animals naturally display themselves regardless of whether there is an eye (human or otherwise) to see them or not. Tying this display to the display of imagination itself, Hillman could confidently state that,

> [A]ll living things are urged to present themselves, display themselves, to show *ostentatio*, which as a common Latin translation for the Greek *phantasia*, or fantasy. Each animal's ostentation is its fantasy of itself, its self-image as an aesthetic event without ulterior function.[40]

Of course, this would also apply to the human animal as well – a natural image among other natural images.

Dream images are no different, and it is within the theatre of the nighttime dreamworld where we are most clearly images among images. These images and scenes appear unbidden, yet they entangle us in dramas that allow for their expression and for ours:

> The dream image is always embedded, a priori, in the entire psyche, is the psyche itself. And, since – as Jung says – you are in the psyche rather than the psyche in you, my personal dream image is webbed into the anima mundi; that vast humus of mycelium fibers, spreading and sprouting everywhere, boundless and unfettered by time.[41]

Stanley Kunitz, while not specifically referencing depth psychology's devotion to the autonomy and mystery of dream images, seemed to echo Hillman's assessment of what dreams do:

> One function of dreams is to inform us that the boundaries of experience are infinitely open and that the limits we perceive in our daily life are in themselves an illusion, that actually to be alive is to occupy territories beyond those we recognize in our physical universe. . . . In the dream, you move beyond [the daytime] dominion into one where the rules have not yet been discovered and never will be.[42]

Attention to dreams involves a type of crafting that mirrors *bricolage*, a collage-like technique of arranging disparate objects, especially castoffs and remnants, into a meaningful whole. Hillman's advocacy for image making as a form of meaning making, and soul-making, includes the actual crafting of artworks, songs, poems, dances, rituals, films, and more. These methods host and honor images as they recognize these living images, as both Jung and Hillman argued, have claims upon us.[43] The work of the *bricoleur* of images follows the movements of attention, inspiration, devotion, and *poesis*/making associated with creators such as Kunitz, but this work is not the exclusive province of any one group. Still, it is the artist who provides the clearest example of welcoming and working with images.

Image as ritual

In an essay celebrating the paintings and installation work of artist Margot McLean, Hillman further refined his ideas on images, stating that "images are like rituals, or, an image is a ritual in brief." To the eye and heart sufficiently both quiet enough to see and feel it, an image created with care can be considered a "slowed epiphany" with the power to reorient time:

> Images arrest. They stop us up, bring us to a standstill. That is their first effect and a prime measure of their success. Interruption, surprise, stopping – the flow of time is invaded by the timeless. . . . Rituals alter time by repetition. They do not move forward and, by repeating movement, they arrest time's progress.[44]

The repeated movements of ritual, and of image making, become acts of ennoblement – not so much by adding value with each repetition but by recognizing, revealing, and honoring the *inherent value* in the root image itself – that particular piece of imagination. In describing the power of poetry, Louise Glück offered a parallel argument for Hillman's conception of the archetypal image with its inexhaustible value, as well as for the Jungian symbol, with its inexhaustible mystery: "Poetry survives because it haunts, and it haunts because it is simultaneously utterly clear and deeply mysterious, because it cannot be entirely accounted for, it cannot be exhausted."[45]

Hillman insisted that when we are touched by – and sometimes haunted by – a dream image, a poem, a film, a painting, or any piece of imagination, we are able to "feel into things" beyond the limits of our personal education and experience, and that by "opening up the essential imagination we also expand our compassion."[46] Hillman continually made clear the importance of expanding our compassion for our animated world of images and for confronting the tragic bias of human superiority over other life-forms. Arguably, this is still our most urgent task as creators and as human beings living *among*, and not over, other beings. One way that Hillman argued for this expansion of compassion was through his advancement and alteration of Jung's notion of a creative instinct.

Instinct and the creative opus

As we have seen, Jung's thoughts on creativity are paradoxical: In many of his lectures and writings, we find him describing the artist as a special type of human being, set apart from "normal man," while elsewhere he argues that creativity itself is akin to an instinct among other vital human instincts – thus, requiring fulfillment in every human life.[47]

Hillman noticed that Jung did not explicitly work out his theory of a creative instinct alongside, or in contrast, with his theories of the creative individual.

94   Archetypal Creativity

Nevertheless, Hillman suggested that Jung's entire psychology was "primarily based upon the creative instinct" and was a "creative psychology."[48] Hillman believed that at least part of the reason that Jung never took this any further was due to an error that we all continue to make – confusing the creative with the artistic.

Jung's theorizing on a creative instinct links it to the process of individuation and to the drive of the self to become realized, thus "we are driven to be ourselves," and "the individuation process is a *dynamis*, not a matter of choice or for a few." The creative instinct, as summed up by Hillman is not a gift or special grace, nor an ability or talent: "Rather it is that immense energy coming from beyond man's psyche which pushes one to self-dedication. . . . Creativity impels devotion to one's person" even as it "brings with it a sense of helplessness and increasing awareness of its numinous power."[49]

Hillman described this lifelong devotion to oneself as an opus. As a *dynamis* akin to an instinct, the creative opus of life is the essential – if oftentimes invisible and unconscious – work of all people. In extending the word "opus" beyond its connection with the arts, Hillman provided an apt metaphor for the creative work of life. Like the classic definition of an artist's work, the opus entails as much destruction as construction, along with a sense of being driven or pulled along by the work itself. The creative opus of one's life may be also described as "psychological creation," the task of "generating psychic reality in one's life, reanimating life."[50] Psychological creation both underpins and permeates all individual callings – it is a universal level of experience, where, as both Jung and Hillman argued, we can confidently declare that everyone is creative, that every life is creative.

Creativity and the *via aesthetica*

One thing that has been missing so far is a definition of creativity or "the creative" itself. In Hillman's assessment, there is no single "creativity" but rather perceptions of creativity driven by archetypal patterns. These "perceptions are filtered through the prism of the psyche. We stand inescapably in the light of one or another color band, giving us a definite perspective and bias."[51] Hillman identified at least seven distinct perspectives on creativity, with the first being shaped by classic myths of creation, such as in Genesis. Here a single powerful creator-god brings order out of chaos with the goal of uniting and stabilizing many differentiated parts – something that Hillman felt could easily fall into a type of sterility and rigidity associated with the shadow side of the *senex* or father image.

The second perspective holds that creativity is novelty and that it must constantly bring about something fresh, young, and absolutely original. In contrast to the *senex*, the *puer aeternus*, or eternal child, rules this notion of mercurial creativity, which looks always to the future. This forward motion toward novelty may override more measured efforts of crafting lending a sense of irresponsibility or even narcissism to creative activity. This sweeping away of the old led Hillman to his third notion of creativity: creativity as primal power. Here, creativity is linked to Dionysian excess and dismemberment and to even more ruthless gods such as Shiva and Wotan who thrive on the frontier between construction and destruction.

Prometheus personifies Hillman's fourth notion of creativity with his theft of fire from the gods, signifying a new level of brash human agency. This notion is perceived primarily through the ego as it views creativity as a means toward enhancement of consciousness and is close to the common understanding of creativity as problem solving. This perspective idolizes willpower and hard work while diminishing the value of intuition, spontaneity, and chance. Hillman's fifth notion is seen through the eyes of the persona and is linked to ambition, fame, and eminence. The persona, or mask, can easily overtake the performer as evidenced by our culture's obsession with celebrities and the details of their lives. The mask, however, is also a reminder of the archetypal patterns that propel the role of "creator," underscoring the ability of artists to allow themselves to be inhabited by powers beyond their own making.

The sixth notion stems from the archetype of the Great Mother and envisions creativity as a type of continuous renewal and rebirth from the indestructible and timeless ground of nature. This notion positions us as devotees to an external "mothering unconsciousness, nourishing and regenerating, at the ground of each human being, and naturally subject to periodic barrenness, like the seasons."[52] The diminishment of human agency within this notion of creativity can lead to passivity but can also act as a corrective for the ego-driven Promethean notion.

Hillman's seventh notion of the creative is perceived through the archetype of the anima and personified through the mythic figures of Psyche and Eros and their tale of longing, separation, suffering, and reunion.

> Anima becomes psyche through love and . . . it is eros which engenders psyche. . . . The creative is an achievement of love. It is marked by imagination and beauty, and by connection to tradition as a living force and to nature as a living body.[53]

Hillman's passion for the myth of Psyche and Eros is contributed greatly to his approach to analysis as a creative act and to the formulation of his ideas around artmaking and soul-making. Of course, more than one of these archetypal notions, or styles of creativity just mentioned, may become dominant in any human life, especially as one moves through different stages of life. The styles may also combine into hybrid patterns that form the prisms through which the *dynamis* of the creative instinct is experienced.

Transcending any given style is the opus of life itself, which can enfold and express any number of creative styles. The opus brings together body, soul, and spirit in a conjunction, which, according to Hillman, is held together by what the Greeks called *aisthesis*, a type of sense perception that also refers to "breathing in." *Aisthesis* is the "gasp" of our aesthetic perception and a type of sensitive and imaginal breathing that "sniffs out" images as they manifest out of imagination.

One does not need artistic talent to approach the world as an ever-changing aesthetic creation – a grand act of *poesis*. One does, however, need a good "nose" as "this approach to living psychologically reconnects us to the ancient meaning of psyche as a breath-soul of the head whose passages were the nostrils."[54]

Hillman called this mode of living the *via aesthetica*, the royal road toward a restoration of the significance of the senses in living creatively as images among images. This restoration begins by recognizing the aesthetic nature of the senses, which is simply their ability to sense significance through a type of close attention that is not far from devotion and prayer: "A significant life does not have to 'find meaning' because significance is given directly with reality; all things as images make sense."[55]

This approach to life underscores archetypal psychology's allegiance to each unique image – each "piece of imagination" – just as it presents itself without need of symbolic support or protracted searches for meaning. This calling toward aesthetic immediacy is echoed in the words of poet Mary Oliver who laid out three lessons for living a life: "Pay attention, Be astonished, Tell about it."[56] Her first lesson is an aesthetic move: being especially alert to what the senses perceive. Lesson two urges us not to move out of the experience too quickly but rather to dwell in astonishment. Lesson three invites us, regardless of artistic skill, to follow the lead of the artist toward *poesis*, toward a telling which is a making – this is precisely what Hillman meant by the act of image making, which is available to all:

> If we imagine ourselves engaged as artists in life, if we use artists as our models . . . then we would work with the daily mess in our lies as the material for psychological creativity. . . . I want to get far, far away from creative in the romantic sense. I mean having gratitude toward what one is given, for out of that one makes one's life, or to say it differently: you don't have to become creative because the psyche is already that; right in its mess there is creation going on. The artist fantasy of oneself accepts the mess, likes it, needs it.[57]

The "artist fantasy" allows everyone to enact the movements of the *bricoleur* who collages together bits of this and that without explicitly trying to be creative on the one hand and without being daunted by a perceived lack of creativity on the other.

The "artist fantasy" also returns us to artists themselves. Even with Hillman's expansive understandings of creativity, we are still left with artistry, "the artistic," and the questions of calling, duty, and destiny in the lives of those people whom we call "artists," "creators," and sometimes "geniuses." Alongside his democratization of creativity, Hillman was still enamored with creators; he marveled at the power of their work and at the inner seeds (the acorns and images) of their lives. Departing from Jung's mostly heroic view of "creative man," Hillman sketched out a more vulnerable and human version of those who hear persistent callings to make and create both through and beyond the *poesis* of one's own opus. Hillman's honest and challenging, yet generous and inspiring, portrait of the creative individual as the quintessential practitioner of *psychopoesis*, or soul-making, is bound up with his kaleidoscopic perspectives on the soul. These are the subjects of the next chapter.

Notes

1 See Dick Russell's *The Life and Ideas of James Hillman* for a thorough account of Hillman's early life, career in Zürich, and break with the C.G. Jung Institute.
2 Hillman, *A Terrible Love of War*, p. 149.
3 Hillman and Ventura, *We've Had a Hundred Years of Psychotherapy and the World Is Getting Worse*, p. 69.
4 Hillman, "Archetypal Psychology: A Brief Account," in *Archetypal Psychology*, pp. 13–14.
5 Ibid., p. 14.
6 See Chapter 5 for Hillman's kaleidoscopic descriptions of "soul," "psyche," and "anima."
7 Corbin, "Mundus Imaginalis: Or the Imaginary and the Imaginal," in *Spring* 1972, pp. 1–19.
8 Hillman, "Plotino, Ficino, and Vico," in *Loose Ends*, pp. 157–159.
9 Ibid., p. 155. Hillman also refers here to Jung's notion of *esse in anima*, or being-in-soul (*CW*6, paras. 66, 77), and the primacy of psychic images (*CW*11, para. 769).
10 Ibid., p. 157.
11 McEvilley, *The Shape of Ancient Thought: Comparative Studies in Greek and Indian Philosophies*, pp. 568–584.
12 Hillman, "Plotino, Ficino, and Vico," in *Loose Ends*, p. 150.
13 Ibid., p. 151.
14 Ibid., p. 153.
15 Ibid., p. 152.
16 Hillman, Foreword to Heraclitus *Fragments: The Collected Wisdom of Heraclitus*, p. xvi.
17 Heraclitus, Fragment 12 in *Fragments: The Collected Wisdom of Heraclitus*, p. 9.
18 Hillman, "Why 'Archetypal' Psychology?," in *Loose Ends*, p. 143.
19 Blake, *The Complete Prose and Poetry of William Blake*, p. 132.
20 Bachelard, *On Poetic Imagination and Reverie*, p. 19.
21 Ibid., p. 84.
22 Ibid., p. 104.
23 Barfield, *Poetic Diction: A Study in Meaning*, pp. 29, 41.
24 Jung, "Commentary" to Richard Wilhelm's translation of *The Secret of the Golden Flower: A Chinese Book of Life*, p. 130.
25 Jung, "Foreword to Suzuki's *Introduction to Zen Buddhism*," in *CW11*, p. 544, para. 889.
26 Hillman, *Inter Views: Conversations with Laura Pozzo on Psychotherapy, Biography, Love, Soul, Dreams, Work, Imagination, and the State of the Culture*, p. 32.
27 Jung, *Memories, Dreams, Reflections*, pp. 336–337.
28 Hillman, "Archetypal Psychology: A Brief Account," in *Archetypal Psychology*, p. 19.
29 Jung, "The Problem of Types in Classical and Medieval Thought," in *CW6*, p. 63, para. 93.
30 Williams, in Bram Dijkstra's *Cubism, Stieglitz, and the Early Poems of William Carlos Williams*, p. 73.
31 Belting, *Likeness and Presence: A History of the Image Before the Era of Art*, p. 6.
32 Psyche, imagination, and the "imaginal" should not be confused with the supernatural.

98 Archetypal Creativity

33 Slater, "From Jung to Hillman," in *Quadrant 2012*, pp. 15–37.
34 Hillman, "An Inquiry into Image," in *Spring 1977*, p. 69.
35 Ibid., p. 75.
36 See W.J.T. Mitchell, *What Do Pictures Want?*
37 Heywood and Sandywell, "Introduction: Critical Approaches to the Study of Visual Culture," in *The Handbook of Visual Culture*, p. 37.
38 Hillman, "An Inquiry into Image," in *Spring 1977*, p. 81.
39 Hillman, *Inter Views*, pp. 132–133, 144.
40 Hillman, "The Animal Kingdom," in *Animal Presences*, p. 51.
41 Hillman, "Amplification as Consecration (for Philip Zabrinskie: In Memoriam)," in *Quadrant*, p. 26.
42 Kunitz, *Wild Braid*, pp. 87–88.
43 See Chapter 5 for more on the autonomy of the image, and Hillman's claim that the work of soul-making is actually directed toward the individuation of the image (or "angel" after Corbin) and not the individual.
44 Hillman, "Ideas I See in Her Work," in *Margot McLean: Ritratti D'Artista*, p. 73.
45 Glück, *American Originality: Essays on Poetry*, p. 162.
46 Hillman, *Inter Views*, p. 116.
47 See Jung's "Psychological Factors Determining Human Behavior," in *CW8*, "On The Relation of Analytical Psychology to Poetry," and "Psychology and Literature," in *CW15*, along with his *Liber Novus/The Red Book* and *Memories, Dreams, Reflections*.
48 Hillman, *The Myth of Analysis*, p. 34.
49 Ibid., pp. 35–36.
50 Hillman, *Inter Views*, p. 61. See also Chapter 5 for similarities between "the opus" and Hillman's conception of "soul-making."
51 Hillman, *The Myth of Analysis*, p. 41.
52 Ibid., pp. 40–49 for Hillman's first six notions of creativity.
53 Ibid., p. 54. See also Chapter 5 for Hillman's closely related insights into the anima and Chapter 6 for more on the creative coupling of Psyche and Eros.
54 Hillman, "Image-Sense," in *Spring 1979*, pp. 142–143.
55 Ibid., p. 143.
56 Oliver, "Sometimes," in *Devotions: The Selected Poems of Mary Oliver*, p. 105. See also Chapter 7.
57 Hillman, *Inter Views*, p. 62.

References

Bachelard, Gaston. *On Poetic Imagination and Reverie*. 1971. Translated by Colette Gaudin. Putnam, CT: Spring Publications. 2005.

Barfield, Owen. *Poetic Diction: A Study in Meaning*. 1928. Middletown, CT: Wesleyan University Press. 1973.

Belting, Hans. *Likeness and Presence: A History of the Image Before the Era of Art*. Chicago, IL: University of Chicago Press. 1996.

Blake, William. *The Complete Poetry and Prose of William Blake*. 1982. Edited by David V. Erdman. Berkeley, CA: University of California Press. 2008.

Corbin, Henry. "Mundus Imaginalis: Or the Imaginary and the Imaginal." In *Spring: An Annual of Archetypal Psychology and Jungian Thought*. New York, NY: Spring Publications. 1972.

Dijkstra, Bram. *Cubism, Stieglitz, and the Early Poems of William Carlos Williams*. 1969. Princeton, NJ: Princeton University Press. 1978.

Glück, Louise. *American Originality: Essays on Poetry*. New York, NY: Farrar, Straus & Giroux. 2017.

Heraclitus. *Fragments: The Collected Wisdom of Heraclitus*. Translated by Brooks Haxton. New York, NY: Viking. 2001.

Heywood, Ian and Barry Sandywell, Eds. "Introduction: Critical Approaches to the Study of Visual Culture." In *The Handbook of Visual Culture*. London: Bloomsbury Academic. 2017.

Hillman, James. "An Inquiry into Image." In *Spring: An Annual of Archetypal Psychology and Jungian Thought*. Dallas, TX: Spring Publications. 1977.

Hillman, James. *The Myth of Analysis: Three Essays in Archetypal Psychology*. 1972. New York, NY: Harper Collins. 1978.

Hillman, James. "Image-Sense." In *Spring: An Annual of Archetypal Psychology and Jungian Thought*. Dallas, TX: Spring Publications. 1979.

Hillman, James. *Inter Views: Conversations with Laura Pozzo on Psychotherapy, Biography, Love, Soul, Dreams, Work, Imagination, and the State of the Culture*. New York, NY: Harper and Row. 1983.

Hillman, James. "Why Archetypal Psychology?" In *Loose Ends*. 1975. Dallas, TX: Spring Publications. 1986.

Hillman, James. "Foreword." In *Fragments: The Collected Wisdom of Heraclitus*. Edited by Heraclitus. Translated by Brooks Haxton. New York, NY: Viking. 2001.

Hillman, James. "Ideas I See in Her Work." In *Margot McLean: Ritratti D'Artista*. Bergamo, Italy: Moretti and Vitali Editori. 2002.

Hillman, James. "Archetypal Psychology: A Brief Account." In *Archetypal Psychology: Uniform Edition of the Writings of James Hillman*. Vol. 1. 1983. Putnam, CT: Spring Publications. 2004.

Hillman, James. *A Terrible Love of War*. 2004. New York, NY: Penguin Books. 2005.

Hillman, James. "Amplification as Consecration (for Philip Zabriskie: In Memoriam)." In *Quadrant: Journal of the C.G. Jung Foundation for Analytical Psychology*. Vol. 37:2. New York, NY: C.G. Jung Foundation. 2007.

Hillman, James. "The Animal Kingdom." In *Animal Presences: Uniform Edition of the Writings of James Hillman*. Vol. 9. Putnam, CT: Spring Publications. 2008.

Jung, Carl Gustav. "Foreword to Suzuki's *Introduction to Zen Buddhism*." 1939. In *Psychology and Religion: CW11*. Edited by Herbert Read, Michael Fordham, Gerhard Adler and William McGuire. Translated by R.F.C. Hull. Princeton, NJ: Princeton University Press. 1969.

Jung, Carl Gustav. "The Problem of Types in Classical and Medieval Thought." 1921. In *Psychological Types: CW6*. Edited by Herbert Read, Michael Fordham, Gerhard Adler and William McGuire. Translated by R.F.C. Hull. Princeton, NJ: Princeton University Press. 1971.

Jung, Carl Gustav. *Memories, Dreams, Reflections*. 1963. Edited by Aniela Jaffé. Translated by Richard and Clara Winston. New York, NY: Vintage Books. 1989.

Kunitz, Stanley and Genine Lentine. *The Wild Braid: A Poet Reflects on a Century in the Garden*. New York, NY: W.W. Norton & Company. 2005.

McEvilley, Thomas. *The Shape of Ancient Thought: Comparative Studies in Greek and Indian Philosophies*. New York, NY: Allworth Press. 2002.

Oliver, Mary. "Sometimes." In *Devotions: The Selected Poems of Mary Oliver*. New York, NY: Penguin Books. 2017.

Slater, Glen. "Between Jung and Hillman." In *Quadrant: Journal of the C.G. Jung Foundation for Analytical Psychology*. Vol. 42:2. New York, NY: C.G. Jung Foundation. 2012.

Chapter 5

Image Making and Soul-Making

The artist and the aesthetic soul

Speaking to a group of artists at the San Francisco Art Institute in 1988, James Hillman began with a provocative question:

> I want to ask all of you who paint and draw and model and sculpt whether soul ever enters your eye or mind or hand, and if it is not a consideration, a perspective in what you're doing, then what are you doing? Why do it? And how do you expect your works to be noticed by the great tradition stretching behind you and in front, or by the soul of the world in which we all live?[1]

Having successfully thrown down a dramatic "gauntlet on behalf of soul," Hillman moved on to a whirlwind tour of the nature of soul itself, along with the idea that some works of art may exhibit either soulfulness or soullessness. While not suggesting that a particular artist's body of work is *always* soulful or *always* soulless, he nonetheless argued that soul must be taken into account when considering the essential role of the arts in communal, political, and ecological life.[2]

Hillman's typed and handwritten notes for this presentation feature some of the primary themes of his life's work: soul, beauty, *aisthesis* or aesthetic wonder, and the image of the cosmos as an exquisitely ordered arrangement of ensouled beings constantly displaying themselves. He circled specific words such as cosmos, image, beauty, and ecology to remind himself to give them proper emphasis.[3]

Aided by a slideshow (including works by Matisse, Rothko, and Pollack) Hillman asked his audience of artists to "let images hit, absorb your eye as opening to soul" as he staked a claim for a type of neoromanticism that would

> restore the dignity and freedom of the image maker in the name of the liberty of the people against the rising tides . . . of commercialism, industrialism, and empire which were the enemies of the first Romantics as they are of us today.[4]

DOI: 10.4324/9780429057724-6

Hillman showed no hesitation in insisting that the contemporary artist has a duty to push back against these tides, for the artist possess the power to,

> open the eye of the human soul to see the soul in the world. To see the cosmos and to feel at home among its adornments, to celebrate and rejoice in existence, recalling the soul of the individual to its participation by means of imagination in its home in this world.[5]

Evoking Keats and Jung, Hillman went on to insist that if psyche is image and vice versa, then "psyche is basically an *image maker*, or an artist, or a poet [and that] *"making images is actually making soul."*[6] Hillman's unapologetically romantic idea of "soul as artist" might have felt deeply ennobling and inspiring to his audience, but possibly confusing as well. His proposition requires further clarification as it opens a host of new questions, such as: If soul is an artist, then is the artist the human exemplar of the soul? What exactly makes someone an artist, and are artists somehow different from everyone else? In response to these questions, this chapter will revolve around Hillman's conception of "soul-making" beginning with his insights into the nature of soul/anima/psyche itself. In addition, Hillman's notion of an "artist's fantasy," a soulful and creative life available to all, will be considered alongside his thoughts on human destiny and purpose, which point toward a unique personal calling or innate image that yearns for fulfillment in each human life.

The kaleidoscopic soul

Unlike any other twentieth-century thinker, James Hillman reintroduced the idea of "soul" back into serious discourse around every manner of human concern: from medicine to city planning, from economics to artmaking, from ecology to personal relationships, from architecture to neuroscience and beyond. Following Jung's own radical reintroduction of psyche/soul into modern thought, Hillman, in his own way, continued the mission of welcoming the soul back from a long exile on the outer fringes of modernity. Hillman challenged his fellow psychologists and analysts to confront the lack of soul in their own profession: Why had psyche been drained out of psychology (*psyche-logos*)? Where had it gone? These provocations were at the heart of Hillman's 1970's Dwight H. Terry Lecture Series at Yale, and at the heart of his groundbreaking book *Re-Visioning Psychology*.

Both the term "soul," and the more obscure "soul-making" are reimagined in this volume in ways that can still amaze, ennoble, humble, and confuse. Acknowledging his debt to Heraclitus regarding the vastness, depth, and mystery of the soul, Hillman built a kaleidoscopic image beginning with the notion that the soul is more a perspective rather than a substance and a "viewpoint toward things rather than a thing itself." This perspective acts as mediator between ourselves and everything that happens around us. In this central position, the soul can be envisioned as a mirror or as the moon "which mediates only borrowed light. But just this peculiar and paradoxical intervening gives one the sense of having or being a soul."[7]

While recognizing that every attempt at a clear definition is futile, Hillman suggested that the word "soul" might also be imagined as "that unknown component which makes meaning possible, turns events into experiences, is communicated in love, and has a religious concern." He then added three further modifications to this multifaceted portrait of the soul:

> First, "soul" refers to the deepening of events into experiences; second, the significance soul makes possible, whether in love or in religious concern, derives from its special relation with death. And third, by "soul" I mean the imaginative possibility in our natures, the experiencing through reflective speculation, dream, image and fantasy – that mode which recognizes all realities as primarily symbolic or metaphorical.[8]

In an earlier book, Hillman listed dozens of ways that the soul has been described and imagined throughout history. He argued that the oftentimes contradictory descriptions found in philosophy, theology, and science are each as valid as the next when these descriptions are understood as the soul's own collection of vantage points about itself: They are "statements about the soul, made the soul in the language of thought," as valid as the way that the soul "images itself in the contradictions and paradoxes in the language of poetry and painting."[9] Much in the way that archetypes are both thematic patterns *and* lenses through which we see and interact with the world, soul itself has a deep repertoire of ways of seeing itself with each stance or view being equal to the next.

Soul and spirit

Even while acknowledging that "soul" and "spirit" had been used interchangeably throughout history, Hillman drew a distinction between these terms – a distinction that is important when considering the soul's relationship to creativity and the call to create. In an early essay titled "Peaks and Vales," Hillman charted the steps that sent soul into exile in the West beginning with the Council of Nicea (787 BCE) and the Council of Constantinople (869 BCE). The ancient tripartite cosmos of body, soul, and spirit was flattened into a dualism of spirit (mind) and body (matter).[10] The later Cartesian split between living subject and dead object only widened the chasm hollowed out in the space of "in between" – the space where soul belongs.

While long being conflated, soul and spirit are not the same. Spirit, according to Hillman, has come to "be carried by the Apollonic archetype," associated with "sublimations of higher and abstract disciplines, the intellectual mind, refinements, and purifications." The world of spirit "blazes with light. . . . Its direction is vertical and ascending: it is arrow-straight, knife-sharp, power-dry, and phallic.

It is masculine, the active principle, making forms, order, and clear distinctions."[11] Soul, on the other hand, has more of an androgynous, or feminine flair, preferring shadows to brightness, moisture instead of dryness, and spiraling indirection rather than direct ascensions:

> Soul involves us in the pack and welter of phenomena and the flow of impressions. . . . Soul is vulnerable and suffers; it is passive and remembers. It is water to the spirit's fire. . . . *Soul is imagination*, a cavernous treasury. . . . Look up, says spirit, gain distance, there is something beyond and above, and what is above is always, and always superior. . . . Soul replies by saying, "Yes, this too has a place, may find it's archetypal significance, belongs in a myth." The cooking vessel of the soul takes in everything, everything can become soul, and by taking into its imagination any and all events, psychic space grows.[12]

The immanence of soul, so connected to the world, tempers the upward drive of spirit, so bound up with transcendence, and even escape. Spirit, however, reminds the soul of those realms beyond knowing. "The job," according to Hillman, "is to keep spirit and soul distinct (the spirit's demand) and to keep them attached (the demand of the soul)."[13] And while long demoted to a place lesser than both spirit and soul, body is the necessary vessel where both spirit and soul intermingle. From an archetypal perspective, "body" does not begin with or stop at the human body; thus offering a much larger and more porous vessel for the play of spirit and soul.

Anima mundi

Hillman's kaleidoscopic imagining of soul went beyond the human and revived an ancient idea of an animated or ensouled world: the *anima mundi*. In this conception, all things may exhibit soul including everything that falls within the category of "nature," such as animals and plants, and even those things thought for so long to be inanimate, such as stones, mountains, and rivers. The archetypal eye goes even further to see soul, with its sufferings, follies, triumphs, and joys, in human-made objects and environments, such as furniture, houses, roads, and entire cities – everything that exists partakes of soul.[14]

Hillman was adamant that soul is not something that we project upon the things of the world. Rather, the things of the world display and announce themselves, offering a soul spark of the *anima mundi* through their unique images. He was quick to point out that what psychology calls "projection," is "simply animation as this thing or that spontaneously comes alive, arrests our attention, draws us to it. . . . The soul of the thing corresponds or coalesces with ours."[15]

Taken seriously, the notion of an ensouled world helps to explain why so many creators maintain personal fixations with some animals, objects, and places in the world. A single painting of a bird, for example, may grow into a multi-year series,

Soul as symbol and prism

The multiplicity and mystery of the soul led Hillman to one of his most insightful portrayals: soul not as concept but as *symbol*. Like the symbol, "*the soul is a deliberately ambiguous concept resisting all definition,*" in the same way that other "root metaphors" such as "matter," "nature," "energy," "justice," and "life" resist fixed definitions while maintaining a sense of meaning, reality, and power.[16] Hillman insisted that like all symbols, "soul," is not under our control and cannot be used without ambiguity. Further, he considered soul to be no more an obfuscation than any other axiomatic first principle. While psyche can be seen as a "concomitant to physical life," soul has "metaphysical and romantic overtones. It shares frontiers with religion."[17]

Hillman purposely used the terms "soul," "psyche," and "anima" interchangeably in his writings depending upon the inflection he wanted to achieve; he also restated and repositioned his core portrayals of the soul throughout his writings and public talks depending upon the urgings of the moment. In this way he enacted the work of soul itself by becoming a mediating "mirror" of shifting vantage points for soul to see itself and say something about itself. While not an artist in the manner of Jung, Hillman's emphasis on the soul as mediator/mediatrix – along with his personal enactment of enlivened mediation – aligns him with the work of the artist and all those who share a shamanic sensibility for working "in the middle."

As described in the previous chapter, archetypal psychology owes a great deal to Henry Corbin and to his interpretation of a *mundus imaginalis* inspired by his decades of immersion in Islamic spiritual thought. According to Corbin, the *mundus imaginalis*, or imaginal world, exists precisely in the middle between the sensible world and the world of spirit. In this tripartite model, the sensible, visible world is perceived through the senses, the intermediate world of soul through the imagination, and the third world of spirit through a visionary type of intellect. Roberts Avens, one of archetypal psychology's most expansive thinkers, described the *mundus imaginalis* or "middle ground" of the soul as acting as an intermediary between worlds of body and spirit, yet always involved in both:

> The soul does not exist in separation from what she does, including her spiritual and material configurations. Neither is she a conglomeration of spirit and matter. The soul *is* precisely, absolutely, unreservedly in the middle. *That* is the *mysterium tremendum et fascinans*: the soul, that strictly *is* not, endows all else with being and meaning.[18]

Imagining a middle realm, or place that is "no-place," is an evocative window into soul and imagination. Yet another is through personification. Like both Jung and Hillman, Avens personified the soul by using the feminine pronoun "she." More clearly than either "psyche" or "soul," the term "anima" *animates* the middle ground as not only "place" but also "person."

Anima and the artist

Hillman's use of "anima" reflects Corbin's influence along with Jung's resurrection of the idea of *esse in anima*, a "being in soul," as a psychological reality occupying the third and central position between *esse in intellectu* (being in spirit) and *esse in re* (being in matter).[19] Anima, as another one of soul's faces, so captivated Hillman that he referred to this figure as his own personal "root metaphor" and as a component that had dominated his thoughts, colored his particular style of being, and "graciously proffered themes" for his attention over many years and many writings, including an entire book contrasting Jung's portrayals of the anima to his own imaginings.[20]

In that book, Hillman demonstrated how Jung's many writings on anima reveal a multifaceted personification who bridges worlds and acts as "a function of relationship to the unconscious."[21] Like Jung, Hillman would oftentimes use feminine pronouns when referring to the anima, although he made it clear that both anima and animus could express themselves in anyone regardless of gender. As we have seen in an earlier chapter, Jung chided an anima figure for suggesting that he was an artist, while Hillman's depictions of the anima closely parallel his depictions of artist themselves. Two of these are particularly valuable to contemporary creators: anima as mediatrix (mediator and guide) and the anima/animus union as a syzygy, or dynamic, hermaphroditic communion or *coniunctio* of polarities.

Anima as mediatrix and *psychopomp* of souls may first bring to mind a benevolent figure acting as a bridge for unconscious contents to cross over into consciousness. Hillman's emphasis, however, is on the opposite journey into unconsciousness mediated by an anima that is mercurial and moody, autonomous and willful:

> Let us not imagine anima bridging and mediating inward only as a sibylline benefactrice, teaching us about all the things we do not know. . . . There is another direction to her movement. . . . for across her bridge roll fantasies, projections, emotions that make a person's consciousness unconscious and collective. . . . As mediatrix to the eternally unknowable she is the bridge both over the river into the trees and into the sludge and quicksand, making the known ever more unknown. . . . By leading whatever is known from off its solid footing, she carries every question into deeper waters, which is also a way of soul-making.

This notion of anima parallels the long-held notions of creative individuals as naturally ambiguous, prone to shifts in moods, irresponsible, difficult to understand (like the ancient oracle and muse who made sense by speaking nonsense), and easily lured into long periods of reflection somewhere outside of, or beneath, full consciousness. Both anima and artist do not bring answers to practical problems, they bring what Hillman called "image answers,"[22] which retain their mystery as they stir a sense of *amor fati* – a love of one's own unknowable fate that performs a double duty of luring us onto the bridge and onto more imaginative quests while entangling us in the world.

So far, we have considered the anima as a singular figure, but one final imagining considers anima to be, much like the artist, a quintessential conjunction of opposites – what Jung called a divine pair or syzygy. Hillman concluded his book on the anima by recognizing that his own writing on the subject was a "mythical activity of anima coming on as a critical activity of animus" – an interpenetration of psyche and logos.[23] Mythical thinking, according to Hillman, connects pairs and couples into tandems rather than dividing them into opposites. The notion of syzygy emphasizes a blending, such as in the mythic union of Aphrodite and Hermes that gave birth to the child Hermaphroditos: "To consider every position in terms of the syzygy reflects a 'hermaphroditic' consciousness in which the One and the Other are co-present, a priori, at all times, a hermetic duplicity and Aphroditic coupling going on in every event."[24] Artists are perfect exemplars of this type of psyche–logos blending, as they must become the bridge that hosts each member of the tandem pairing of unconscious inspiration and conscious crafting – a duo that Stanley Kunitz called "incantation and sense."[25]

While dualities are essential to the idea of syzygy, the primarily gendered polarities are limiting to many contemporary creators. Along with imagining the creator as a bridge between two shores, imagining the creator as an intersection or as a crossroads allows for a multiplicity of influences beyond dualities (yin and yang, sol and luna, king and queen, anima and animus). Multiple archetypal energies and personifications (many gods) may congregate from any number of directions for the same result: moments of creation in time achieved with and through a human vessel. This reimaging beyond opposites retains the essence of the magic that occurs "in the middle" while expanding the playing field for contemporary creators who are weary of binaries presented as fact.[26]

Artists, *angelos*, and anxiety

What is an artist, anyway? It's not difficult to imagine Hillman throwing out this question during one of his provocative lectures. If we take Jung seriously (as Hillman did) and agree that creativity is akin to an instinct, then creators, like everyone else, participate first and foremost in the creative opus of their own human lives. As described in the previous chapter, Hillman called for a separation of creativity from artistry as the first step toward understanding two things: 1) That there is not a single type of creativity, rather, there are many *creativities* powered by different archetypal styles; and 2) that these styles of creativity are universal potentials and not solely expressed by those among us called artists. However, these distinctions do not diminish the artist/creator – on the contrary, Hillman suggested that living by means of the "artist fantasy" could bring anyone into a deeper relationship with psychic creativity. We look to artists to see this fantasy played out into life.[27]

Hillman's "artist fantasy" fleshes out a vibrant, multidimensional – yet quite human – picture of those called to create. As part of his separation of creativity from artistry, Hillman sought to untangle our common understanding of the artist with the image of the so-called creative genius. The makings of a "genius" include any number of factors that come together in the right way at the right time, such as a talent that is noticed and nourished; a particular historic, geographic, and cultural setting; opportunities for apprenticeship, mentorship, and exposure; and dedication to one's work. Added to these factors is the possibility of a "more direct and uncomplicated relation" to the creative instinct shared by all. Hillman argued that even with this enhanced relationship, artists and those who live "largely in terms of the creative instinct" should not be separated out from common humanity through the limiting notion of "genius."[28]

Hillman noted how creators such as Eliot, Mann, Freud, and Matisse insisted upon their unexceptional regularity – their human normality – even when lauded as geniuses. Notable creators in our own time, such as poet Ursula K. Le Guin, have also eschewed the label of "creative genius," insisting instead upon their everyday humanness. Le Guin was as devoted to mothering, housekeeping, and cooking as she was to her writing.[29] Her balance of devotions offers a more accurate portrait of an artist, without the burdens of being a genius nor the banishment from one's human community.

For Hillman, living in close relation to the creative instinct entails being particularly open to what Jung called "non directed," imaginative, or fantasy thinking. In collaboration with artist Margot McLean, he explored this openness as a sense of permeability, further distancing the artist from the notion of genius:

> The composer, the painter, the writer are not special human exceptions. They are the subtle, more vulnerable examples – not of "weak ego," but of the essential nature of the human mind, that it is membranous, osmotic, susceptible, suggestible, seducible, seditious, hysterical.[30]

Enhanced subtleness and vulnerability allow creators to come into relationship with images – those "pieces of imagination" that continually search for places of manifestation.[31] A willingness to become a transparent meeting ground for images exposes artists to the vast range of life's themes (from the glorious to the horrifying) beyond what many people would find attractive or even endurable. Reflecting on these same themes of vulnerability and openness, Kunitz suggested that each of us is a "very sensitive keyboard" and that artists display a further heightening of receptivity and susceptibility.[32]

108   Image Making and Soul-Making

These related metaphors of "unprotectedness" align the artist with one of Hillman's perspectives on the nature of the soul: that it has a special closeness to mortality and death, to ancestors and to the dead. Not "walled off" in the land of the living, with its denial of uncertainty, mystery, and death, the artist is a *psychopomp* who is able to move between the upper world and the underworld. Unprotected, yet undaunted, the artist is the "emissary of the strange, the alien. The artist is the *angelos* of anxiety"[33]

Hillman may have had the Romantic poets in mind when coining the phrase, "angelos of anxiety." The permeability that he and McLean explored is reminiscent of the idea of "negative capability" put forth by Keats. Writing to his siblings, Keats described this attribute displayed by great artists (particularly Shakespeare) as a manner of "being in uncertainties, Mystery, doubt, without any irritable reaching for fact and reason."[34] Negative capability is also quite similar to Jung's theory of the transcendent or symbolizing function, the holding of the tension between opposites that allows for something new to emerge in the middle.

If, as Hillman suggested, artists are not special human exceptions, but in fact simply more vulnerable, susceptible, and porous human beings (*angelos* of anxiety), then questions still remain about how they do their work: What allows them to risk a heightened level of openness – how do they shift into what Keats called "negative capability"? How do they manage to survive their encounters with what Jung called the unconscious, what Hillman called the imagination *and* the world of the dead, and what other cultures have called the spirit world?

One answer to all these questions may be found through the writings of Roberts Avens, who compared creative individuals to visionaries and dreamers "not because they are prone to reveries or capricious and erratic fancy, but precisely because they do not lose themselves in the act of vision." This type of vision requires the maintenance of ordinary consciousness even in the midst of extraordinary experiences. Avens suggested that this ability is "analogous to dreaming with one part of ourselves and at the same time knowing with another part that we are dreaming."[35] In this model, there is not so much a shift into the receptive and patient state of negative capability but a more or less constant nimble balancing between *and in* both consciousness and the unconscious.

In a similar manner, Henry Corbin described a type of dual vision where a sensitive seeing through "eyes of fire" is contrasted with the more practical vision made possible by "eyes of flesh." The latter see the world as densely material, focusing on details and relationships between objects, people, and situations, but they do not generally perceive beyond that. "Eyes of fire," however, see the things of the world as "outer signs of inner facts," where nothing is "lonely matter," and where everything is "caught up in a mysterious, ultimately divine whole." While Corbin elevated "eyes of fire" beyond "eyes of flesh," both ways of seeing come together in what art historian Roger Lipsey called "eyes of art."[36] Here, just as with Avens's description, the creative individual's "eyes of art" balance conscious and meticulous crafting of matter (eyes of flesh), with a constant attunement to those epiphanic moments that reveal what lies beyond the material (eyes of fire).

Image Making and Soul-Making   109

This brings us back once again to a shamanic sensibility seen in healers, prophets, and creators who sacrifice enough of their personal control and defenses in order to meld with, and move through, more than one world at a time – to dream with eyes open. This ability carries more than personal importance since the shamanic sensibility entails a call to service. Hillman recognized this in his consideration of the artist as engaged citizen:

> If art moves out, then why not the artist too? Why not imagine the artist first of all as a citizen, a member of the polis, whose life, as with any other citizen is partly in service to the polis? We would no longer regard the artist as the most independent of all persons, but rather as the one most involved, most engaged in the meeting the needs of the soul and therefore most caught himself and herself in the issues of community.[37]

Far from the image of the artist as a special type of outsider, Hillman's image of the artist is that of a devoted *insider*; one who wholeheartedly participates in the mess of everyday life – the place where soul is made. Kunitz underscored the fact that this participation is not a strictly personal endeavor but one with potential communal benefit:

> Art must have a social sense, a sense of the society in which we live and thrash. As an artist, you are a representative human being – you have to believe that in order to give your life over to that effort to create something of value. You're not doing it only to satisfy your own impulses or needs, there is a social imperative.[38]

Devotion to one's art as an act of devotion to the world in which we all "live and thrash" is at the heart of the "artist fantasy," a way of life that is modeled with clarity by the artist. If, as both Jung and Hillman stated, an instinctual creativity impels devotion to one's life regardless of artistic talent, then what we see in artists is a heightened sense of openness and risk taking related to a dual calling – the call of life itself and the call to create. These types of heightened sensibilities beg two deeper questions: If all are called into the creative making of their own lives, then what is involved in the more specific call to create – the call that is answered through *poesis*, the making of songs, dances, paintings, films, plays, poetry, sculpture, novels, rituals, ceremonies, and more? And the perennial question underlying creativity and artistry: Are artists born or are they made?

The artist in the acorn: the call to create

Hillman addressed these questions with his work on calling, character, and destiny in his most commercially successful publication: *The Soul's Code: In Search of Character and Calling*. Of the dozens of well-known people profiled in this book, the majority are creators, such as Ingmar Bergman, Judy Garland, Pablo

Picasso, Bette Davis, Yehudi Menuhin, Josephine Baker, and Jackson Pollock. Hillman was clear that his aim was not to elevate the lives of these already famous individuals above our own. On the contrary, Hillman found that by examining these seemingly extraordinary lives for evidence of an inner calling, we too could more easily examine our own lives for traces of destiny and calling – even though those traces might not show themselves with the same vivid clarity. The unfolding of each individual's inner image over time mirrors the same process seen in nature – a process that Hillman called the "acorn theory."

The acorn theory proposes that just like the oak tree that is given and embedded within each acorn, so too are our callings, our inner images: They are given and embedded within us before they can be lived. The acorn theory does not deny the importance of genetic inheritance combined with environmental factors on the unfolding of a life, although it insists that a third factor exists – a factor that at various times has been called fate, destiny, calling, and image. Hillman's acorn theory questions our understandings of the nature of time, since the innate image exists in the past, present, and the future simultaneously – the image reveals itself, but *it does not develop*, it is complete at all times.[39]

In building his acorn theory, Hillman looked back to the "Myth of Er" found in the last pages of Plato's *Republic*. In this tale, the soul selects the human life that will host its image and is accompanied into life by a daimon, a guardian spirit, who remembers the soul's image. Plato's emphasis was on the importance of choosing wisely to live a life that is meaningful, compassionate, wise, and just. Setting aside the ultimately unanswerable question of whether the soul is eternal, along with questions surrounding the meaning of life itself, Hillman's acorn theory focuses on the *very real* feelings of purpose felt by all human beings at various times and to various degrees. These feelings encourage us to believe that there is a reason for our existence, that there are things that we must attend to beyond the daily round of life, that the world somehow requires our unique presence, and that we are "answerable to an innate image," which we animate and actualize day by day.[40]

The biographies of artists add support to Hillman's theory; they so often clearly reveal a third determining principle (a calling or image) that is even more important to an artist's life (or any human life) than the contributions of the nature–nurture pairing: nature (our genetic inheritance) and nurture (the helpful and/or harmful conditions of our lives). Hillman found confirmation for this third principle in the lives and writings of Pablo Picasso and Wallace Stevens; these two creators somehow understood that they themselves were acts of imagination, or images – not developing, but unfolding into history:

> In a poem called "The Plain Sense of Things," Stevens says we can't get beyond imagination: "the absence of the imagination had/Itself to be imagined." So your life is the ongoing operation of imagination; you imagine yourself into existence, or let's say, an image is continuing to shape itself into the oak tree you consider your reality.[41]

Artists' lives offer an illuminating window into the many ways in which the image/calling may announce itself – there is no "one size fits all" to any calling, especially a creative calling. Sometimes the call to create can be seen in early childhood as an obsession with the tools of a particular art form, or conversely, with an initial aversion to the craft that would eventually come to define the mature artist. The childhoods of creators oftentimes do reveal early signals, and occasional unmistakable annunciations, of an innate image as it begins to seek fulfillment. This is not always the case, however, and an overreliance on identifying flashes of "the artist" in childhood can dampen the response to one's calling when that calling is only heard and witnessed with clarity later in life.

Western culture's worshipful fascination with youth has come to diminish the so-called late bloomer, yet the lives of creators such as sculptor Louise Nevelson (who began her distinctive assemblage work only in her fifties) and poet Sharon Olds (who did not write seriously until she was in her late thirties) show the patience and persistence of the innate image, even against difficult odds. It is critical to remember, however, that while the innate image is persistent, it is not omnipotent. The image must work with conditions and situations in the world that are beyond its control. Just as we witness in nature, not every acorn will flourish, and as Olds stated regarding her own life as a creator, "Anyone who blooms at all, ever, is very lucky."[42]

Luck cannot be underestimated in returning to the question of whether artists are born or whether they are made. If, as Hillman insists, we are all born with an innate image, calling, and sense of purpose, then the artist is given in the acorn. But this is not enough, as an artist must also be "made," as the innate image requires actualization and animation. Chance, both lucky and unlucky, plays as large a role as anything in determining whether an image will be individuated, just as in nature, conditions and circumstances matter. What matters too is the courage that allows an individual to overcome the ego's fear of yielding to the image, which Hillman alternatively described as soul, daimon, genius, and angel: "A calling may be postponed, avoided, intermittently missed. It may also possess you completely. . . . It makes its claim. The daimon does not go away."[43]

Realizing that the daimon's desires supersede our own upends our blind and faulty allegiance to human will and control: "The job of life becomes one of making its moments accord with the image, or what might once have been called 'being guided by your genius,' or daimon or angel."[44] This is the job of soul-making as image making or image making as soul-making – a job that artists have described in various ways, including Kunitz's stirring example of being guided by what he called the "Dark Angel":

> The Dark Angel doesn't bring death with him. He brings with him an aura, an intuition. And his contact with you . . . is an overbearing weight, you're being smothered. At the same time it's like a cloud passing over you that you engage, and it's combined with exhilaration. You meet your destiny, and there is a sense of being given power at the same time. . . . It's a transcendent visit,

112   Image Making and Soul-Making

a universal phenomenon, one of those deep images, and that's what makes it so overwhelming.[45]

Kunitz not only solidifies Hillman's arguments about the desires and demands of the daimon, but his words bear an uncanny resemblance to Jung's account about being driven through his life by the daimon of creativity – not to mention Plato's writings on the *daimonion* who guided Socrates.[46] This is not to suggest that Kunitz was directly influenced by either Hillman or Jung's writings. What it does suggest, however, is the very real affinity between creators and depth psychological thinkers when it comes to the idea of a daimon, image, genius, or angel that is wholly "other" and at the same time deeply invested in a particular creative individual. Martha Graham provided yet another striking description of what it feels like to realize the demands of an innate image – demands that superseded her own:

> There is a vitality, a life force, an energy, a quickening that is translated through you into action, and because there is only one of you in all of time, this expression is unique. And if you block it, it will never exist through any other medium and it will be lost. . . . It is your business to keep it yours clearly and directly, to keep the channel open. . . . No artist is pleased. . . . There is only a queer divine dissatisfaction, a blessed unrest that makes us more alive than the others.[47]

Like Jung, Graham sets the artist apart from others. Hillman's work, on the other hand, invites all into the "artist fantasy" as a means of soul-making.[48]

Soul-making and the soul as maker

The "artist fantasy" that accepts, works with, and ultimately *requires* the daily mess of our lives is analogous to what Hillman called "soul-making," a phrase that originated with Keats:

> The common cognomen of this world among the misguided and superstitious is a "vale of tears" from which we are to be redeemed by a certain arbitrary interposition of God and taken to Heaven – What a little circumscribed straightened notion! Call the world if you please "The vale of Soul-making" Then you will find out the use of the world . . . soul as distinguished from an Intelligence – there may be intelligences or sparks of divinity in millions – but they are not /souls till they acquire identities, till each one is personally itself.[49]

For Keats, as well as for Hillman, the soul requires a comprehensive range of worldly experience for its actualization – including those types of experiences that would lead those whom Keats referred to as the "misguided" to simply consider the world a "vale of tears" from which rescue is sought. These same experiences take on an entirely different meaning, and a profound sense of value, when the world is considered a place of soul-making.

Hillman expanded upon Keats's insights into the lifelong opus of patient, and oftentimes difficult, individuation of the soul/image by emphasizing that it is not we who craft the soul – on the contrary, it is we who are constantly *being crafted by* the soul as the soul crafts itself. It is worth quoting Hillman at length on this critical idea:

> The act of soul-making is imagining, since images are the psyche, its stuff, and its perspective. Crafting images . . . is thus an equivalent to soul-making. This crafting can take place in the concrete modes of the artisan, a work of the hands, and with the morality of the hands. And, it can take place in sophisticated elaborations of reflection, religion, relationships, social action, so long as these activities are imagined from the perspective of soul, soul as the uppermost concern. In other words, only when imagination is recognized as an engagement at the borders of the human and a work in relation with mythic dominants can this articulation of images be considered a psycho-poesis or soul-making. Its intention is the realization of the images – for they are the psyche – and not merely of the human subject. As Corbin has said: "It is their individuation, not ours," suggesting that soul-making can be most succinctly defined as the individuation of the imaginal reality.[50]

As we have seen, Hillman and Corbin were not alone in advocating for the soul's autonomy and the primacy of the soul's own desires. This decentering of the human subject recognizes the soul as the central actor; this positioning is evident in Plato and Plotinus, Ficino and Vico, in the Romantic poets such as Keats, the Islamic mystics important to Corbin, and in Christian mystics such as Meister Eckhart, who grouped human beings among all creatures, or images, through which the soul lives and thereby comes to know itself:

> For whenever the powers of the soul make contact with a creature, they set to work and make an image and likeness of the creature, which they absorb. . . . the soul never approaches a creature without having first voluntarily taken an image of it into herself. . . . Whether it is a stone, a horse, a man, or anything else that she wants to know, she gets out the image of it that she has already taken in, and is thus enabled to unite herself with it.[51]

Eckhart's thirteenth-century description of the imagining activity of the soul is another branch of the ancestral root system of thought that informed both Jung's proclamation that image is psyche, and Hillman's depiction of the soul as a mirror, a prism, and especially as an artist who delights in enlivening individual human beings and all manner of worldly creatures and objects.

The enlivening work of *psychopoesis*, or soul-making, entails a sense of relationship and imagines, "the opus of the soul as a work that is like a craft, [with] the models for it [coming] from the arts."[52] The soul and human pairing of this opus is reflected in the daily rituals of the artist, even with the inevitable lost hours that feel like wasted time:

> Work is a ritual, and part of the ritual is waste, repetition, boredom, the sense of this-is-a-whole-morning-wasted. . . . Those senses of inferiority, of waste, of being blocked, of being unable . . . are tremendously important. . . . Maybe the psyche needs to stay longer where it is, in the dark, or as a lump.[53]

Eventually, the interplay of feelings of inferiority and yearnings for perfection yield concrete results: The "lump" becomes an artwork, a creation which introspective creators from every culture have long declined to describe as totally their own. Instead, many have insisted that their role is one of willing servant, or partner at best, with mysterious forces beyond their control – forces that offer inspiration or even fully formed ideas that still must be made manifest in the world by the human partner. There is an exchange of gifts between the soul and the human maker, an exchange that Lewis Hyde has articulated with passion and precision:

> Out of what the soul has offered him, the poet makes the work. And in this interior commerce the finished work is a return gift, carried back into the soul. . . . The artist makes a soul, makes it real, in the commerce of gifts. As when the Roman sacrifices to his *genius* on his birthday so that it may grow and become free spirit . . . the point of the commerce is a spiritual increase and eventual actualization of the soul.[54]

Hyde offers yet another aspect of the "artist's fantasy": the recognition that the actualization of the genius/image/angel/soul requires sacrifices. The first sacrifice is to dehumanize (to take the human out of the center) and to reimagine that our personalities – and our lives themselves – as not totally our own but rather as shared with a soul. To personify the soul envisions this entity as a person with claims that supersede our own. We can go further (as Hillman did and as artists have always done) to consider the possibility that we are "psychic vessels" and carriers of soul: "Not I personify, but the anima personifies me, or soul-makes herself through me."[55] Or as D.H. Lawrence knew: "Not I, not I, but the wind that blows through me."

Art, pathologizing, and the shamanic soul

Lawrence's poem, "Song of a Man Who Has Come Through," describes those moments when the artist must find the courage to yield and be "borrowed" by a superior power, what Lawrence called a "fine, fine wind" that takes its course through "the chaos of the world." He envisioned himself as the eager blade of an axe ready to be driven by an unknown hand and as a fountain or wellhead ready to unselfishly issue forth those wonders that bubble into his soul.[56]

Sacrificing the ego's heroic notions of control is essential to artmaking. Sometimes the sacrifice is made consciously and with intention, but more frequently, the sacrifice comes as part of a struggle with loss, melancholy, failure, illness, and all other manner of afflictions. An archetypal orientation to soul recognizes this process as natural and necessary since the soul "pathologizes" as it seeks experiences of every kind. By pathologizing, Hillman meant the psyche's autonomous ability to create a sense of suffering in "any aspect of its behavior and to experience and imagine life through this deformed and afflicted perspective."[57] Again, it is the creative individual who provides the most striking example of this work of the soul:

> The soul sees by means of affliction. . . . The crazy artist, the daft poet, and mad professor are neither romantic clichés nor antibourgeois postures. They are metaphors for the intimate relation between pathologizing and imagination. Pathologizing processes are a source of imaginative work, and the work provides a container for the pathologizing processes. . . . The wound and the eye are one and the same.[58]

Insight through woundedness is one of the hallmarks of the shaman and a key component of a shamanic sensibility that is so often displayed by artists who endure and are continually remade by their "creative illnesses."[59] Seeing by means of the wound is a sympathetic vision that penetrates through divisions of "I" and "other." Not driven by will, but by surrender, artists come to know themselves as devotees of imagination and as *psychopomps*, guides of soul.

Through their lives and work, artists offer us frequent and potent reminders that connecting to the "spontaneous images of the psyche is essential for the ailing world as well as for the individual."[60] All image-work – not only artmaking, but also dreamwork and the soul work done in therapeutic settings – invites a reorientation of self to world and self to soul. When undertaken by artists and non-artists alike, this service to imagination has the power to connect us to sources of wisdom, compassion, and healing as it connects us to each other and to the *anima mundi*.

Of course, the art that is made (regardless of whether it is considered professional) is evidence of this service. Hillman went so far as to attribute a sense of autonomy and mission to the art object/art experience itself: "Art intends to restore the fallen world. It has a program – a program, however, that does not stem from the will of the artist, but emerges from the image as the image develops in the artist's service to it."[61] Poet Edward Hirsch paralleled Hillman's thoughts about an artwork's autonomy and intention when he proposed that works of art possess the power to generate new acts of creativity: "Works of art initiate and provoke other works of art, the process is a source of art itself."[62]

These are astounding declarations that challenge our rational sensibilities: The image itself wants to be made known, and the resulting artworks or experiences are themselves provocateurs of art yet to come. Powered by "the image," an autonomous force with intention, those things that we call "art" may also be described as emissaries of imagination and as faces of the soul.[63]

Having intentionally aligned itself from the start with the arts and humanities, archetypal psychology, with its emphasis on a "poetic basis of mind," is itself "archetypal" in Hillman's own definition: It never ceases to yield layer after layer of value and insight, especially for those called to create. Its mode of moving through the world is *poesis*, the never-ending dance of making, unmaking, and making again that creators perform each day – thus artists are its best models. With its bold advocacy for image-makers of all kinds, archetypal psychology returns great gifts to the creators who inspired its own emergence. If, as Hillman insisted, "we are lived by powers we pretend to understand," then our task is one of relationship and not understanding.[64] These powers are images or souls, and artists, as initiates of imagination, continue to be our guides for the making of soul.

Notes

1 Hillman, "The Art of the Soul," in *Philosophical Intimations*, p. 338.
2 Ibid.
3 Hillman's personal notes for this talk are housed at OPUS Archives on the campus of Pacifica Graduate Institute, Carpinteria, CA.
4 Ibid. from Hillman's personal notes and from "The Art of Soul," in *Philosophical Intimations*, p. 341.
5 Ibid., p. 343.
6 Ibid., p. 339.
7 Hillman, *Re-Visioning Psychology*, p. xvi. See also Chapter 1 for Philip Wheelwright's complimentary perspectives on the complex nature of the Heraclitian soul.
8 Ibid., p. xvi.
9 Hillman, *Suicide and the Soul*, pp. 45–46.
10 Hillman, "Peaks and Vales," in *Spring 1979*, p. 54.
11 Hillman, *Re-Visioning Psychology*, p. 68.
12 Ibid., pp. 68–69.
13 Hillman, *Anima: A Personified Notion*, p. 183.
14 See Chapters 4 and 7 for more on the nature of the soul as related to the type of art that we call "commercial" as opposed to "fine," as both contribute to the soul of the world.
15 Hillman, *The Thought of the Heart and the Soul of the World*, pp. 101–102.
16 Hillman, "Peaks and Vales," in *Spring 1979*, p. 46.
17 Hillman, *Suicide and Soul*, pp. 46–47.
18 Avens, *Imagination is Reality: Western Nirvana in Jung, Hillman, Barfield & Cassirer*, p. 8.
19 See Chapter 2 for a review of Jung's various descriptions of the soul and ensoulment including the notion of *esse in anima*. See also Hillman's "Peaks and Vales," in *Spring 1979*, p. 56.
20 Hillman, *Anima: A Personified Notion*, p. ix.
21 Jung, qtd. in Hillman, *Anima: A Personified Notion*, p. 128.
22 Hillman, *Anima: A Personified Notion*, p. 139.
23 Ibid., p. 171.

24 See Chapter 6 for more on Hermaphroditos and the hermaphroditic sensibility.
25 Kunitz, "Table Talk: A Paris Review Interview with Chris Busa," qtd. in Brown, Finch and Kumin, *Lofty Dogmas: Poets on Poetics*, p. 208.
26 See Chapter 7 for more on the idea of the artist as a crossroads and a place of transformation.
27 See Chapter 4.
28 Hillman, *Myth of Analysis*, p. 39.
29 Phillips, "The Subversive Imagination of Ursula K. Le Guin," in *The New Yorker*.
30 Hillman and McLean, "Permeability," in *ARAS: Art & Psyche Online Journal*, p. 4.
31 See Chapter 4 for Glen Slater's description of an image as a piece of imagination.
32 Kunitz and Lentine, *The Wild Braid: A Poet Reflects on a Century in the Garden*, p. 64. See also Chapter 7 for parallel thoughts on the "sensitive keyboard" and "radio receiver" by Leroy Little Bear and John Lennon.
33 Hillman and Mclean, "Permeability," p. 21.
34 Keats, "Letter to George and Tom Keats, Dec. 1817," in *John Keats: Selected Letters*, pp. 77–80.
35 Avens, *Imagination Is Reality*, p. 22.
36 Lipsey, *An Art of Our Own: The Spiritual in Twentieth Century Art*, pp. 17–18.
37 Hillman, Notes for a lecture titled "Soul and Beauty in Today's Urban World," at Konan University, Kobe, Japan, 1991. OPUS Archives.
38 Kunitz and Lentine, *The Wild Braid*, p. 103. See also Chapter 7 where Kunitz's insights are brought into conversation with Franz Kafka.
39 See Hillman's *The Soul's Code: In Search of Character and Calling*, pp. 6–7 for his explanation of the timelessness of the innate image or calling.
40 Hillman, *The Soul's Code: In Search of Character and Calling*, p. 4.
41 Hillman and Ventura, *We've Had a Hundred Years of Psychotherapy and the World Is Getting Worse*, p. 63.
42 Olds, qtd. in Keillor, *Good Poems, American Places*, p. 470.
43 Hillman, *The Soul's Code: In Search of Character and Calling*, p. 8.
44 Hillman and Ventura, *Hundred Years*, p. 64.
45 Kunitz, *Wild Braid*, pp. 128–129.
46 See Chapter 2 for Jung's accounts of his creative daimon compared to Plato's writings on the *daimonion* associated with Socrates.
47 Graham, in Agnes De Mille's *Martha: The Life and Work of Martha Graham*, p. 264.
48 See Chapter 4 for an introduction to Hillman's proposition of an "artist fantasy."
49 Keats, "Letter to George and Georgiana Keats, April, 1819," in *John Keats: Selected Letters*, pp. 337–364.
50 Hillman, *Archetypal Psychology*, pp. 38–39.
51 Eckhart, *The Complete Works of Meister Eckhart*, p. 31.
52 Hillman, *Inter Views*, p. 169.
53 Ibid., p. 173.
54 Hyde, *The Gift: Imagination and the Erotic Life of Property*, p. 191. The most recent version of this classic book is now titled, *The Gift: Creativity and the Artist in the Modern World*.
55 Hillman, *Re-Visioning Psychology*, p. 51.
56 Lawrence, "Song of a Man That Comes Through," in *The Complete Poems of D.H. Lawrence*, p. 250.
57 Hillman, *Re-Visioning Psychology*, p. 57.
58 Ibid., p. 107.
59 See Chapters 1 and 2 for an extended discussion of the shaman as the archetypal ancestor of artists, philosophers, and healers, including Ellenberger's concept of "creative illness" as related to a shamanic sensibility evident in Freud and Jung.
60 McConeghey, *Art and Soul*, p. 11.
61 Hillman, "Ideas I See in Her Work," in *Margot McLean: Ritratti D'Artista*.

118 Image Making and Soul-Making

62 Hirsch, *Transforming Vision: Writers on Art*, p. 10.
63 See Chapter 7 for more on the autonomy and intentions of art objects, artifacts, and experiences.
64 Hillman and Shamdasani, *Lament of the Dead: Psychology After Jung's Red Book*, pp. 227–228.

References

De Mille, Agnes. *Martha: The Life and Work of Martha Graham*. New York, NY: Vintage. 1992.

Eckhart, Meister. *The Complete Works of Meister Eckhart*. Edited and translated by Maurice O'C. Walshe. New York, NY: Crossroads Publishing. 2009.

Hillman, James. "Peaks and Vales: The Soul/Spirit Distinction as Basis for the Differences Between Psychotherapy and Spiritual Discipline." In *Spring 1979*. Irving, TX: Spring Publications. 1979.

Hillman, James. Personal notes for the talk titled "The Art of Soul." Presented at the symposium on Embodying the Spiritual in the Art of the Future. San Francisco Art Institute, Sept. 1988. Notes housed within the James Hillman Collection at OPUS Archives, Carpinteria, CA.

Hillman, James. Personal notes for a talk titled "Soul and Beauty in Today's Urban World." Presented at Konan University, Kobe, Japan. Notes housed within the James Hillman Collection at OPUS Archives, Carpinteria, CA. 1991.

Hillman, James. *Re-Visioning Psychology*. 1976. New York, NY: Harper Perennial. 1992.

Hillman, James. *The Thought of the Heart & the Soul of the World*. 1981–1982. Woodstock, CT: Spring Publications. 1995.

Hillman, James. *The Soul's Code: In Search of Character and Calling*. New York, NY: Warner Books. 1996.

Hillman, James. *Suicide and the Soul*. 1965. Putnam, CT: Spring Publications. 1997.

Hillman, James. "Ideas I See in Her Work." In *Margot McLean: Ritratti D'Artista*. Bergamo, Italy: Moretti and Vitali Editori. 2002.

Hillman, James and Sonu Shamdasani. *Lament of the Dead: Psychology After Jung's Red Book*. New York and London: W.W. Norton and Co. 2013.

Hillman, James. "The Art of the Soul." In *Philosophical Intimations: Uniform Edition of the Writings of James Hillman*. Vol. 9. Edited by Edward S. Casey. Thompson, CT: Spring Publications. 2016.

Hillman, James and Margot McLean. "Permeability." In *ARAS: Art and Psyche Online Journal*. Vol. 4. 2009.

Hillman, James and Michael Ventura. *We've Had a Hundred Years of Psychotherapy and the World Is Getting Worse*. New York, NY: Harper Collins. 1992.

Hirsch, Edward. *Introduction to Transforming Vision: Writers on Art*. The Art Institute of Chicago. Boston, MA: Bulfinch Press. 1994.

Hyde, Lewis. *The Gift: Imagination and the Erotic Life of Property*. London: Vintage. 1999.

Keats, John. *John Keats: Selected Letters*. Edited by John Barnard. New York, NY: Penguin Books. 2014.

Keillor, Garrison. *Good Poems, American Places*. New York, NY: Viking. 2011.

Kunitz, Stanley. "Table Talk: A Paris Review Interview with Chris Busa." In *Lofty Dogmas: Poets on Poetics*. Edited by Deborah Brown, Annie Finch and Maxine Kumin. Fayetteville, AK: University of Arkansas Press. 2005.

Kunitz, Stanley and Genine Lentine. *The Wild Braid: A Poet Reflects on a Century in the Garden*. New York, NY: W.W. Norton & Co. 2005.

Lawrence, D.H. *D.H. Lawrence: The Complete Poems*. Edited by Vivian De Sola Pinto and F. Warren Roberts. New York, NY: Penguin Books. 1993.

Lipsey, Roger. *An Art of Our Own: The Spiritual in Twentieth Century Art*. Boston, MA: Shambhala. 1989.

McConeghey, Howard. *Art and Soul*. Putnam, CT: Spring Publications. 2003.

Phillips, Julie. "The Subversive Imagination of Ursula K. Le Guin." In *The New Yorker*. 25 Jan. 2018.

Chapter 6

Mythopoesis

The Archetypal Ancestors of the Modern Creator

Artmaking and mythmaking

Artmaking of any kind is a "storying," – an assemblage of existing elements into a unique whole that, with luck, holds the power to revel and transform. Mythmaking is no different, although myths are generally thought of as lies – harmless, powerless, and sometimes captivating, lies. Myths *are* lies – just as every poem, song, painting, and film is a lie. Myths *do* captivate, but they are far from being harmless and powerless. Myths are timeless and necessary fictions emerging from psyche's ceaseless imaginings; they are exquisitely flexible lies that refashion themselves for every age in order to story (and re-story) our realities for better – or for worse. "Myths" according to poet, scholar, and painter, Dennis Patrick Slattery, "give back to an individual or even an entire people a felt sense, through images, of what matters and of what is at stake if what matters is lost, trivialized and muted."[1]

While myths are powerful modes of orientation and reorientation, they are certainly not all good; nor are they above being twisted and wielded as tools of oppression. Philip Wheelwright's lamentation on the degradation of humankind's relationship with myth is eerily prophetic of our modern social and political instability:

> This loss of myth-consciousness I believe to be the most devastating loss that humanity can suffer; for . . . myth-consciousness is a bond that unites men both with one another with the unplumbed Mystery from which mankind is sprung and without reference to which the radical significance of things goes to pot. Now a world bereft of radical significance is not long tolerated; it leaves men radically unstable, so that they will seize at any myth or pseudomyth that is offered.[2]

Wheelwright went on to assert that it is the artist who is tasked with leading us into a generative and conscious relationship with the stories that drive our lives. More recently, author, storyteller, and conservationist, Barry Lopez observed: "Everything is held together with stories. That is all that is holding us together, stories, and compassion."[3]

DOI: 10.4324/9780429057724-7

Sensitive creators, like Lopez, have always recognized the power of myth and the universal archetypal themes that propel all stories, including their own. Ursula K. Le Guin employed Jung's concepts of symbol and archetype in her homage to myths, likening them to dreams:

> The great fantasies, myths, and tales are indeed like dreams: they speak *from* the unconscious *to* the unconscious, in the *language* of the unconscious – symbol and archetype. Though they use words, they work the way music does: they short- circuit verbal reasoning, and go straight to the thoughts that lie too deep to utter.[4]

Le Guin added that even though myths cannot be accounted for in the "language of reason," they are nonetheless "profoundly meaningful" and even quite practical and useful in regard to what they reveal to us about ourselves and our place in the world.[5] Le Guin's fluency with Jungian theory speaks to the value that depth psychology offers creators as they negotiate their calling – a calling that can feel quite urgent, large, and transpersonal – the makings of something mythic.

The various branches of depth psychology have always looked to myth as the clearest and most potent manifestation of archetypal themes that appear in every age and in every culture. Jung believed that the numinous quality of myths – the sense that they arrived to us from some force beyond the reach of our own will – revealed the "divine life in man."[6] In this same vein, Joseph Campbell argued that myth and art show us our own divinity: "We are all phenomenal manifestations of a divine will to live, and that will and the consciousness of life is one in all of us, and that is what the artwork expresses."[7] No matter our advancements in science and technology, Jung insisted that humankind would *always* need "mythic statements" to satisfy our constant yearning for meaning as individuals enmeshed in a mostly mysterious cosmos: "Meaninglessness inhibits fullness of life and is therefore equivalent to illness. Meaning makes a great many things endurable – perhaps everything. No science will ever replace myth, and a myth cannot be made out of any science."[8]

Jung lamented the fact that the West's modern scientist biases had all but completely cut us off from the great communal well of mythic insight. He believed, however, that creative individuals could correct these biases and imbalances by revivifying eternal and necessary stories for the collective.[9] Just as Le Guin observed, any art that speaks at the mythic level of symbol and archetype holds the potential to leap over the rational mind forming a bridge from one's unconscious to the unconscious of another – a nonrational soul-to-soul connection that may lead to authentic rebalancing and transformation. Jung emphasized *both* the "unconscious to unconscious" bridging power of myth and the role that myth plays in uniting *conscious and unconscious*:

> Myth and fairytales give expression to unconscious processes, and their retelling causes these processes to come alive again and be recollected, thereby

> re-establishing the connection between conscious and unconscious. . . . a supraordinate "third" is always required, in which the two parts can come together. And since the symbol derives as much the conscious as from the unconscious, it is able to unite them both.[10]

The conscious portion of symbolization includes the actual crafting or refashioning of the myth, or the artwork, that becomes a symbol suited to the needs of the present moment. Those who are stirred by the symbol participate in yet another union of unconscious to consciousness when incorporating the story or artwork into their lives.

In her concise history of myth, Karen Armstrong underscored the need for incorporation by insisting that myth must lead to imitation and participation, not simply passive contemplation.[11] This advice, encouraging mimesis – or embodied reenactment – is especially valuable for artmakers in their capacity as modern-day mythmakers. Mimesis, according to Slattery, follows the inherent "motion or action of psyche" which is *poesis* or making. This action moves "towards imitation, representation, and duplication in another register so to deepen the possibilities of an original event, person, object, or image." Mirroring Eckhart's insights into the soul, Slattery has developed the idea of "psychopoetics," which views psyche as always being engaged in "creating simulacra of its experiences, often with an aesthetic design."[12] The creation of stories (whether in words, paint, or dance) follows the motions of psychopoetics, which lead to,

> a synthesis or a constellation of the visible and invisible realms that narratives have the capacity to unite to shape our lives' past events into formed and coherent experiences that integrate these two realities, one more attuned to the facts of our past, and the other to the mythopoetic truth of our stories.[13]

Contemporary creators can forget that the creation of their work is mimetic; that it follows mythic patterns and is akin to what Eliade called a repetition of primordial acts.[14] Navigating between the inherently incompatible demands of the studio and those of the marketplace, they may find themselves adrift without adequate touchstones and reminders of these patterns and of their own mythic ancestry as creators. Campbell observed this same dynamic among many of the artists whose worlds intersected with his: "They are at sea because the traditions don't tell them that their inspirations come from divine, transcendent sources . . . They think [technical] studio problems are what it's all about."[15] Creators may also lose touch with what is so clearly illustrated in myth: that there is no singular "creativity" nor singular manner of creating. As Hillman explained, there are many "creativities," many faces of the creative, each with its own archetypal style and guiding figures.[16]

Tales of creation and creators inspired and confirmed Hillman's claims of humankind's inherent multiplicity as they demonstrate a myriad of styles of creative living and making – styles that we imitate and relive regardless of whether we are aware of them or not.

Getting acquainted with these tales – or reacquainting oneself with them – is an important step toward a conscious embodiment, or mimesis, of the storylines that call to us and claim us. A depth psychological approach to the individual gods, goddesses, and other supernatural figures in many of these tales maintains the position that these figures are not *real* in a literal sense, although as manifestations, or personifications, of archetypal themes that are *real* in a psychical sense. Ginette Paris has argued that gods and goddesses in particular have long influenced, illuminated, and enriched human lives, even though they have always been (and continue to be) *imaginal*:

> [The gods of the Greeks] did not require a credo, "I believe." The religious myths belonged to them just as my dreams belong to me; they knew that the myths were collective "dream images" not to be taken literally. If a dream (a myth) brings me fresh understanding of a personal situation, why turn my back on it?[17]

The imaginal has its own reality, and we are impoverished by modernity's misunderstanding and diminishment of myths as "imaginary" and as childish fantasies. Paris's focus on the gods of the Greeks was mirrored by Octavio Paz's focus on the ancient civilizations of Mexico:

> The privileged expression of change, as in poetry, are metaphors, as in rituals and masks. The gods are metaphors of the rhythm of the cosmos; for each date, for each measure of the dance of time, there is a corresponding mask.[18]

While the realm of myth is not literal, Hillman insisted that "our lives follow mythic figures: we act, think, feel only as permitted by primary patterns established in the imaginal world."[19] We ignore the imaginal and the mythical at our peril, as Jung, Hillman, Corbin, Hopper, Paris, and Paz, each warned in their own way.[20] With their perspectives in mind, this chapter now turns to a group of mythic creators whose tales illustrate the varied mythopoetic patternings of life as a creative individual.[21]

Tricksters, magicians, and cosmic flux: Hermes, Thoth, Isis, and Coyote

Tricksters and magicians are trespassers and shape-shifters; they are also inspired storytellers who can easily enchant us with their fictions – they are the very best liars. Appearing in multiple guises within the mythologies of many cultures, these figures are mercurial transformers, smooth talkers, and enemies of boundaries; they share many of the same transgressive qualities as bandits, thieves, and of course, artists. The Greek mythic figures Proteus and Prometheus are certainly tricksters, as is the god Hermes (known to the Romans as Mercury). As evidenced in the *Homeric Hymns*, and in many hundreds of subsequent appraisals, Hermes is one of the best examples of the collection of archetypal character traits associated with the trickster.

The "Homeric Hymn to Hermes" begins with the birth of the clever infant who immediately embarks on a startling streak of creativity and trickery. Hermes does not pause at the prospect of sacrificing life in order to transform it into something new; in the glossy-shelled turtle he sees the possibility of a musical instrument that will enchant the gods. From this he moves on to cattle theft and extortion, which eventually leads to an exchange of wondrous gifts and reconciliation with his half-brother, Apollo. In exchange for the enchantment of the lyre, Hermes is gifted with his signature golden caduceus and installed as messenger of the gods and guide of souls; in the latter role he is known as Hermes *Psychopompos*. Hermes's good fortune continues as Apollo happily offers him lessons in divination and magic; skills that Apollo has gained through his special relationship with three-winged "bee sisters" whose powers of divination are now at his sibling's disposal. As the god of communication, Hermes may offer his gifts to mortals in moments of unexpected inspiration and clarity that the Greeks called *hermaion* or lucky finds. He is just as quick, however, to sow confusion and miscommunication.

Contemporary creators have enjoyed comparisons to Hermes and to the trickster's rebellious boundary-defying powers – although most would not readily claim the full range of his character traits. Like all tricksters, Hermes is neither good nor bad; he is an amoral figure, as prone to deception and robbery as he is to dispensing gifts. The "artist as thief" is not necessarily attractive, but some creators, like Martha Graham, have understood and embraced this aspect of themselves:

> I am a thief – and I glory in it – I steal from the present and from the glorious past – I stand in the dark of the future as a glorying and joyous thief – There are so many wonderful things of the imagination to pilfer – so I stand accused – I am a thief – but with this reservation – I think I know the value of that which I steal and I treasure it for all time – not as a possession but as a heritage and as legacy. . . . Because I am a twentieth century pirate, I steal what I need for this time in which I live.[22]

More than a combination of clever thief and helpful guide, Hermes has been known by a host of names, including *kathochos* (the spellbinder), *enodios* (at the crossroads), and *onieros* (god of the dream). Hermes is more than an individual mythic figure – he is "an experience of multiplicity," of "the many in the one."[23] The mythic Hermes mirrors the historic human shaman-like figures of the Mediterranean who combined the roles of healers, seers, artists, and philosophers into one before those roles were separated.[24] Paris linked early shamanistic medicine/healing practices such as fasting, pilgrimages, charms, potions, ritual, and dream incubation to a Hermetic sensibility that valued the irrational – what today we might call "magic."[25] While these practices eventually gave way to less communal and less esoteric healing sensibilities and techniques, Hermes's links to magic and to the magician continue to offer valuable insights for today's artists, healers, and hybrid artist/healers as they find their places in a world in need of magic.

Hermes the magician echoes earlier mythic figures such as the Egyptian god Thoth. Equal to Hermes in his multiplicity, Thoth was god of the arts, speech, writing, astronomy, medicine, and magic and was credited with authoring the *Book of the Dead*; in short, he influenced every significant manner of knowledge and creative practice, both human and divine. Thoth was regarded as the "heart" and the "tongue" of the supreme divinity, Ra/Re, and presided over the final judgment of souls; his magic was thought to assist souls on their perilous journeys through the underworld.[26]

In his theriomorphic form, Thoth was pictured with the body of a human male and the head of an ibis. In his purely animal form, he was pictured as a seated baboon wearing a crescent moon as a headdress and sometimes holding a stylus and writing tablet. Freud's beloved collection of Egyptian antiquities included a marble Thoth in his baboon form, which commanded a prominent place among the many statues of mythic figures that faced him as he wrote. Seated on a throne close by was a bronze figurine of Imhotep, an Egyptian master builder and sage, also associated with writing, magic, and medicine.[27] It is important to note that early magician/trickster figures were not exclusively male. The Egyptian goddess Isis was known as "the mistress of magic" for her creative and healing powers which she used in various tales, most notably to reassemble and revivify the dismembered body of her husband, Osiris. Isis attained her most potent powers by tricking the sun god Ra into revealing his secret name.[28]

The figures of Hermes, Thoth, Isis, and Imhotep are related to the legend of the magician and alchemist Hermes Trismegistus (Thoth/Hermes Thrice Blessed).[29] The blending of magician and healer with alchemist, maker, and prophet leads to the Hermit. As a prominent figure within Tarot's major arcana, the Hermit wears the blue cloak of the initiate, which reveals only three panels of a six-paneled lantern shielded within. This symbol of wisdom both illuminates and conceals, and the hidden panels must

> remain an inward light and cannot be used to blind or dazzle those for whom it is not destined. . . . The Hermit is a secret master who works invisibly to mould the future as it comes into being.[30]

Like the Hermit, artists are also "moulders" whose work is not totally their own. Recall that Jung suggested that the artist was less an individual than a "collective man" serving as a "vehicle and moulder of the unconscious psychic life of mankind."[31] The Hermit, the mystic, and the artist all share a prophetic heritage, and each must also be cautious about what to reveal and what to conceal. In his classic book *Trickster Makes This World: Mischief, Myth and Art*, Lewis Hyde observed that across cultures,

> [S]ome special insight is regularly attributed to tricksters, implying that they might have a touch of the prophet about them. . . . [they] break through the crust of mundane affairs and conventional morality to real higher truths . . . or the plentitude and complexity of this world.[32]

Further describing this shared inheritance, Lewis Hyde utilized the Hebrew word for prophet (*nebi'im*), which has two senses: the first refers to "those who bring forth, unmediated, the revelation of the most high," the second "to those who speak to the people through the medium of the imagination."[33] It is the second sense that relates best to the archetypal trickster and to the human creator – neither are enlightened beings set apart from others due to unmediated powers of revelation. Trickster stories and biographies of artists remind us that they certainly are not saints, even with their prophetic abilities expressed through imagination; the magician is also the fool, the jester, and the clown – the trickster is always a paradox.

Humor, including the most earthy and graphic varieties, links trickster figures from multiple traditions including the Norse Loki, African Eshu and Legba, Chinese Monkey, Indian Krishna, Mayan twins Hunahpu and Xbalanque of the *Popol Vuh*, as well as the Native American Raven and Coyote. As a type of bungling, yet adaptable survivor, Coyote is one of the most beloved examples of trickster creativity.[34] Highlighting Coyote's multiplicity, linguist and anthropologist William Bright collected generations of stories (both Native and non-Native) focusing on various aspects of this shape-shifter's character: Coyote is a wanderer, glutton, lecher, thief, cheat, outlaw, spoiler, loser, clown, pragmatist, horny old man, survivor – and of special interest to artists – Coyote is a *bricoleur*.[35] Coyote makes, and makes due, just as in Hillman's notion of the artist as *bricoleur*.[36]

Coyote has even been credited with primal creation itself, albeit a very imperfect creation cobbled together as a *bricolage*. Comparing Native American cosmology to modern theoretical physics, Blackfoot scholar Leroy Little Bear has described the trickster as a manifestation of a primordial chaos, or the ever-creating flux itself, out of which all things emerge and eventually return. In this worldview, the trickster is the ultimate creator and transformer, as well as a teacher who reminds us that no life-forms are distinct or everlasting, they are simply recombinations of the same "energy waves" or "spirit" – simply put, "all creation is a spirit." Little Bear has emphasized the fact that what we think of as "reality" is more accurately a "temporary reference point" within an eternal flux; thus the need for the cyclical ceremonies of renewal common to indigenous peoples of the Americas enacted as a means of maintaining the present configuration lest it be enfolded back into the flux.[37] Complimenting this worldview is another face of the creative symbolized by Shiva, Dionysus, and other figures that not only welcome but also actively

Mythopoesis 127

bring forth the destructive movements of the flux, which do not so much destroy as transform and recreate.

Creators and destroyers: Shiva, Dionysus, Kali, and Coatlicue

As part of his theorizing about a "creative instinct," Jung turned to the workings of nature and the cosmos itself, arguing that "creation is as much destruction as it is construction."[38] The dynamic of breaking down in order to build up again is a prominent theme in myths of various cultures and is beautifully symbolized by the East Indian Shiva/Siva: a god of many forms and appellations, including Shiva Nataraja, the Lord of the Dance. In this widely recognizable form, Shiva dances within a ring of flames simultaneously destroying the current manifestation of the world and as he brings forth a new one:

> The upper right hand . . . carries a little drum, shaped like an hour-glass. . . . This connotes sound, the vehicle of speech, the conveyer of revelation, tradition, incantation, magic, and divine truth. . . . The opposite hand, the upper left . . . bears on its palm a tongue of flame. Fire is the element of the destruction of the world. . . . The "fear not" gesture . . . is displayed by the second right hand, while the remaining left lifted across the chest, points down to the uplifted foot. . . . The divinity is represented as dancing on the prostrate body of a demon . . . symbolic of life's blindness [and] man's ignorance. . . . A ring of flames and light . . . issues from and encompasses the god. This is said to signify the vital process of the universe and its creatures, nature's dance as moved by the dancing god within.[39]

Dance itself is an ancient form of magic, existing side by side in India with practices of austerity such as meditation, fasting, and hermetic introversion.[40] Dance can induce trance and forms of ecstasy that are meant to enchant the dancer; once that state is attained, the dancer is then able to enchant others. Shiva as Nataraja illuminates the artist's affinities with the shaman, as both must undergo a type of preparation, or "self-enchantment," which burns away enough of the personal to make room for the more than personal. Contrasting Shiva's enthused movements is the serene face of the god; he is a true unity of opposites simultaneously symbolizing life's frantic, playful, and destructive energies, intertwined with an underlying inner calm. Shiva is both the cosmos and the chaos that Jung identified in world mythologies and in alchemy. The image of Shiva Nataraja offers an epiphany of how everything is dependent upon its opposite; destruction takes on a necessary and even sacred meaning:

> This is the teaching: Destroy, destroy, destroy. Destroy within yourself, destroy all around you. Make room for your soul and for other souls. Destroy, because all creation proceeds from destruction. . . . For all building up is done

128 Mythopoesis

> with debris, and nothing in the world is new but shapes. But the shapes must be perpetually destroyed . . . Break every cup from which you drink.[41]

Shiva's archetypal energies are shared in large part by the Greek god Dionysus/ Dionysos, the patron of dance, ritual, theater, festival, and every communal pathway toward a type of ecstatic primal oneness. The Dionysian sensibility encourages risk taking and the dismemberment, or dissolution, of the self into the wildly creative, but equally dangerous, realm of the eternal flux.[42] The archetypal patternings of the Dionysian, so prominently displayed by creative individuals, have in many ways become a stereotype – a type of shorthand for a certain type of the frenzied figure prone to excess, flamboyance, and all manner of intoxication. Behind the stereotype, however, lie the archetypal impulses that are seen so clearly in biographies of artists who loved dancing on the edges of the volcanic unconscious – of course, some danced too close and were consumed. As Jung came to know during his early years of training at the Burghölzli Mental Hospital, the creative psyche is the same bubbling cauldron that invites and ignites both artists and madmen.

Representing both artists and madmen, Friedrich Nietzsche reveled in the Dionysian depths, going so far as to call himself Dionysus. While pulled toward self-oblivion, he understood that the Dionysian must be tempered by the Apollonian–creative ecstasy or creative intoxication must be accompanied by a measure of consciousness and discernment:

> If intoxication is nature playing with human beings, the Dionysiac artist's creation is a playing with intoxication. . . . It if rather like dreaming and at the same time being aware that the dream is a dream. Thus the attendant of Dionysos must be in a state of intoxication and at the same time he must lie in ambush, observing himself from behind. Dionysiac art manifests itself, not in the alternation of clear- mindedness and intoxication, but in their co-existence.[43]

Ray Bradbury has offered a contemporary take on this same sentiment but insists on alternation between the Dionysian with the Apollonian rather than coexistence: "This afternoon, burn down the house. Tomorrow, pour cold critical water upon the simmering coals. Time enough to think and cut and rewrite tomorrow. But today – explode – fly apart – disintegrate!"[44] The contemporary creator would not need to be familiar with the various tales associated with Dionysus to understand what Bradbury is advocating, but even a casual level of engagement with the Dionysian myths reveals their universality, their rootedness in the human psyche, and their continual reappearances in modern life.

The origins of the Greek cult of Dionysus and its related rituals (such as the Eleusinian Mysteries) are not completely known, but its primary thematic movement of dismemberment/dissolution as a necessity for regeneration was already present in earlier societies, particularly in Egypt and India. As the son of Zeus and the mortal Semele, the tales of Dionysus begins with the god's birth from the thigh of his father. Shortly thereafter, the infant is attacked, torn apart, and consumed by the Titans; only his tiny heart remained intact, and out of this precious organ he was reconstituted. This pattern mirrors multiple Egyptian tales of mutilation and reconstitution including the dismemberment of the body of Osiris by Set and its restoration by Isis and Anubis, along with the beheading of Isis by Horus and Thoth's bestowal of a new bovine head for the goddess. In many cases, the dismemberment/mutilation followed by a restoration leads to greater powers for the gods and goddesses concerned.[45]

Unlike the tales of tricksters and magicians, myths involving destroyers and creators include a healthy number of female protagonists. Presiding over slaughter and plagues, the striking lion-headed Egyptian Sekhmet/Sakhmet is one manifestation of a complex of goddesses including Isis and Hathor, who were all enfolded within the Great Goddess.[46] At the behest of Ra, Sekhmet sets out on a bloody rampage against mankind as punishment for disrespecting the gods. She goes too far, however, and is finally deceived into ending her frenzied killing spree when Ra/Re sets vats of red pomegranate-tinted beer in front of her, mimicking the blood that she craves. In contrast to the Dionysian tales, where intoxication is aimed at loosening limbs and conscious control, Sekhmet's intoxication puts her to sleep before she can completely destroy any chance of a new beginning for mankind. Hers is a cautionary tale of excess and imbalance where the powerful impulses to destroy and clear the way for transformation threaten to overtake those of reconstruction.

Like the Egyptian Sekhmet, the Indian goddess Kali is a manifestation of a multifaceted creator/mother goddess: She is at once Devi, Durga, Kali, Parvati, Uma, and Sati, to name just a few of her forms. The Mother Goddess is the consort of all the male gods and the origin of their shakti/sakti or creative power.[47] Kali herself has multiple aspects, including goddess of the cremation grounds. In this well-known guise, she is "surrounded by corpses, jackals, and terrible female spirits. From Her mouth flows a stream of blood, from Her neck hangs a garland of human heads and around Her waist is a girdle made of human hands." Kali is a paradox – even in her most terrifying form, she exemplifies the Tantric concept of *lila*, or the eternal play of the gods, as she simultaneously destroys, creates, and preserves. Kali delights equally in each aspect of her game, but unlike Sekhmet, Kali's playful destruction is never meant to be final: "After the destruction of the universe, at the end of a great cycle, the Divine Mother garners the seeds for the next creation."[48]

The Great Mother as destroyer/creator is manifested in the Americas in the figure of the Aztec/Mexica Coatlicue, "Goddess of the Serpent Skirt." Echoing Kali's fearsome visage, Coatlicue wears a necklace of human hearts and hands, with a human skull as a medallion over her prominent and sagging breasts; her skirt is made of interwoven rattlesnakes, and her own dismembered head has been replaced by two large multi-fanged coral snake heads.[49] Sometime prior to the Spanish conquest, a Mexican sculptor carved a monumental Coatlicue in the form of an aging warrior woman. Buried for centuries, this homage to the goddess was resurrected in the eighteenth century and has since become one of the most recognizable symbols of Mexican history and culture. Coatlicue has also been seen as a symbol of feminine strength, the dark reaches of the unconscious, and as a model of the creative–destructive cosmos itself.

In his *Essays on Mexican Art*, Octavio Paz identified the principle of metamorphosis as essential to Mesoamerican gods and goddesses, who like Coatlicue, were so often depicted as dismembered, beheaded, flayed, or otherwise destroyed:

> The universe is time, time is movement, and movement is change, a ballet of masked gods dancing the terrible pantomime of the creation and destruction of worlds. . . . And human beings? They are one of the signs that universal movement traces and erases, traces and erases. "The Giver of Life," according to an Aztec poem, "writes with flowers."[50]

Figures like Coatlicue, Dionysus, and Kali jolt the contemporary creator into an embodied recognition, *beyond* an intellectual understanding, of the necessary destructive acts that they must somehow find the courage to commit. Also, they must deal with the guilt that comes from these acts of plowing under and tearing apart. As Rollo May observed:

> A dynamic struggle goes on within a person between what he or she consciously thinks on the one hand and, on the other, some insight, some perspective that is struggling to be born. The insight is then born with anxiety, guilt, and the joy and gratification that is inseparable from the actualizing of the new idea or vision. The guilt that is present . . . has its source in the fact that the insight must destroy something. . . . As Picasso remarked, "Every act of creation is first of all an act of destruction."[51]

This dismembered gods and goddesses also point to remembrance and renewal. Gloria E. Anzaldúa, queer Chicana poet, writer, and feminist, wrote about developing her own "Coatlicue consciousness" in order to find the courage to "straddle the various borders of her own ancient-modern, patriarchal-feminist, and southern/northern Hispanic heritage."[52] Coming into relationship with the mother and daughter goddesses Coatlicue and Coyolxauhqui allowed Anzaldúa to deal with the guilt of burning the old to forge the new, as she simultaneously re-membered the many parts of herself.

Wounded healers and oracles: Asclepius, Chiron, Persephone, and *duende*

In Thornton Wilder's short play titled "The Angel that Troubled the Waters," two sufferers climb the stone steps leading to a healing sanctuary built around a large pool of water; there are already many others assembled around the pool.

Occasionally, an angel, the god of the waters, appears and transforms the water into a sacred substance that heals all wounds and afflictions. Fortunately for the supplicants, the spectacular angel does appear and begins to move the waters. Only one of the two sufferers, however, is allowed to dive into the waters for healing; the other is a physician, himself a healer, to whom the angel speaks these words:

> Without your wound where would your power be? It is your very remorse that makes your low voice tremble into the hearts of men. The very angels themselves cannot persuade the wretched and blundering children on earth as can one human being broken on the wheels of living. In love's service only the wounded soldiers can serve. Draw back.[53]

The physician's fellow sufferer, his injury now healed, wishes the same healing for the physician, but the angel has departed. The healed man implores the physician to accompany him to his home where his son has withdrawn into silence, and his daughter has slipped into despair from the loss of her own child. This physician has tended to these young people before, and the healed man insists that it is only this physician who can relieve their suffering now. The play ends at this very point, as the audience realizes why the angel did not dispense healing to the physician: Only the wounded healer can heal.

As has become clear through the past chapters, those who tend to the bodies and souls of others are not exclusively physicians. The physician in Wilder's play is revealed to be more of a therapist at the end, as his wisdom and counsel are what is sought for the psychic suffering of the healed man's grown children. As McEvilley, Tucker, and others have uncovered, the artist and the physician were not always specialists – they were at one time both melded together with the philosopher, seer, and magician into a multifaceted shaman-like figure.[54]

Like the trickster, the wounded healer has long been recognized as an archetypal image, or pattern of enactment, taking shape from the formless archetype(s) that power it. Far from a one-dimensional figure of woundedness made whole, the wounded healer combines aspects of a *therapeutes* (healer/servant/attendant), a creator, and a prophet/oracle. The wounded healer is well represented in Greek myth, with figures such as Chiron, Asclepius/Asklepios, Oedipus, Orpheus, Odysseus/Ulysses, Hephaestus, Athena, and Persephone offering moving examples of healing, creative, and prophetic powers that were honed through suffering. But to have suffered is not enough – the wounded ones must also dedicate themselves to a type of service uniquely their own. The individual path of service is revealed through an initiatory ordeal or a series of ordeals. Here again, we witness the shamanic pattern of "creative illness."[55]

In her appraisal of the wounded healer in Greek mythology, Christine Downing suggested that the initiation into service generally comes about either through significant physical illness or through another threat to normality such as a significant loss. A certain level of healing is accomplished when one accepts the

132 Mythopoesis

mantle of healer, although Downing was quick to point out that not all wounds heal. Indeed, the wound itself becomes a portal into the psychic depths (at times called the spirit world) as well as an aperture for seeing the world anew; it is the humbling source of healing power.[56] For Downing, the ultimate wounded healer of the Greek pantheon was, and is, Persephone. This goddess of the underworld addresses the most serious illness of all: our fear of woundedness, loss, finitude, and death. Persephone dissolves our fantasies of wellness without wounds, of contentment without loss, and of life without death.

Paradoxically, the mystery that works its curative power through the wound (sometimes personified as a god, goddess, spirit, or daimon) may also be responsible for the wounding in the first place. Federico García Lorca called this mystery *duende*. Ultimately defying translation, *duende* is neither angel nor muse but a power that pulses in the bloody "marrow" of all art forms, particularly music, dance, and spoken poetry which require a living body as an ephemeral interpreter:

> The *duende* does not come at all unless he sees that death is possible. . . . With idea, sound, or gesture, the *duende* enjoys fighting the creator on the very rim of the well. . . . The *duende* wounds. In the healing of that wound, which never closes, lie the strange, invented qualities of a man's work. . . . The *duende* loves the rim of the wound, and . . . he draws near places where forms fuse together into a yearning superior to their visible expression.[57]

Lorca's haunting ode to the *duende* recalls Jung's haunting insistence upon an "alien will" that seizes the artist in order to press that individual into service. Hillman too could be haunting when he spoke of the angel/image whose yearnings and needs overtake our own.[58] In his essay, "Puer's Wounds and Ulysses's Scar," Hillman, like Lorca, emphasized the embodied nature of a type of woundedness linked to creative expression: "A wound may be a mouth that speaks spirit, but the spirit is in the flesh."[59]

In this same essay, Hillman addressed various types of mythic wounding, including laming, maiming, and bleeding. He argued that "building the psychic vessel of containment, which is another way of soul-making, seems to require bleeding and leaking as its precondition." Hillman's work continues to remind us that the wounded healer, like all archetypal figures, "is not a human person, but a personification presenting a type of consciousness." He mirrored Downing in suggesting that "healing comes [to the wounded one] not because one is whole, integrated and all together, but from a consciousness breaking through dismemberment."[60] Neumann went even further to claim that the curative power is a *creative* power – it is the creative process itself.[61]

Hillman's most stirring insight into the wounded healer relates this figure to the *puer* or eternal child; linking both directly to "creativity," a word that he felt was too nebulous for the task assigned to it:

> That word creativity dulls and blunts the spirit of inquiry; it covers over more than it reveals, and is, in fact, a most uncreative word. The usual misty-eyed

reverence with which it is spoken is an invocation to the fresh, spontaneous, unreflecting, and beautiful, though tortured spirit, that is, it refers us back again to the puer, which it is supposed to explain.[62]

This tortured, yet jubilant and fresh, *puer* spirit of the creative is reflected in poet Amanda Gorman who has described her poetry as her "pathology."[63] The wound is an eye, as well as the mouth that sings, and the hands that make, and remake again and again.

Lovers, hermaphrodites, and alchemists: Eros and Psyche, fire and desire

The creative reveals itself in myth through any number of singular protagonists – but the creative is not exclusively singular. Neumann proposed that the creative individual was closely aligned with a natural bisexuality or original wholeness of the self.[64] This paradox of multiplicity as wholeness is illustrated by mythic figures from numerous cultures, which bolsters the idea of psyche as multiple and relational.

For example, the glorious image of Shiva Nataraja (The Lord of the Dance) discussed earlier is but one of Shiva's manifestations, as he is also known as Ardhanarisha (The Half-Woman Lord). In this aspect, Shiva has been depicted with a striking dual, or hermaphroditic, body: an ascetic male god on one side and a luxuriant goddess on the other. The goddess side is Shakti or Parvati, the potent feminine creative force that is inseparable from every manifestation of the god. As an indivisible couple, Shiva and Parvati are known as the "Two-in-One"; their beloved elephant-headed son Ganesha displays his own multiplicity as one of his aspects is a devouring monster called Kirtimukha.[65] Campbell saw parallels between Shiva/Shakti as Ardhanarisha in the Greek figure of Tiresias, the blind mystic of Sophocles' Theban trilogy of tragic plays. Both are seers and hermaphrodites.[66]

The etymology of "hermaphrodite" leads us directly to Hermaphroditos/Hermaphroditus, the son of Aphrodite and Hermes.[67] As the myth goes, the youth Hermaphroditos was quite beautiful, with an adventurous nature that led him to leave home and wander in far-off lands. Deep in a lush forest, he rests near a crystal-clear pool where he encounters Salmacis, a nymph who is immediately filled with desire for the young man. Her advances embarrass Hermaphroditos, and Salmacis eventually agrees to leave so that he may enjoy a private swim in the enticing pool. Instead of leaving, however, she hides in the tall grasses near the pool and her desire only grows as she watches the naked Hermaphroditos enter the water. She dives into the pool and wraps herself around the young man as she calls out to the gods to join them forever. The gods grant her wish as Salmacis and Hermaphroditos are fused into one. They are neither man nor woman but a melding of both.

Rafael López-Pedraza described the hermaphrodite as a "hermetic paradox," whose bisexuality reconciles the conflict of opposites.[68] As a "type of consciousness," the hermaphrodite, like the *psychopomp*/trickster is a world-bridger and uniter who embodies an expanded, fluid, and nuanced awareness of multiplicity. The hermaphrodite counters modernity's prevailing notion of the artist as a singular (usually male) heroic figure, opening new pathways of self-knowledge for contemporary creators who do not identify exclusively with male or female sensibilities. López-Pedraza went further to state that within the "archetypal longing and rejection" inherent in the myth "can be seen the dynamism which makes psyche and life move."[69] A hermaphroditic consciousness is a creative consciousness, one that arises and moves in *desire*.

Desire is the archetypal fuel that drives so many of the world's creation myths. The passion in the Egyptian coupling of Nut and Geb is mirrored in the union of the Native American Changing Woman and the Sun, and in the love, loss, and refound love underpinning the Greek myth of Psyche and Eros. In Hillman's explorations of the various archetypal styles of the creative (types of consciousness that he called the Senex, the Puer, the Creator/Destroyer, the masked Persona, the Promethean, and the Great Mother) most of his attentions were focused on gazing at the creative through the prism of the anima, with its "psychosexual ambivalence," and attunement to beauty and those realms considered to be "feminine." Unlike Jung, Hillman made it clear that the archetypal prism of the anima is a structure of consciousness shared by every gender.[70]

Unlike Neumann who looked to the tale of Psyche and Eros as an archetypal expression of the development of the feminine, Hillman found the myth to be of great importance for demonstrating the inherent creativeness in the archetypal expressions and rituals of analysis and of depth psychology itself. The myth holds the same value for illuminating the creative longings, trials, and pleasures of the artist.

The tale begins in a hermaphroditic state of playful attraction between the mortal Psyche and the immortal Eros. Their coupling is tested, disrupted, and ultimately strengthened through episodes of insecurity, envy, longing, rejection, suffering, courage, and reunion.[71] Hillman perceived the story through the earlier writings of the Romantic poets; through his empirical observations of the creative work of analysis, and through the prism of the personified anima herself, a figure that is always awakening and always becoming:

> *Anima becomes psyche through love* and that *it is eros which engenders psyche. . . . The creative is an achievement of love.* It is marked by *imagination* and *beauty*, and by connection to *tradition* as a living force and to *nature* as a living body.[72]

The myth of Psyche and Eros is a tale of initiation and transformation; it is a tale powered by love and plenty of drama illuminating the creative as relational, needy, impulsive, and drawn to the chaotic. Hillman came to the conclusion that soul is made through love (Psyche engendered via Eros) and that "Eros is born of chaos":

> Out of every chaotic moment . . . creativity can be born. Furthermore, eros will always hearken back to its origins in chaos and will seek it for its revivification. . . . Eros will attempt again and again to create those dark nights and confusions which are it nest. . . . it thrives close to the dragon.[73]

Chaos is the *prima materia*, the term that the alchemists used for the messy starting point of every transformational series of operations. Sharing the movements of Psyche and Eros, alchemy brings matter and psyche together into a *heiros gamos*, or sacred marriage, which inspired Jung's notion of sygyzy or tandem pairings.[74] The rich and mysterious visual imagery associated with alchemy is replete with images of intertwined hermaphroditic couples, and conjoined figures of queens and kings, of sun and moon (sol and luna), united in divine marriage. Alchemy, as Hillman professed, begins in desire, the fiery principle that propels the style of creative consciousness shared by mythic lovers, hermaphrodites, alchemists, and of course, many artists.[75]

Marie-Louse von Franz called this principle *emotio* or emotion, likening it to fire, libido, desire, and creativeness. Emotion is that which "moves one out of something, which makes one move. . . . the absolute basic factor in all creation myths together with its concomitant psychological feelings and physical reactions."[76] The principle of *emotio* for the artist as alchemist is felt and lived through the soul *and* the body – united in a collaborative relationship of making soul and transforming matter.

The myths explored here (a representative handful selected from many dozens from across the world) offer creators an array of styles of consciousness through which creativity, or the creative, manifests in the world. All these figures, along with those profiled earlier, are made real through the human creator, as a maker, craftsperson, *artifex*, and *therapeutes* of soul. Like the human creator, each of these figures has its own pathologies and its own shadows. Deepening one's mythic awareness brings creative individuals into relationship with these figures and with the many facets of their archetypal heritage. Ultimately, mythic awareness leads to better mythmakers.

Living mythopoetics: mirroring, mythmaking, and soul-making

A good mythmaker is a maker of mirrors. From the Latin *mirare* (to wonder at or become astonished) come both "mirror" and "miracle." Myths, like dreams, are mirrors; they reflect timeless dramas enacted by a rotating cast of characters that never seem to tire of taking their turn upon the stage. Myths and dreams are closely related as dreams have been described as personal myths, while mythic tales have been described as collective dreams. Dreams "are the mirror that the unconscious throws up at us."[77] The artist, working as a type of daylight dream-crafter for the collective, creates mirrors in the form of literature, dance, film, song, painting, and much more. Campbell referenced Shakespeare's belief that "art is a mirror held up to nature," to assert that the nature outside ourselves is the same as the nature within ourselves – art, of all types, offers opportunities for revelation.[78]

To gaze into these mirrors is to see our lives reflected as wondrous and wounded montages – assemblages of stories in constant flux. When we not only reflect upon what we see in these mirrors but also set about to actually craft these mirrors of self and world, we participate in what Hillman called the "artist fantasy."[79] Regardless of artistic ability, artmaking as mythmaking is a type of *psychopoesis* – an engendering of soul, a deepening of our participation with the creative cosmos, and a "stirring of an emotional and living factor of overwhelming importance" for every life and for every death.[80]

Tales of mythic creators, such as those highlighted earlier, act as mirrors for the contemporary creator, as enactments of soul-making. To understand oneself as creative is to understand that the archetypal dynamisms that power one's call to create are the same archetypal dynamisms powering the tales of mythic creators the world over. As we have seen, there is no single style of "creativity." In fact, creators may see themselves reflected in multiple styles – a trickster *and* a wounded healer or a hermaphrodite *and* a magician. No matter their hybrid natures, creators have always been our mythmakers and our guides in a never-ending project of renewal and re-storying. As James Hollis so eloquently stated: "The artist is often the carrier of the mythological project, the one who, from the intersection of conscious intent and unconscious patterning, makes the myth of the age – mythopoesis."[81]

Mythopoesis requires the embodied and intentional acts of making and enactment. Like ancient wells fed from an underground river made up of all the world's stories, myths must also be tended to, recharged, and rejuvenated in every era. As essential as water, "myth draws us near the profound depths of love and hate, life and death – precincts of the gods, the mysteries, where categories of thought falter and slip into dumbfounded silence. Myth is a way of talking about the ineffable."[82] Those called toward making, toward *poesis*, are the *therapeutes* of the mythic imagination. Karen Armstrong has gone so far as to suggest that our artists and writers should be called upon to step into the priestly role of instructors in mythic lore to bring fresh insight into our damaged world, particularly when professional religious leaders fail to do so.[83]

In a short poem, William Butler Yeats wrote how he had made his song a beautiful coat embroidered with bits of old mythologies, but the coat was taken, worn carelessly, and ruined by others who lacked an understanding of the origins and power of the old stories. In the proliferation of pseudomyths in the contemporary world we see the power of a storyline to concretize into what Harari called "imagined orders," worldviews comprising damaging mythologies which benefit one group at the expense of others.[84] The old cloaks made of stories need continual mending and refashioning. Those who create and tend to these garments deserve our praise, for everything – as poets like Yeats and Lopez have always known – is held together with stories.[85] That is how we as human beings have always survived our dark nights and stormy seas: with cloaks embroidered with stories and compassion.

Notes

1 Slattery, "Psyche's Silent Muse: Desert and Wilderness," in *Depth Psychology: Meditations in the Field*, p. 48.
2 Wheelwright, qtd. in Romaine Hopper, "Myth, Dream, and Imagination," in Campbell, *Myths, Dreams, and Religion*, pp. 114–115.
3 Lopez, "Author's Website and Facebook Page."
4 Le Guin, "The Child and the Shadow," p. 141.
5 Ibid., p. 141.
6 Jung, *Memories, Dreams, Reflections*, p. 340.
7 Campbell, "Creativity," in *The Mythic Dimension: Selected Essays 1959–1987*, p. 187.
8 Jung, *MDR*, p. 340.
9 See Chapter 2 for a thorough discussion of Jung's insights into the powers and duties of the creative individual.
10 Jung, "Background to the Psychology of Christian Alchemical Symbolism," in *CW9ii*, p. 180, para. 280. See also Chapter 3 for Rosemary Gordon's insights into "symbolizing."
11 Armstrong, *A Short History of Myth*, p. 135.
12 Slattery, "Mimesis, Neurology, and the Aesthetics of Presence," in *Psychological Perspectives: A Quarterly Journal of Jungian Thought*, p. 270.
13 Ibid., p. 273.
14 Eliade, "The Eternal Return," in *The Inner Journey: Myth, Psyche, and Spirit*, p. 12.
15 Campbell, qtd. in McConeghey, *Art and Soul*, p. vi.
16 See Chapters 4 and 5.
17 Paris, *Pagan Grace: Dionysos, Hermes, and Goddess Memory in Daily Life*, p. 95.
18 Paz, *Essays on Mexican Art*, p. 50.
19 Hillman, "Pothos: The Nostalgia of the Puer Eternus," in *Loose Ends*, p. 50.
20 See in particular Henry Corbin's essay, "Mundus Imaginalis: Or the Imaginary and the Imaginal."
21 The profiles that follow are not meant to comprise an exhaustive survey of mythic creators from all cultures; rather, the selected figures have been included for their relevance to contemporary creators.
22 Graham, "Center of the Hurricaine," in *The Notebooks of Martha Graham*, p. 303.
23 Doty, "Hermes Heteronymous Appellations," in *Facing the Gods*, pp. 115–133.
24 See Chapter 1 for an in-depth discussion of early Greek shamanism.
25 Paris, *Pagan Grace*, p. 97–98.
26 Mercatante, "Thoth," in *Who's Who in Egyptian Mythology*, pp. 189–190; Mark, "Thoth," in *Ancient History Encyclopedia*.
27 See *Sigmund Freud and Art: His Personal Collection of Antiquities*, edited by Lynn Gamwell and Richard Wells, pp. 45–45, 56–57.
28 Pinch, *Egyptian Myth: A Very Short History*, pp. 35, 42, 96–97.
29 See later for more on Hermes Trismegistus and the artist as alchemist.
30 Chevalier and Gheerbrant, "The Hermit," in *The Penguin Dictionary of Symbols*, p. 501.

138   Mythopoesis

31 Jung, "Psychology and Literature," in *CW15*, p. 101, para 157.
32 Hyde, *Trickster Makes This Word: Mischeif, Myth and Art*, p. 289.
33 Ibid., p. 295.
34 See Hyde, *Trickster Makes This World*, p. 43.
35 Bright, *A Coyote Reader*, pp. 19–23, 35–55.
36 See Chapters 4 and 5 for Hillman's notion of the *bricoleur* inspired by Claude Levi-Strauss, and Chapter 7 for more on this figure from Levi-Strauss.
37 Little Bear, "Preface," in David Bohm's *Bohm: On Creativity*, pp. vii–xiv.
38 Jung, "Structure and Dynamics of the Psyche," in *CW8*, p. 118, para. 245.
39 Zimmer, *Myths and Symbols in Indian Art and Civilization*, pp. 152–153.
40 Ibid., pp. 151–152.
41 Marcel Schwob qtd. in Coomaraswamy, *The Dance of Shiva: Fourteen Indian Essays*, p. 180.
42 For more on Dionysus and his continued relevance for both creative practice and therapy, see Susan Rowland's *Remembering Dionysus: Revisioning Psychology and Literature in C.G. Jung and James Hillman*; Ginette Paris, *Pagan Grace: Dionysos, Hermes, and Goddess Memory in Daily Life*.
43 Nietzsche, "The Dionysiac World View," in *The Birth of Tragedy and Other Writings*, p. 121.
44 Bradbury, *Zen in the Art of Writing*, p. 7.
45 Pinch, *Egyptian Myth*, pp. 96–97.
46 Rundle-Clark, *Myth and Symbol in Ancient Egypt*, p. 266.
47 Zimmer, *Philosophies of India*, p. 569.
48 Ibid., pp. 564–566.
49 Read and Gonzalez, *Mesoamerican Mythology: A Guide to the Gods, Heroes, Ritual, and Beliefs of Mexico and Central America*, p. 151.
50 Paz, *Essays on Mexican Art*, pp. 38, 42.
51 May, *The Courage to Create*, pp. 59–60.
52 Read and Gonzalez, *Mesoamerican Mythology*, p. 152. See also Andazlúa, *Border-lands/La Frontera: The New Mestiza* and *Light in the Dark/Luz en lo Oscuro: Rewriting Identity, Spirituality, Reality (Latin America Otherwise)*.
53 Wilder, "The Angel That Moved the Waters," in *The Collected Short Plays of Thornton Wilder*, p. 74.
54 See Chapter 1 for more on this early multidimensional figure, particularly in ancient Greece and the surrounding Mediterranean cultures.
55 See Chapter 1 for more on "creative illness" as related to destiny and the artist.
56 Downing, "Only the Wounded Healer Heals: The Testimony of Greek Mythology."
57 Lorca, "Play and Theory of the Duende," in *In Search of Duende*, pp. 48–62.
58 See Chapter 2 for Jung on the "alien will," and Chapters 4 and 5 for Hillman's theories on image, angel, soul, and soul-making.
59 Hillman, "Puer Wounds and Ulysses' Scar," in *Puer Papers*, p. 118.
60 Ibid., pp. 115–117.
61 See Chapter 3 for a thorough discussion of Erich Neumann's theories about the creative individual.
62 Hillman, "Puer Wounds," p. 101.
63 Gorman, "How Poet Amanda Gorman Prepared for Inauguration Day," Interview with Jeffrey Brown for PBS.
64 See Chapter 3.
65 See Campbell, *Hero with a Thousand Faces*, p. 154; Zimmer, *Myths*, pp. 184, 197, 216.
66 Ibid.
67 Kerényi proposed that Aphrodite and Hermes were twins (already a duality before the birth of Hermaphroditos) and that Aphrodite herself was worshipped as Aphroditos – a hermaphroditic goddess. See Kerényi's *Gods of the Greeks*, pp. 171–173.

68 López-Pedraza, *Hermes and His Children*, p. 39.
69 Ibid., p. 50.
70 Hillman, *Myth of Analysis*, pp. 49–50.
71 See the original myth in Apuleius's *Golden Ass* and Neumann's analysis of the tale in *Amor and Psyche: The Psychic Development of the Feminine*.
72 Ibid., p. 54.
73 Ibid., pp. 98–99.
74 See Chapter 5 for more on the notion of sygyzy in relation to Hillman's reflections on the myth of Psyche and Eros.
75 See Hillman, "The Alchemy of Psychology," *Better Listen*. Audio.
76 von Franz, *Patterns of Creativity Mirrored in Creation Myths*, p. 138.
77 Edinger, *The Eternal Drama: The Inner Meaning of Greek Mythology*, p. 86.
78 Campbell, *The Power of Myth*, p. 68.
79 See Chapters 4 and 5 for Hillman's conception of an "artist's fantasy."
80 Hillman, *Myth of Analysis*, p. 52.
81 Hollis, *Tracking the Gods: The Place of Myth in Modern Life*, p. 30.
82 Ibid., p. 23.
83 Armstrong, *A Short History of Myth*, p. 149.
84 See the Introduction for Harari's explanation of "imagined orders."
85 See Yeats's poem "The Coat," and the Introduction for Barry Lopez's insights into stories and compassion.

References

Armstrong, Karen. *A Short History of Myth*. New York, NY: Cannongate. 2005.

Bright, William. *A Coyote Reader*. Berkeley, CA: University of California Press. 1993.

Campbell, Joseph. *The Hero with a Thousand Faces*. 1949. Princeton, NJ: Princeton University Press. 1968.

Campbell, Joseph. *The Mythic Dimension: Selected Essays 1959–1987*. New York, NY: Vintage. 2007.

Campbell, Joseph and Bill Moyers. *The Power of Myth*. Edited by Betty Sue Flowers. New York, NY: Doubleday Books. 1988.

Chevalier, Jean and Alain Gheerbant. *The Penguin Book of Symbols*. 1969. Translated by John Buchanan-Brown. New York, NY: Penguin Books.

Coomaraswamy, Ananda K. *The Dance of Shiva: Fourteen Indian Essays*. New York, NY: Noonday Press. 1957.

Doty, William. "Hermes Heteronymous Appellations." In *Facing the Gods*. Edited by James Hillman. Dallas, TX: Spring Publications. 1988.

Downing, Christine. "Only the Wounded Healer Heals: The Testimony of Greek Mythology." A talk delivered to the San Diego Friends of Jung, 15 Oct. 1993. Audio Recording. jungsandiego.org.

Edinger, Edward. *The Eternal Drama: The Inner Meaning of Greek Mythology*. Edited by Deborah A. Wesley. Boston and London: Shambhala Press. 1994.

Eliade, Mircea. "The Eternal Return." In *The Inner Journey: Myth, Psyche, and Spirit*. Edited by Martha Heyneman. Sandpoint, ID: Morning Light Press. 2008.

Gorman, Amanda. "Poet Amanda Gorman on How She Prepared for Inauguration Day." Interview with Jeffrey Brown. 18 Jan. 2021. pbs.org/video-inaugural-poet.

Graham, Martha. *The Notebooks of Martha Graham*. New York, NY: Harcourt, Brace, Jovanovich, Inc. 1973.

140 Mythopoesis

Hillman, James. "The Alchemy of Psychology." In *Better Listen*. Audio Series. BetterListen.com.

Hillman, James. *The Myth of Analysis: Three Essays in Archetypal Psychology*. 1972. New York, NY: Harper Collins. 1978.

Hillman, James. "Pothos: The Nostalgia of the Puer Eternus." In *Loose Ends*. 1975. Dallas, TX: Spring Publications. 1986.

Hollis, James. *Tracking the Gods: The Place of Myth in Modern Life*. Toronto, Canada: Inner City Books. 1995.

Hillman, James. "Puer Wounds and Ulysses' Scar." In *Puer Papers*. Dallas, TX: Spring Publications. 1979.

Hopper, Stanley Romaine. "Myth, Dream, and Imagination." In *Myths, Dreams and Religion*. Edited by Joseph Campbell. Dallas, TX: Spring Publications. 1970.

Hyde, Lewis. *Trickster Makes This World: Mischief, Myth, and Art*. 1998. New York, NY: Farrar, Straus and Giroux. 2010.

Jung, Carl Gustav. "Background to the Psychology of Christian Alchemy." 1950. In *Aion: Researches into the Phenomenology of the Self. CW9ii*. Edited by Herbert Read, Michael Fordham, Gerhard Adler and William McGuire. Translated by R.F.C. Hull. Princeton, NJ: Princeton University Press. 1968.

Jung, Carl Gustav. "Psychological Factors Determining Human Behavior." 1937. In *The Structure and Dynamics of the Psyche: CW8*. Edited by Herbert Read, Michael Fordham, Gerhard Adler and William McGuire. Translated by R.F.C. Hull. Princeton, NJ: Princeton University Press. 1969.

Jung, Carl Gustav. "Psychology and Literature." 1930/1950. In *The Spirit in Man, Art, and Literature: CW15*. Edited by Herbert Read, Michael Fordham, Gerhard Adler and William McGuire. Translated by R.F.C. Hull. Princeton, NJ: Princeton University Press. 1978.

Jung, Carl Gustav. *Memories, Dreams, Reflections*. 1963. Edited by Aniela Jaffé. Translated by Richard and Clara Winston. New York, NY: Vintage Books. 1989.

Kerényi, C. *The Gods of the Greeks*. 1951. London: Thames and Hudson. 2010.

Le Guin, Ursula K. "The Child and the Shadow." In *The Quarterly Journal of the Library of Congress*. Vol. 32, No. 2. Apr. 1975, pp. 139–148.

Little Bear, Leroy. "Preface." In *Bohm: On Creativity*. 1966. Edited by David Bohm. London and New York, NY: Routledge. 2004.

Lopez, Barry. "Author's Website." BarryLopez.com.

López-Pedraza, Rafael. *Hermes and His Children*. 1989. Einsiedeln, Switzerland: Daimon Verlag. 2003.

Lorca, Federico García. "Play and Theory of the Duende." In *In Search of Duende*. Edited and translated by Christopher Maurer. New York, NY: New Directions Publishing. 1998.

Mark, Joshua J. "Thoth." In *Ancient History Encyclopedia*. www.ancienthistory.eu/thoth.

May, Rollo. *The Courage to Create*. 1975. New York, NY: W.W. Norton and Company. 1994.

McConeghey, Howard. *Art and Soul*. Putnam, CT: Spring Publications. 2003.

Mercatante, Anthony S. "Thoth." In *Who's Who in Egyptian Mythology*. 1978. Edited by Robert Steven Bianchi. New York, NY: Metro Books. 2002.

Nietzsche, Friedrich. *The Birth of Tragedy and Other Writings*. Edited by Raymond Guess and Ronald Speirs. Translated by Ronald Speirs. Cambridge and New York, NY: Cambridge University Press. 2009.

Paris, Ginette. *Pagan Grace: Dionysos, Hermes, and Goddess Memory in Daily Life*. 1990. Translated by Joanna Mott. Putnam, CT: Spring Publications. 2006.

Paz, Octavio. *Essays on Mexican Art*. Translated by Helen Lane. New York, NY: Harcourt, Brace and Company. 1993.

Pinch, Geraldine. *Egyptian Myth: A Very Short Introduction*. Oxford and New York, NY: Oxford University Press. 2004.

Read, Kay Almere and Jason J. Gonzalez. *Mesoamerican Mythology: A Guide to the Gods, Heroes, Rituals, and Beliefs of Mexico and Central America*. Oxford and New York, NY: Oxford University Press. 2000.

Rundle-Clark, R.T. *Myth and Symbol in Ancient Egypt*. 1959. London: Thames and Hudson. 1991.

Slattery, Dennis Patrick. "Psyche's Silent Muse: Desert and Wilderness." In *Depth Psychology: Meditations in the Field*. Edited by Dennis Patrick Slattery and Lionel Corbett. Einsiedeln and Carpinteria: Daimon Verlag. 2000.

Slattery, Dennis Patrick. "Mimesis, Neurology, and the Aesthetics of Presence." In *Psychological Perspectives: A Quarterly of Jungian Thought*. Vol. 56, No. 3. Sept. 2013.

Von Franz, Marie-Louise. *Patterns of Creativity Mirrored in Creation Myths*. Zürich: Spring Publications. 1972.

Wilder, Thornton. "The Angel That Troubled the Waters." In *The Collected Short Plays of Thornton Wilder*. Vol. 2. Edited by Tappan Wilder. New York, NY: New York Theater Communications Group. 1998.

Zimmer, Heinrich. *Myths and Symbols in Indian Art and Civilization*. 1946. Edited by Joseph Campbell. Princeton, NJ: Princeton University Press. 1974.

Zimmer, Heinrich. *Philosophies of India*. 1951. Edited by Joseph Campbell. Princeton, NJ: Princeton University Press. 1974.

Chapter 7

The Soul, the Creative, and the Archetypal Artist

Crossroads and crosscurrents of the creative

The soul, the creative, and the artist are all residents of the crossroads. More accurately, they *are* the crossroads, the places of movement, exchange, revelation, manifestation, and transformation. Human beings have long recognized the power of the crossroads by erecting altars, shrines, obelisks, chapels, and stone statuary at the spot where two or more roads come together; this place, when entered, becomes the *axis mundi* or center of the world. The phallic stone *hermae*, or herms, erected at crossroads in ancient Greece recognized Hermes (patron of artists, liars, and thieves) as the lord of the crossroads, the ruler of the "in-between." The crossroads is a symbol of both possibilities and dangers, of endings and beginnings, it is a place that implies relationship as the poet Novalis knew: "The seat of the soul is where the inner and outer worlds meet."[1]

In a series of radio interviews from the 1970s, structural anthropologist Claude Lévi-Strauss utilized the idea of the crossroads to describe both the generation of myth in the human psyche and the generation of his own creative work:

> I have written that myths get thought in man unbeknownst to him. This has been much discussed and criticized. . . . But for me it describes a lived experience, because it says exactly how I perceive my own relationship to my work. That is, my work gets thought in me unbeknown to me. . . . Each of us is a kind of crossroads where things happen. The crossroads is purely passive; something happens there. A different thing, equally valid, happens elsewhere. There is no choice, it is just a matter of chance.[2]

Lévi-Strauss made it clear that his particular "idiosyncrasy" of feeling himself to be a crossroads was no more valuable an insight than what others had proposed in describing the making of myth, the making of a book, or the making of any new idea or thing. He continued by stating that every approach to how things get made, to how creativity happens, has the potential for expanding our relationship to the creative. While this is true, not every approach holds the potency

DOI: 10.4324/9780429057724-8

The Soul, the Creative, and the Archetypal Artist 143

of the crossroads for correcting our contemporary biases toward the supremacy of human willpower and control with its accompanying dismissal of the role of chance, or acausal factors, in every act of creation.

Lévi-Strauss described feeling as though his books were written "through him" and not by him; for this reason, he oftentimes could not easily recall what he had written in the past. This observation places him in excellent company, as similar observations across the centuries from Plato to Jung, from John Keats to John Lennon attest. Many of these observations have populated the pages of this book including Sir Herbert Read's articulation of the artist as a "field of operation," and Erich Neumann's description of the creative principle as cutting through the axis of chaos and rigidity forming a crossroads at the center.[3]

Just as clarifying and inspiring as the symbol of the bridge associated with Jungian ideas around creativity, the crossroads is inherently more complex than the place of creative tension between two polarities or the bridge between two shores. The crossroads, with its potential for multiplicity and inclusiveness, is an essential symbol for the contemporary creator. With its sparks of possibility radiating from a supercharged center, the crossroads shares symbolic resonance with the mandala and with the many-sided, brilliant star, which are equally evocative faces of the creative. As one of the key figures of Tarot's major arcana, the Star has been described as representing the "intercommunication between different worlds; as the soul linking the spirit to matter"; as a "passage to guided development"; and as an emblem of "creation, birth, and transformation."[4]

Ideas about linking spirit with matter and intercommunication between worlds or types of realities return us once again to the shaman, the multifaceted archetypal ancestor of the artist who was a combined maker, healer/physician, magician, philosopher, and seer. More importantly, we are once again reminded of a pattern of shamanic sensibilities that continue to course through the lives of contemporary creators. These patterns are demonstrated by a heightened attunement to the living cosmos that is oftentimes born out of wounding, illness, or significant loss; the courage to surrender to imagination or what has also been called the unconscious or the spirit world; the use of aesthetic means of expression; and the sense of calling to be of service to others and to the earth in a never-ending project of renewal and re-creation.

When asked to connect the poets of the present with the mythmakers of the past, Joseph Campbell did not hesitate to name the shaman as the equivalent of today's artists.[5] Recall as well Jean Erdman Campbell's observation that the artist and the mystic are very much alike, although the mystic does not have a craft; the act of *poesis*, or making, keeps the artist connected to humanity as if dreaming with eyes open.[6] In this same vein, Anaïs Nin described the affinities between artists and their archaic ancestors:

> The primitive and the poet never parted company. . . . Music, the dance, poetry, and painting are the channels for emotion. It is through them that experience penetrates our blood stream. Ideas do not. . . . Each generation

144 The Soul, the Creative, and the Archetypal Artist

must create its own reality and its own language, its own images. Each one of us must re-create the world.[7]

Like Jung, who professed that the artist who speaks in primordial images speaks in a thousand voices, Nin realized that the personal, when traversed to the deepest levels, becomes "universal, mythical, and symbolic." She eschewed "intellectualizing," and turned instead to the "primitive instruments" of discovery employed by the archaic artist: seeing, hearing, and feeling.[8]

Echoing Nin, iconic jazz musicians John and Alice Coltrane each felt called to the task of remaking the world through their music. In his sweeping survey of the shamanic spirit in twentieth-century art and culture, Michael Tucker observed that both artists believed that music was an emanation of a universal spirit; a sentiment that other musicians in their circles of influence also shared. "Like a shaman of old," wrote Tucker,

> John Coltrane was inexorably drawn to the archetypal intuition that the world's ills cannot be healed exclusively in the profane realm so to speak. For the world – the sacred *cosmos* which dominated Coltrane's imagination in the last years of his life – must be periodically recharged with primal energy from the *ur-* domain of mythopoesis.[9]

More recently, poet and novelist Sandra Cisneros has reiterated the shamanic power of artworks to transform and to heal by describing books as medicine. Her use of the word "medicine" is not metaphorical – the absolute seriousness of her statement attests to the fact that the right book (or film, or song, or poem, or painting) at the right time can be a lifesaving grace.[10] What these creators came to understand about the crossroads where art and soul are made is the same thing that archaic creators knew: Art (in a myriad of forms) does things, art has powers, art is alive, art transforms, art *works*.

Anima mundi and *anima ars*: art has its own desires

As we have seen, Jung made dozens of bold and influential statements about art, creativity, and the creative individual over the course of his long life. One of his boldest came very close to conferring true autonomy to artworks themselves, as he compared the artist to the soil in which an artwork (out of its own inherent agency) emerges:

> The plant is not a mere product of the soil, it is a living, self-contained process which in essence has nothing to do with the character of the soil. In the same way, the meaning and individual quality of a work of art inhere within it and not in its extrinsic determinants. One might almost describe it as a

The Soul, the Creative, and the Archetypal Artist   145

living being that uses man only as a nutrient medium, employing his capacities according to its own laws and shaping itself to the fulfillment of its own creative purpose.[11]

The notion of the artwork as a living being existed long before Jung, with creators such as Rainer Marie Rilke having expressed similar sentiments in their own way. In his poem, "Archaic Torso of Apollo," Rilke recounts an encounter with an artwork that does not merely glow with life – but is, in a rather shocking way, alive. The ancient statue startles the poet into attention, as it penetrates the depths of Rilke's soul. The poet is left with an unsettling feeling that he is being personally addressed and that he must change his life: "For here there is no place that does not see you."[12] A world away from Rilke, a Navajo poet known as Old Torlino expressed the same eerie feeling of being held to account by the nonhuman faces of nature such as the sun, the sky, the dawn, and the evening twilight: "Some of these things are always looking at me/I am never out of sight/Therefore I must tell the truth."[13]

The idea that everything is alive and ensouled in some way has been called animism; a way of orienting oneself to the cosmos that has primarily been associated with societies of the past. Modernity has for the most part dismissed this type of orientation toward life as primitive and has smugly moved on. Just as Jung argued for the reality and autonomy of the psyche and psychic images, Hillman argued for the reality and autonomy – for the soul – of images as they display themselves in the world, including those human-made images that impact our lives for better and worse such as our homes, office buildings, highways, furniture, clothing, and of course, every kind of art. The word "image," as commonly used, refers to the object crafted or made manifest, but as we have seen, an archetypal understanding extends the meaning of "image" to include a deep interiority or essence that is synonymous with soul.

As we have seen, Hillman imaged the *anima mundi* not as something transcendent and remote nor as "unifying panpsychic life-principle," but rather,

that particular soul-spark, that seminal image, which offers itself through each thing in its visible form. . . . Not only animals and plants ensouled as in the Romantic vision, but soul is given with each thing, God-given things of nature and man-made things of the street. . . . The soul of a thing corresponds or coalesces with ours.[14]

In making these arguments, Hillman extended a sense of belonging and responsibility to those creators that we group under the categories of "commercial artists" or "designers," as their type of creative work, along with every other type, becomes part of the soul of the world.

With his revivification of the idea of the *anima mundi*, Hillman returned to his philosophical familial tree where Plato, Plotinus, and Ficino reside. Each made similar arguments in their own time about an interrelatedness of the human soul and the soul of world:

> The Platonic cosmos [always recognized] that the soul of the individual can never advance beyond the soul of the world, because they are inseparable, the one always implicating the other. Any alteration in the human psyche resonates with a change in the psyche of the world.[15]

This worldview of ensouled interconnection and interdependence corresponds with indigenous ways of knowing, with ancient philosophies of both East and West, and with an enduring shamanic sensibility that has woven its path through the previous chapters. In addition, it parallels ideas proposed by theoretical physicists such as David Bohm, who stressed the participatory nature of the so-called objective observer in what we call reality. Each of us is a co-producer of the world – each of us is a place of transformation.[16]

Of course, Bohm meant that *every* human being is a place of transformation not just artists. However, his assertion is a particularly revelatory and even sobering reminder of the powers of the creative individual – powers that have been described as a type of magic. Art, ritual, religion, and magic all stem from the same yearnings for communion with what Neumann termed the "unitary reality," and what others have termed the numinous, the sacred, the spirit world, the miraculous, or the ineffable – a force that is ultimately beyond all attempts at naming. This communion is not only aimed at creating relationship, but it is also aimed at influence. The magician, the artist, and the ritualist create objects and experiences in hopes of satisfying two primary desires of human existence: the preservation of certain favorable orders of reality and the transformation of non-favorable orders into more generative orders.

The Paleolithic ancestors of today's creators have been described as magicians, whose drawings, paintings, and carvings approximated magic spells or incantations. Their artmaking was aimed at honoring, enchanting, and influencing the invisible powers of both preservation and transformation – these were acts of prayer.[17] Creative actions aimed at maintenance are still seen in the ceremonies of the Lakota and other indigenous peoples. Leroy Little Bear has described these actions as the making of objects and experiences that are focused on maintaining the world so that it is not subsumed – at least not yet – into the eternal flux.[18]

The transformational power of magic, art, and ritual is especially valid for today's creators as they wrestle so often with a calling that feels necessary, urgent, even sacred, contrasted against Western culture's limited expectations of the artist, which generally do not include the idea of "artist as magician." Creators have had to proclaim these powers, and *reclaim* them, for themselves, even if these acts of reclamation and proclamation remain private – a proclamation does not need to be public to be real. In fact, the archetypal figure of the Hermit reminds us to keep our inner lamps shielded and to use discernment when offering that light, or magic, to the world. The humble Hermit is also a corrective against the shadowy aspects of the Magician, which can include ego inflation and misuse of one's powers.[19]

No matter how the creative calling is announced, those who hear the call are faced with the tasks of recognizing, proclaiming, and fulfilling their destinies. In an essay focused on Walt Whitman, D.H. Lawrence articulated the transformational power and moral imperative of art and artmaking:

> The essential function of art is moral. Not aesthetic, not decorative, not pastime and recreation. . . . But a passionate, implicit morality, not didactic. A morality which changes the blood, rather than the mind. Changes the blood first. The mind follows later, in the wake.[20]

What Lawrence described is a kind of alchemy, an operation that bypasses the intellect to transform "the blood," which, in other words, is a transformation of the individual soul and the soul of the world – nothing less than a work of magic. Playwright and actor Lin Manuel Miranda has said very much the same regarding the powers of art and artist, and more specifically the power of literature: "To engender empathy and create a world using only words is the closest thing we have to magic."[21] To feel empathy one needs to somehow be transported into the lives of others; this is a type of magic that our fractured world desperately needs. All art forms are capable of this type of transport and transformation when crafted by the caring voices, bodies, and minds of the artist.

To equate artmaking with magic is to also consider the artwork (whether a physical object like a painting or an experience like a theatrical performance) itself as a magical object, a manifestation of imagination that is alive, ensouled, and not dependent upon its maker. Octavio Paz understood what we so often misunderstand today: that a work of art is capable of becoming a *talisman* – a medium for transmission of "forces and powers that are sacred, that are *other*. The function of art is to open for us the doors that lead to the other side of reality."[22] This is magic.

The Western world's long history of iconoclasm and distrust of art, particularly visual and sacred art, acts as a convincing argument *for* the autonomy and power of the artwork. Why have artworks been feared to the point of desecration and destruction if not for fear of their power? Do we fear what Rilke came to know; that they *behold us* just as we behold them?

Camille Paglia has argued that a type of Puritanism lingers in "conservative suspicions about the sorcery" of beauty.[23] We turn to the word "beautiful" to describe everything from a building to a sunset, from a song to a smile. The "soul" of a thing, including an artwork, could be described as its "beauty." The souls of things touch our own souls, and the resulting sensation is aesthetic: We are moved and at the same time reminded of our vulnerability as souls among souls. This is

148 The Soul, the Creative, and the Archetypal Artist

the effect of *aesthesis*, the gasp of recognition that both Campbell and Hillman returned to over and over again in their writings. For Slattery, "*aesthesis* is a moment of both anticipation and fulfillment. . . [which] engages a noticing and a being noticed by. . . . It is an instant of sudden making, which is the original sense of *poesis*."[24]

In its splendor, the aesthetic encounter with an artwork as a soul can guide us back to the *via aesthetica* – the path of beauty. As with Rilke, these encounters may startle and unsettle us into changing our lives as there is nothing that does not see us. No wonder we put up defenses against beauty, against the soul. Poet Claire Lejeune clarified this strange phenomenon: "The ultimate object of human fear is Beauty. Nothing is more disarming, more ravishing, than its eruption in our lives."[25]

To consider the possibility that an artwork (whether a poem, painting, film, novel, dance, or other object or experience) is alive and ensouled is not an archaic nor overly romantic idea. As already noted, contemporary scholars of culture and the arts have gone so far as to describe art objects and artifacts as having "their own lives and fortunes."[26] In a similar manner, artists have long described their creations as their children – creations birthed by the artist but also independent beings, like any child. In conversation with Rollo May, the poet W.H. Auden once said that "the poet marries the language, and out of this marriage the poem is born."[27] May followed this with his own observation that the language of a poem is an equal spouse to the poet: Language uses the poet to the same degree that the poet uses language. The poet is not the only member of this trio with desires; the language (the artform) and the poem/child (the artwork) have their own desires, their own souls.

Hillman's sustained preoccupation with soul and image and with image *as* soul offers an eye-opening collection of insights into sincere discussions into the ensoulment of all the things around us, as beings in their own right.[28] Recall that an archetypal understanding of images begins with imagination; anything from a dream figure to an animal, to a poem, to a person, may reveal its innate living image (its soul) when approached with fascination and care. As we have seen, the word "image" defies a single meaning: Images are emanations of imagination, they are the *thing* crafted or made manifest, *and* the deep interiority or essence that is synonymous with soul.

All of the relational movements that Hillman advocated for as steps toward getting to know dream images on their own terms are just as valid for encountering images in the world:

> If, as Jung says, "image is psyche," then why not go on to say, "images are souls," and our job with them is to meet them on that soul level. . . . This is indeed different from interpretation. No friend or animal wants to be interpreted, even though it may cry for understanding. We might as well call the unfathomable depth in the image, love, or at least say we cannot get to the soul of the image without love of the image.[29]

Eros at the crossroads: what the artist knows

Nothing can happen at the crossroads without risk, openness, communion, and without some type of love. As Jung stated in a talk devoted to the sixteenth-century physician, alchemist, astrologer, and philosopher Paracelsus: "where there is no love, there is no art."[30] Jung was speaking about the art of healing, seeing little distinction between the physician, the philosopher, and the artist, as they all turn to the same universal sources for their powers – powers that are not actually theirs but are instead expressed through them as intermediaries. Moreover, these powers will not "work" properly if the practitioner's "heart is false."

Jung was moved by Paracelsus's insistence upon healing being a work of a true heart properly situated to receive the earth's medicine. The readiness of the heart is akin to the Zen notion of *shoshin*, or "beginner's mind," where openness, eagerness, and humility are fostered and egoic control is recognized and diminished. Amplifying this readiness further is Keats's notion of "negative capability" where dwelling in uncertainties, mystery, and doubt is endured without grasping for fact and reason. This is the experience of the artist as crossroads, which combines patience with insecurity and humility. Creators, healers, and teachers have commented upon this experience utilizing metaphors complimentary to the crossroads, such as picturing the artist as a type of radio receiver as expressed by Leroy Little Bear:

> It's almost as though you act simply as a conduit, like a radio, picking up energy waves that are always there and flowing through you. . . . it just depends where you're tuned. . . . That's the reason why our people go on a vision quest. That is why I call upon the bears. I call upon the eagle. I call on the rocks, the plants, and so on to tell us knowledge that we would not otherwise pick up – the knowledge that is beyond our frequency range.[31]

Mirroring this same sentiment, John Lennon spoke about his own turning away from the grind of the music industry during a period of creative illness to truly hear again and to heal:

> The real music, the music of the spheres, the music that surpasses understanding comes to me, I'm just the channel. But in order to get that channel clear again, I had to stop picking up every radio station in the world, in the universe. So turning away from it is how I began to heal.[32]

What these insights reveal is the advantage – the necessity, really – of "not knowing," as a prerequisite for creating. Creation is more accurately *reception and recognition* made possible through preparation, *plus* a readiness that is akin to devotion, to shape what is received and recognized at the crossroads. It is a type of dreaming with eyes open that is counterintuitive to our prevailing notions of personal will and control. It is dreaming with a combination of what Corbin termed "eyes of fire" and "eyes of flesh." Mary Oliver put it even more simply: "Pay attention/Be astonished/Tell about it."[33]

In the telling and making, we do not make anything absolutely new; rather, as *bricoleurs*, we combine and recombine in the manner of psyche itself; which as Jung observed is the quintessential creator: "Our souls as well as our bodies are composed of individual elements which were all already present in the ranks of our ancestors. The 'newness' of the individual psyche is an endlessly varied combination of age-old components."[34]

In this book's introduction, the "artist" was described as one who feels a need to "make" beyond necessity, to recombine what is given into new forms, and to create something extraordinary out of the ordinary. The *poesis* practiced by the creative individual was described as a type of making, or bringing forth, that implies a heightened sense of devotion to a creative potential and service to what Jung called the "creative spirit." Along the way, a few more layers have been added to this description including: the artist as a *psychopomp* or guide who bridges the material and spiritual worlds; the artist as a magician or alchemist with powers to preserve and to transform; the artist as one who expresses a shamanic sensibility with its underlying attunement to an interconnected and ensouled cosmos; and the artist as a valued soul worker. These are noble and soul-stirring descriptions, and contemporary creators could use some ennobling and stirring of the soul.

Lest they lead to inflation and hubris, however, these descriptions should be combined and tempered with other more vulnerable and all-too-human depictions that have also been introduced. Jung depicted the creative individual as being driven by a daimon, as a servant to an alien will, and as a nutrient or medium utilized by the artwork. Hillman described the artist as an "angelos of anxiety," one who lives a particularly susceptible and permeable existence with affinities to a type of consciousness linked to the *puer* (the eternal youth) and the hermaphrodite that is typified by desire and disappointment, longing, and love.

Similar to Hillman's notions, Martha Graham portrayed the artist as one who embodies a paradox of "divine dissatisfaction," melding a type of exhilarating exceptionality with deep frustration and a sense of duty.[35] Kunitz balanced on this same edge when describing creators as "representative human beings," who are also linked to their fellow human beings as "sensitive keyboards" always reacting to the world's "weather" with songs of loss and loneliness, alternating with songs of harmony and companionship. Believing that one is "representative" is not a reflection of a large ego, it is a necessary support for giving one's life over to create things of value.[36]

Turning to Hillman's assessment of the creative individual, we can say that artists are models of soul-making, which is not a romantic or ethereal designation but one that places them firmly into the muck of life – the *prima materia*. They show us how to take the scraps, the driftwood, the rags, and the bones, and alchemize them into something valuable and necessary for the soul. Hillman's artist's fantasy allows all to be artists of soul:

> If we imagine ourselves engaged as artists in life, if we use artists as our models . . . then we would work with the daily mess in our lies as the material

The Soul, the Creative, and the Archetypal Artist   151

for psychological creativity. . . . I mean having gratitude toward what one is given, for out of that one makes one's life. . . . you don't have to become creative because the psyche is already that; right in its mess there is creation going on. The artist fantasy of oneself accepts the mess, likes it, needs it.[37]

To approach one's life as artists approach their work is to realize that the opus of the soul is a continual crafting onto a surface that becomes a palimpsest – movements of addition and of building up alternate with movements of subtraction and scraping away. Most importantly, we realize that it is the soul who is doing the making: "Not I but the wind," wrote D.H. Lawrence. Hillman offered the same revelation in different words:

Not I personify, but the anima personifies me, or soul-makes herself through me, giving my life her sense – her intense daydream is my "me-ness": and "I," as a psychic vessel whose existence is a psychic metaphor, an "as-if being," in which every single belief is a literalism except the belief of soul whose faith posits me and makes me possible as a personification of psyche.[38]

Creation happens at the crossroads of desire and dissatisfaction, longing and love – the place where we ourselves are being created.

The good host and the coming guest

Jung never gave up arguing for the vital necessity of listening to psyche's messages, which he saw most clearly expressed through the artist:

We have simply got to listen to what the psyche spontaneously says to us. . . . What the dream, which is not manufactured by us, says is just *so*. Say it again as well as you can. . . . It is the great dream, which has always spoken through the artist as a mouthpiece. All his love and passion (his "values") flow towards the coming guest to proclaim his arrival.[39]

Writing to his friend, Herbert Read, Jung explained that the "coming guest" was no less than "the future and the picture of the new world, which we do not understand."[40] von Franz concurred as she emphasized the role of the creative individual for the collective:

It is generally the creative artist who creates the future. A civilization that has no creative people is doomed. So the person who is really in touch with the future, with the germs of the future, is the creative personality.[41]

Jung and von Franz knew the importance of consciously hosting the psyche and of paying attention to the guests who arrive carrying with them their own immediate desires and intentions, as well as intimations of the future. To approach the mysteries of creativity is not so much to seek them – and definitely *not* to try to harness them – but to ready oneself to host the guests that psyche sends forth. Over his long lifetime as a poet, Kunitz came to understand that,

> [T]he more you enter into the unconscious life the more you believe in its existence and know it walks with you, the more available it becomes and the doors open faster and longer. It learns you are a friendly host.[42]

To prepare for the coming guest is to anticipate, oftentimes with more than a bit of dread, that the intentions of the guest will supersede our own. To use words that Hillman used interchangeably: The guest is the image, the soul, the acorn, the angel – and our task is to determine what the guest expects from us. The realization (making real) of the image is the primary act of individuation – not my will, not my individuation but that of the *imagine del coeur*, the image of the heart.[43]

To consider (along with Jung, Hillman, Lawrence, Nin, Oliver, Paz, Kunitz, and so many others) that art may have a mission that aims at what Hillman termed, "restoring a fallen world," we must also consider art itself as a guest with its own intentions: "[Art] has a program – a program, however, that does not stem from the will of the artist, but emerges from the image as the image develops in the artist's service to it."[44] This challenges the prevailing and deadening modern understanding of art and artmaking that denies claims to any sort of mission. Sensitive artists know better; like poet Lawrence Ferlinghetti who believed that "art is capable of the total transformation of the world, and of life itself, and nothing less is really acceptable."[45]

The dark rainbow, the blessing hand, and the archetypal artist

A hundred years ago, two office mates (Franz Kafka and Gustav Janouch) would walk the streets of Prague during their lunch hours. The younger associate, Janouch, would take notes and would later set down their conversations in his notebooks. The topics that they explored are the same topics that creators, philosophers, theologians, and psychologists have always explored and that have been explored here: How does one deal with the call to create? What is an artist? What does art do? What is the nature of the soul and what does it want?

Born just a decade after Jung, Kafka did not live beyond forty years of age. Like so many of today's creators, he spent his weekdays working a regular job that he needed; a job that he did very well and one that made a difference in the lives of many. Kafka's nights and weekends were spent writing stories and thinking deeply about the power of art. His efforts yielded insights into creativity and the lives of creators that are rich with uncanny parallels to those that we have seen from Jung, confirming Read's observation that poets and philosophers had long been exploring the same territory that psychologists claimed to have discovered.[46]

The Soul, the Creative, and the Archetypal Artist   153

The notion of dwelling in "not knowing" while awaiting the "coming guest" was poignantly expressed by Kafka as he reflected upon his own calling as a poet:

> I try to be a true attendant upon grace. Perhaps it will come – perhaps it will not come. . . . I do not know. But that does not disturb me. In the meantime, I have made friends with my ignorance.[47]

Both Kafka and Jung brought art and science back together as fellow servants of what Jung called the "creative spirit." Each in their own way, both men intuited an endlessly creative middle ground of soul (*esse in anima*) between all sets of polarities:

> Man throws himself into the dark rainbow, which spans living and dying in order to offers existence a home in the cradle of his little ego. That is what science, art and prayer all do. So that to sink into oneself is not to fall into the unconscious, but to raise what is only dimly divined into the bright surface of consciousness.[48]

This is what Jung meant by "say it again as well as you can" in regard to psyche's dream language. This is what artists do: We wait, we notice, we attend, we are astonished, and we do our best to restate and redraw, to raise to the surface, what psyche has offered. Many times we fail, but we are driven to keep trying by a type of devotion that sometimes feels like servitude, and just as often like an overflowing love: "the creative" according to Hillman, "is an achievement of love."[49] This is the destiny of the archetypal artist; whether shaman, *sourcier*, *artifex*, *bricoleur*, *psychopomp*, trickster, wounded healer, or any combination of terms both mythic and ordinary – terms which ultimately *mean nothing* in and of themselves. What matters is what artists can do, what they love and attend to, and what they can bring forth and bestow from the "dark rainbow."

Resting outside of a church on one of their walks, Janouch asked Kafka to explain the nature and purpose of art. Kafka replied that "art, like prayer, is a hand outstretched in the darkness, seeking for some touch of grace that will transform it into a hand that bestows gifts."[50] Deep in our collective imagination, the rhizome that once fused art with magic, divination, philosophy, alchemy, science, medicine, prophecy, and prayer for our archaic ancestors is still intact, although we have forgotten that the disparate shoots that emerge into the daylight are all siblings. These shoots, like small and hopeful hands emerging from the earth, all reach for the same thing: for the grace to bestow gifts.

Notes

1 Qtd. by Campbell, *The Power of Myth*, p. 69.
2 Lévi-Strauss, "An Introduction," in *Myth and Meaning: Cracking the Code of Culture,* pp. 3–4.

3 See Chapter 3 for profiles of both Read and Neumann, including their advancement of Jungian theories and their unique contributions to the nature of creativity.
4 Chevalier and Gheerbrant, *The Penguin Dictionary of Symbols*, p. 929.
5 Campbell, *The Power of Myth*, pp. 85–89.
6 See Erdman Campbell's statement in the Introduction.
7 Nin, *The Diary of Anaïs Nin*, p. 154.
8 Ibid., p. 153. See Chapter 2 for Jung's thoughts on the artist as one capable of speaking in a thousand voices.
9 Tucker, *Dreaming with Eyes Open: The Shamanic Spirit in Twentieth Century Art and Culture*, p. 229. After John Coltrane's death, Alice Coltrane continued her career as a solo artist, composer, and bandleader, eventually taking vows as a *swamini* and leading her own congregation.
10 J.R. Ramakrishnan, "Books as Medicine: A Conversation with Sandra Cisneros," in ElectricLiterature.com.
11 See Chapter 2 and also Jung's "The Relation of Analytical Psychology to Poetry," in *CW15*, p. 72, para 108.
12 Rilke, "Archaic Torso of Apollo," in *Ahead of All Parting: Selected Poems and Prose by Rainer Maria Rilke*, p. 67.
13 Old Torlino, qtd. in Kenneth Lincoln, *Native American Renaissance*, p. 37.
14 Hillman, *Thought of the Heart and Soul of the World*, p. 101. See also Chapter 5 for Hillman's articulation of the *anima mundi*, which encompasses the man-made objects of the world.
15 Ibid., p. 105. See also Hillman and Michael Ventura's *We've Had a Hundred Years of Psychotherapy and the World Is Getting Worse* for more on Hillman's views on the *anima mundi* and the sufferings of soul in the man-made environment.
16 See Bohm's *On Creativity* as well as the 2020 film titled *Infinite Potential* by filmmaker Paul Howard.
17 See Chapter 1 for contributions on these theories from Bazin, Tucker, Dissanayake, and others.
18 See Chapter 6 for Little Bear's description of ceremony in regard to the idea that creation consists of both construction and destruction, plus Jung's assertions on the latter on Chapter 2.
19 See Chapter 6 for more on the figure of the Hermit and his relationship to Hermes and other trickster/magician figures.
20 Lawrence, "Whitman," in *D.H. Lawrence: Studies in Classic American Literature*, p. 180.
21 Miranda, "Lin Manuel Miranda: By the Book," in *the New York Times*.
22 Paz, *Essays on Mexican Art*, p. 40.
23 Paglia, "Introduction," in *Glittering Images: A Journey Through Art from Egypt to Star Wars*, p. xii.
24 Slattery, "Mimesis, Neurology and the Aesthetics of Presence," in *Psychological Perspectives: A Quarterly Journal of Jungian Thought*, p. 275.
25 Lejeune qtd. in Paris, *Pagan Meditations: Aphrodite, Hestia, Artemis*, p. 17.
26 See Chapter 4 for Heywood and Sandywell as part of an expanded discussion on the idea of image as proposed by Hillman.
27 May, *The Courage to Create*, p. 85.
28 See Chapters 4 and 5 for more on archetypal perspectives on image and soul. See also the work of Ginette Paris, Dennis Patrick Slattery, Roberts Avens, Glen Slater, Safron Rossi, Michael Meade, Mary Watkins, Edward Casey, and Thomas Moore for sensitive appraisal of Hillman's work on many topics, especially image and soul.
29 Hillman, "An Inquiry into Image," in *Spring 1977: An Annual of Archetypal Psychology and Jungian Thought*, p. 81.

30 Jung, "Paracelsus the Physician," in *CW15*, p. 29, para. 42.

31 Little Bear, qtd. in Hill, "Listening to Stones," in *Alberta Views*.

32 Lennon, qtd. in Graustark, "For John Lennon Isolation Had a Silver Lining," in *the New York Times*.

33 Oliver, "Sometimes," in *Devotions: Selected Poems by Mary Oliver*, p. 105.

34 Jung, *Memories, Dreams, Reflections*, p. 235.

35 See the Introduction for more on Graham's notion of "divine dissatisfaction."

36 Kunitz and Lentine, *The Wild Braid: A Poet Reflects on a Century in the Garden*, pp. 64, 103. See also Chapter 5 for more insights from Kunitz brought together with Hillman's.

37 Hillman, *Inter Views: Conversations with Laura Pozzo*, p. 62.

38 Hillman, *Re-Visioning Psychology*, p. 51.

39 Jung, "Letter to Herbert Read," in *Letters, Vol. 2, 1951–1961*, pp. 591–592.

40 Ibid.

41 Von Franz and James Hillman, *Lectures on Jung's Typology*, p. 43.

42 Kunitz and Lentine, *The Wild Braid*, p. 87.

43 Hillman and Ventura, *We've Had a Hundred Years of Psychotherapy and the World Is Getting Worse*, p. 62.

44 Hillman, "Ideas I See in Her Work," in *Margot McLean Ritratti Di Artista*, p. 68.

45 Vitale, "Lawrence Ferlinghetti Beat Poet and Small-Press Publisher Dies at 101," in *NPR Morning Edition*.

46 See the Introduction and Chapter 3 for more in-depth assessments of Sir Herbert Read's contributions.

47 Kafka, qtd. in Janouch, *Conversations with Kafka*, p. 116.

48 Ibid., p. 113.

49 Hillman, *The Myth of Analysis*, p. 54. See also Chapters 4 and 5.

50 Ibid., p. 48.

References

Armstrong, Karen. *A Short History of Myth*. New York, NY: Cannongate. 2005.

Campbell, Joseph and Bill Moyers. *The Power of Myth*. Edited by Betty Sue Flowers. New York, NY: Doubleday Books. 1988.

Chevalier, Jean and Alain Gheerbant. *The Penguin Book of Symbols*. 1969. Translated by John Buchanan-Brown. New York, NY: Penguin Books.

Graustark, Barbara. "For John Lennon Isolation Had a Silver Lining." In the *New York Times*. 8 Dec. 2020.

Hill, Don. "Listening to Stones: Learning in Leroy Little Bear's Laboratory: Dialogue in the World Outside." In *Alberta Views*. 1 Sept. 2008. albertaviews.ca/listening-to-stones.

Hillman, James. "An Inquiry into Image." In *Spring 1977: An Annual of Archetypal Psychology and Jungian Thought*. New York, NY: Spring Publications. 1977.

Hillman, James. *The Myth of Analysis: Three Essays in Archetypal Psychology*. 1972. New York, NY: Harper Collins. 1978.

Hillman, James. *Inter Views: Conversations with Laura Pozzo on Psychotherapy, Biography, Love, Soul, Dreams, Work, Imagination, and the State of the Culture*. New York, NY: Harper and Row. 1983.

Hillman, James. *Re-Visioning Psychology*. 1976. New York, NY: Harper Perennial. 1992.

Hillman, James. *The Thought of the Heart and the Soul of the World*. Woodstock, CT: Spring Publications. 1995.

Hillman, James. "Ideas I See in Her Work." In *Margot McLean: Ritratti D'Artista*. Bergamo, Italy: Moretti and Vitali Editori. 2002.

Hillman, James and Michael Ventura. *We've Had a Hundred Years of Psychotherapy and the World Is Getting Worse*. New York, NY: Harper Collins. 1992.

Janouch, Gustav. *Conversations with Franz Kafka*. Translated by Goronwy Rees. 1968. New York, NY: New Directions Books. 2012.

Jung, Carl Gustav. "Paracelsus the Physician." 1941. In *The Spirit in Man, Art, and Literature: CW15*. Edited by Herbert Read, Michael Fordham, Gerhard Adler and William McGuire. Translated by R.F.C. Hull. Princeton, NJ: Princeton University Press. 1966.

Jung, Carl Gustav. *Letters*. Vol. 2. 1951–1961. Edited by Gerhard Adler and Aniela Jaffé. Translated by R.F.C. Hull. Princeton, NJ: Princeton University Press. 1975.

Jung, Carl Gustav. *Memories, Dreams, Reflections*. 1963. Edited by Aniela Jaffé. Translated by Richard and Clara Winston. New York, NY: Vintage Books. 1989.

Kunitz, Stanley and Genine Lentine. *The Wild Braid: A Poet Reflects on a Century in the Garden*. New York, NY: W.W. Norton and Company. 2005.

Lawrence, D.H. "Whitman." In *D. H. Lawrence: Studies in Classic American Literature*. 1923. New York, NY: Penguin Books. 1977.

Lévi-Strauss, Claude. *Myth and Meaning: Cracking the Code of Culture*. 1979. New York, NY: Shocken Books. 1995.

Lincoln, Kenneth. *Native American Renaissance*. Berkeley, CA: University of California Press. 1983.

May, Rollo. *The Courage to Create*. 1975. New York, NY: W.W. Norton and Company. 1994.

Miranda, Lin Manuel. "Lin Manual Miranda: By the Book." In *New York Times*. 5 Apr. 2016.

Nin, Anaïs. *The Diaries of Anaïs Nin: Volume Four, 1944–1947*. Edited by Gunther Sthulmann. New York, NY: Harvest Books. 1971.

Oliver, Mary. "Sometimes." In *Devotions: The Selected Poems of Mary Oliver*. New York, NY: Penguin Books. 2017.

Paglia, Camille. *Glittering Images: A Journey Through Art from Egypt to Star Wars*. New York, NY: Pantheon. 2012.

Paris, Ginette. *Pagan Meditations: Aphrodite, Hestia, Artemis*. Translated by Gwendolyn Moore. Dallas, TX: Spring Publications. 1987.

Paz, Octavio. *Essays on Mexican Art*. Translated by Helen Lane. New York, NY: Harcourt, Brace and Company. 1993.

Ramakrishnan, J.R. "Books as Medicine: A Conversation with Sandra Cisneros." *ElectricLiterature.com*. 2 Nov. 2015.

Rilke, Rainer Maria. "Torso of Apollo." In *Ahead of All Parting: Selected Poetry and Prose of Rainer Maria Rilke*. Edited and Translated by Stephen Mitchell. New York, NY: Modern Library. 1995.

Slattery, Dennis Patrick. "Mimesis, Neurology, and the Aesthetics of Presence." In *Psychological Perspectives: A Quarterly of Jungian Thought*. Vol. 56, No. 3. Sept. 2013.

Tucker, Michael. *Dreaming with Eyes Open: The Shamanic Spirit in Twentieth Century Art and Culture*. San Francisco, CA: Aquarian, Harper. 1992.

Vitale, Tom. "Lawrence Ferlinghetti, Beat Poet and Small-Press Publisher Dies at 101." In *NPR Morning Edition*. 23 Feb. 2021.

von Franz, Marie-Louise and James Hillman. *Lectures on Jung's Typology*. 1971. Thompson, CT: Spring Publications. 2020.

Epilogue as Testament and Talisman

The astute reader will have noticed that this book does not contain a single "I" or direct first-person assertion amidst the many circumambulations around its main questions – but of course, there *is* an "I" behind the scenes. I have somehow attempted here, outside of my initial intent, to embody Lévi-Strauss's idea of the artist as the crossroads of unknowing, with its embedded elements of patience and chance, to which I would add doubt, fear, foolhardiness, courage, and devotion. This effort, accomplished over too many years with too many delays, took everything that I had within me – yet none of it originated with me. I simply (or not so simply) became a crossroads where travelers began to arrive bringing with them tales of their encounters with the mysteries of the soul and of creativity. I'm honored to have been their host and their scribe. This book has emerged as both a testament and a talisman – again, not something totally intended – but something now recognized and held in gratitude and awe. May it now deliver gifts and blessings to all who are called to create.

DOI: 10.4324/9780429057724-9

Index

acorn theory (Hillman) 12, 33n32, 96, 109–112, 152
aesthesis 148
aisthesis 95, 100
alchemy, alchemist 3, 8, 79, 153; artist as 68, 71, 135, 150; artistic process as 147; desire (Eros) and 133–135; European 27, 78; Hermes Trismegistus and 125; hermit and 125; Jung's forays in 42, 55–57; Neuman's ideas on 66; Paracelsus 149; Read's views on 68, 71, 73; Rowland's ideas on 11; synchronicity and 79; *unus mundus* of 78
amor fati 106
analytical psychology 6, 44, 85
angel 3, 111–112, 152; "dark" 38, 111; sacrifice required by 114
angelos (vulnerable emissaries) 11, 106–109
angelos of anxiety 108, 150
"Angel that Troubled the Waters, The" (Wilder) 130–131
Anima (feminine voice that spoke through Jung) 37, 105
anima: animus and 106; as archetypal prism 134; artist and 106; *esse in anima* 55, 105, 153; Hillman's understanding of 104, 105–106; Jung's thinking regarding 38, 42, 43, 51, 52–55; as personification of self 114; Read's understanding of Jung's position on 69–70; vitalism in relationship to 11
anima ars 144–148
animalism 71

animal magnetism 27
animals: helpful 20; human 92; hybrid 18; as images 91–92; painter and 19; rights of 84; soul in form of 22
anima mundi (world soul) 10, 12, 115; *anima ars* and 144–148; Hillman's concept of 84, 91, 103–104; Jung's relationship with 56, 92; personal dream image webbed into 92; Western denial of 27
animism 77
animus 51, 55, 105–106
Anubis 129
Anzaldúa, Gloria 130
Apollo 102, 124; "Archaic Torso of Apollo" (Rilke) 145
Apollonian 128
archetypal ancestors of modern creators 120–137; shaman as 3, 12, 19–20, 65
archetypal artist *see* artist
archetypal creativity 83–97
archetypal eye 87–88, 91, 103
archetypal figures *see* Hermit; magic and magicians; shaman; Trickster
archetypal images 10, 45; symbols as 78
archetypal imagination 85–87
archetypal poetics 87–88
archetypal potentials 41
archetypal psychology 6, 7, 8, 22, 53, 83, 96; as archetype in itself 116; Corbin's influence on 104; Heraclitus's influence on 18; *see also* Hillman, James
archetypal, the 11
archetypal theory 8
archetypes: Apollonic 102; art and 48–50;

Index   159

artist and 44–48; as contrasexual forces 51; of God-image 54; Great Mother as 63, 95; ideas around 8–9, 10; Jung and 67, 70, 72, 79; Le Guin's understanding of 121; power of 64; Read's understanding of 71; *see also* anima; animus

Ardhanarisha (The Half-Woman Lord) 8, 133

Armstrong, Karen 7, 12, 122, 136

art 4; archetype and 48–50; desires of 144–148; as face of the soul 117; Freud's model of 28–32; as "guest" with its own intentions 152; Hillman's writing on 11; Paglia's view of 9; power of 147; akin to prayer 10, 153; prehistoric 19; psychological or visionary, Jung's delineation between 11, 48–50; soulful 32; as talisman 147; *see also* artmaking

art historian *see* Read, Herbert (Sir)

artifex 7, 12, 135; Jung as 55–57, 83

artist: acorn theory (Hillman) and 109–112; aesthetic soul and 100–101; "alien will" seizing 132; *angelos* and 106–109; anima and 105–106; archaic 144; archetypal 142–153; archetypal images used by 90; archetypal model of 8–9, 19, 44–48; born or made 109; daily ritual of 114; defining 2–3; "divine frenzy" of 45; "education of the age" as activity of 66; eye of 88, 91; first 18; Freud's description of 28, 31; inner life as explored by 6; Jung as reluctant 11, 37–57; Jung's views of 93; hermaphrodite 134; Hermes and 124, 125; Hillman's view of 84, 100–101, 104–116; images and 92, 93; Neumann on 63–64, 65; Read's understanding of 69; psyche as 87, 101; soul as 12, 101; *sourcier*, shaman and 9–10; Wheelwright's understanding of 120; *see also* Leonardo da Vinci; Michelangelo; Kandinsky; McLean, Margot; Picasso, Pablo

artist as alchemist 68, 71, 135, 150

artist as bisexual being 65, 74, 133

artist as bricoleur 7, 126

artist as craftsperson 7

artist as "daylight dreamer" 136

artist as engaged citizen 109

artist as "field of operation" 143

artist as insider 109

artist as madman 128

artist as magician 150

artist as outsider 109

artist as psychopomp 108, 115, 150, 153

artist as shaman 16, 17, 19–20, 46, 66, 68, 79, 127

artist as thief 124

artist fantasy (Hillman) 12, 96, 107, 109, 112, 114, 136

artistic ability 2, 4, 136; creativity unlinked from 52

artistic calling 50

artistic continuum of soul 26

artistic creation 20, 73; magic power of 66; as mission and service 73; two categories (Jung) 48

artistic expression 47, 68; ancient 21

artistic practice 6; depth psychology and 72

artistic, the 73, 96

artistic voices 10

artistic wholes 78

artistry 96; as separate from creativity 11, 52, 85, 94, 106–107, 109

artmaking 7, 76, 152; "creation in time" as definition of 78; ego-control and 115; Hillman's ideas regarding 95, 101; by Jung 41, 44; as magic 147; mythmaking and 120–123, 136; Paleolithic 146; power of 147; Read's understanding of 68

Asclepius, Asklepios 8, 21, 56, 130–131

astrologer 86, 149

astrology 76, 79

astronomy 125

Athena 29, 131

Auden, W.H. 148

Augustine *see* Saint Augustine

"autonomous psychic complex" 88

Avens, Roberts 7, 104, 105, 108, 154n28

Bachelard, Gaston 7, 88

Bair, Deirdre 38

160 Index

Baker, Josephine 110
Barfield, Owen 7, 88
Baroque era 27
Bazin, Germain 19
Berger, John 19
Bergman, Ingmar 109
Berk, Tjeu van den *see* van de Berk, Tjeu
Berry, Pat 85, 90
Berry, Thomas 9, 56–57
Bettelheim, Bruno 31
bisexuality (in Neumann's notion of the
    artist) 65, 74, 133
Blake, William 26, 49, 88, 89
bricolage 8, 56; dreams and 92; primal
    creation as 126
bricoleur 7, 12, 92; archetypal artist as
    153; "artist fantasy" of 96; Coyote
    trickster figure as 126; psyche and 150;
    of soul 84
Bright, William 126

calling 7, 20, 56, 121; announcing of 111;
    artistic 50, 146; daimonic 11; human
    52; individual 94; inner 110; Oliver on
    96; sense of 143; shamanic 65; *see also*
    creative calling
call to create 109–112
Cambray, Joseph 7
Campbell, Joseph 3, 7, 12, 133; on
    aesthesis 148; on "aesthetic arrest" 66;
    on "art as mirror held up to nature" 136;
    on myth, art, and divinity 121–122; on
    shaman as artist 143
Campbell, Jean Erdman 3; on kinship
    between poet and mystic 143
Casey, Edward 154n28
cave painting 18–20, 26, 68
Changing Woman (Native American
    creation figure) 8, 134
Charot 27
Chiron 130, 131
Chuang Tzu/Zhuangzi 51
Cisneros, Sandra 144
Coatlicue and Coatlicue consciousness
    127–130
Coleridge, Samuel Taylor 18, 88
collective dreams 136

collective unconscious: Jung's concept
    of 5, 8, 10, 22, 39, 41, 45–49; animus,
    anima, and 55; Neumann's emphasis
    on 64; Plotinus' "universal psyche"
    compared to 87; psyche and 53; Read's
    work on 67, 72; symbols and 78
Coltrane, John and Alice 144, 154
complex (Jungian notion of) 10, 44–45, 47
Complexity Theory ("Emergence"
    theory) 76
Complex Psychology 45
Copernicus 27
Corbin, Henry 7, 11, 85, 88, 123; advocacy
    for the soul's autonomy 113; dual vision
    described by (eyes of flesh or fire) 108,
    149; influence on Hillman 105; on the
    imaginary world 104
Cornford, F.M. 22
Coyote 8, 123, 126
Coyolxauhqui 130
creative act 1; analysis as 95
creative calling 3, 5, 6, 32, 111, 147;
    Jung's ideas regarding 63; Riklin 43
creative condition 19
creative consciousness 134–136
creative cosmos 136
creative expression 16, 32; woundedness
    linked to 132
creative fire 11, 48
creative flux 17
creative genius 107; *see also* genius
creative illness 28, 30, 131; Hillman 83;
    Jung 41–42; Lennon 149
creative illumination 76
creative individual 7, 11, 20; creative man
    as 65–66; Dionysian patterns displayed
    by 128; "eyes of art" 108; Jung's
    writings and observations on 31, 45–48;
    natural ambiguity of 106; Neumann's
    writing on 65; power of 146; value of
    67; work of the soul performed by 115;
    as world-bridger 75; *see also* bisexuality
creative inspiration 23
creative instinct 84, 86, 93–94; Jung's
    theorizing of 127; *see also* instinct
"creative man": Jung 96; Neumann 65–66
creative play 4, 39, 75

Index   161

creative power 129, 131
creative practice: archaic healing and 21; human and divine 125; numinous with 11
creative principle 143
creative process 5, 24; Jung's articulation of 25; Neumann's ideas regarding 64; Read's contributions to 70–71
creative psychology 94
creative spirit 3, 150; Jung as servant of 37–57
creative, the 1; archetypal styles of 134; destructive potential of 126–127; Gordon's distinction between "the artistic" and 73; crossroads and crosscurrents of 142; Hillman's seventh notion of 95; longing for 4; multifaceted nature of 12, 122; as revealed by myth 133; service to 52; soul as 2
creativity 1; artistry and 52; crossroads faced by 4–5; as instinct or nature 50–52; as primal power 95; reimagining 10; *via aesthetica* and 94–97
crossroads 12; artists as 142–144; artists working at 64, 157; creativity at 4–5; creativity in and with the world at 79; creators arriving at 48, 106; between desire and dissatisfaction 149; *enodios* as 124; Eros at 149–151; between psyche and matter 78; soul, creative, and artist as residents at 142

Dadaism 42
daimon 2, 3; artist and (Jung) 37–38; *duende* and 132; Hillman's understanding of 111; Jung's notion of 10, 11, 43, 44, 47, 57, 89; "Myth of Er" (Plato) 110; Plato's understanding of 23
daimonion 38, 57n6, 112, 117n46
"daimon of creativity" 43, 44, 47, 57, 112
Dante [Alighieri] 26, 49
Darwin, [Charles] 27
da Vinci *see* Leonardo da Vinci
Davis, Bette 110
death 41; Dark Angel and 111; goddess of 132; life and 64, 75, 136; life without 132; rebirth and 74; soul and 102, 108

Death: Eros and 30
death drive 31
de Nerval *see* Nerval, Gérard de
depth psychology: archetypes in 71; artistic practice and 72; as/at crossroads 32; daimon in 112; dream images in 92; founding figures of 26–27; gods and goddesses approached through the lens of 123; Greek culture as providing foundational ground for 21, 25; Heraclitus' importance to 18; Hillman's return to 83; "image" in 90; "imagination" in lieu of "the unconscious" 89; Jung's understanding of work of 56; Le Guin's familiarity with 121; overview of 6–7, 20–28; philosophical continuum informing 26; Plato's Academy as beginning of 25, 26; psychic reality, insistence on 20; Vico as being poised between ancient and modern concerns of 86; *see also* Hillman, James; Rowland, Susan
Dilthey, [Wilhelm] 18
Dionysus/Dionysos 8, 95, 126–130
Dissanayake, Ellen 4
divination and divinatory practices 7, 24, 32, 79, 124, 153
Dodds, E.R. 22, 23
Doolittle, Hilda ("H.D.") 31
Downing, Christine 30–31, 132
duende 130, 132
dying 153
dying and creating 74
Dying and Creating (Gordon) 73

Earth Mother creation myth 77
Eckhart *see* Meister Eckhart
Eliade, Mircea 7, 12; on repetition of primordial acts 122; on rites of initiation 74; on shamans 16, 56; von Franz and 56
Ellenberger, Henri F. 20–21, 27; "creative illness," concept of 28, 30, 117n59
Empedocles 21–22, 39
Enlightenment 27
enodios (at the crossroads) 124
epistrophé 9, 80

162 Index

Er *see* Myth of Er (Plato)
Eranos conferences 67
Eros 8; artist and 149–151; Death and
    30; death drive and 31; Psyche and 95,
    133–135
Eros principle 38
Eshu 8, 126
esse in anima 55, 105, 153
eye *see* archetypal eye
"eyes of art" 108
eyes of flesh or fire 108, 149; *see also*
    Corbin, Henry

feminine consciousness 77
feminine creative force 133
feminine, the 27, 63, 79, 134; *see also* yin
    and yang
feminine Soul 103, 105
feminine strength 130
feminine voice *see* Anima
Ferlinghetti, Lawrence 152
Ficino, Marsilio 7, 18, 26, 86, 113, 145
Fliess, Wilhelm 29
Freud, Sigmund: art and soul in the work
    of 28–32; depth psychology and 18,
    20, 25–27, 28; Fliess and 29; Hillman's
    observations regarding 107; Jung's
    relationship with 41; Nazism and 32;
    Neumann's essays on 65; Oedipus,
    association with 30; psychoanalysis
    associated with 6; Romanticism's
    influence on 27; *Seele* and *seelisch*,
    concept of 31, 54; shamanic sensibility
    of 117n59; tripartite conception of the
    psyche 23; *see also* Downing, Christine
Freud as collector 29, 125

Gamwell, Lynn 29
García Lorca, Federico *see* Lorca, Federico
    García
Garland, Judy 109
Geb (Egyptian figure of) 8
genius: artist as 96, 107; Hillman's
    understanding of 96, 107, 111, 112;
    Jung as 38; muse as 2; myth of 107;
    Neumann as 67; sacrifice required
    for 114

Glück, Louise 5, 93
God-image 54
Goethe 26, 29, 49; *Faust* 39
Gordon, Rosemary 11, 63, 73–76, 80
Gorman, Amanda 5, 133
Graham, Martha 5, 112, 124; "divine
    dissatisfaction" of 3, 38, 150, 155n35
Great Mother 63, 95

Harari, Yuval Noah 7; on "imagined
    orders" 9, 136
Hatab, Lawrence 21, 22
H.D. *see* Doolittle, Hilda
Hephaestus 131
Heraclitus 7, 21, 26; "flux" in the writing
    of 78; Jung's interest in 39, 51;
    Hillman's debt to 101; Hillman's views
    of 17–18, 87; soul, understanding of
    17–18
hermae (herms or phallic stones) 142
hermaion (lucky finds) 124
hermaphrodite, Hermaphroditos/
    Hermaphroditus 8, 12, 105–106,
    133–135; artist and 150; etymology of
    133; magician and 136
Hermes 8; Aphrodite and 106, 133,
    138n67; "Homeric Hymn to" 124;
    as magician 125; as Mercury 123; as
    patron of artists, liars, and thieves 142;
    as trickster 123–127
Hermes Trismegistus 125
Hermit, the 125, 146–147
Heywood, Ian 91
Hillman, James 28; on alchemy and *artifex*
    56; anima, views of 95; *anima mundi*,
    view of 103–104; on archetypal eye 91;
    archetypal psychology associated with
    6, 22; on archetypes 8, 11; on artists and
    creators 7; on "artist's fantasy" 12; on
    creative instinct 4, 93–94; on creativity
    unlinked from artistic ability 52; on
    epistrophé 80; on *esse in anima* 105; fifth
    notion of creativity 95; first notion of
    creativity 94; fourth notion of creativity
    95; Heraclitus and 18; on hexagrams
    of *I Ching* and dreams 90; on image as
    ritual 93; Jung and 49, 50, 53, 55, 62,

Index   163

83–97; *Lament for the Dead* 43; on
Margot McClean 93; on Prometheus 95;
seventh notion of the creative 95; second
notion of creativity 94; seventh notion of
creativity 95; on six notions of creativity
95, 98n52; soul as a perspective 17; on
soul as symbol 2; on soul-making 4, 7,
11, 57n5, 92, 95, 97, 98n43, 100–119,
132, 150; *Soul's Code* 23, 109; on
via aesthetica 94–97; third notion of
creativity 95; *see also* acorn theory
Hollis, James 7, 10, 136
Horus 129
Howard, Brittany 5, 25
Howard, Paul 154n16
hun, Chinese principle of 51
Hunahpu and Xbalanque 126
hunger 4, 50, 86
Hyde, Lewis 12, 114, 126

image: animal 18; archetypal 8, 11, 45–46,
50, 78, 131; archetypal creativity and
83–97; crafting of 7; definition of 145;
dream 92, 123; father 94; God 54;
Hillman's championing of 83, 91, 148;
images among 96; inner 110; Jung's
understanding of 44, 48, 62; living 32,
88, 90; living reality of 48; personal 12;
primal 70; primordial 46, 144; psyche
as 6, 53, 55, 77, 88–91, 100; psychic
87, 145; Read's understanding of 68;
realization of (making real) 152; *Red
Book* (Jung) 70; as ritual 93; sensuous
91–92; soul as 148, 152; soul force of
20; speaking in 62; universal 47, 86
image answers 106
image as ritual 93
image makers: shaman as 9, 19
image making: soul making and 100–116
imagery 87; guided 21; visual 135
imaginal breathing (Hillman) 95
imaginal figures of the unconscious (Jung)
37, 43
imaginal meeting place (Jung) 76
imaginal, the 123
imaginal work (Jung) 79
imaginary, the (Bachelard) 88

imagination: archetypal 85–87; archetypal
creativity and 83–; archetypal models
of 8; collective 153; creative 4, 55,
134; creativity and 5–7, 62; display
of 92; Hillman as champion of 83, 84,
89, 92, 108; image and 11; images as
emanations of 146; Jung as performer
of 62–63; mythic 136; mythopoetic 44;
"piece of" 93, 96; poetic 22; soul as 103,
105, 116
imaginative process 2
"imagined orders" 9, 136
imagining 53
instinct 4, 27, 83; basic 86; creative 72, 84,
86, 93–95, 107, 109; creative opus and
93–94; creativity as 50–52, 64, 71, 106;
hunger 50; sexual 50; universal 11
Isis (goddess) 8, 123, 125, 129

Jaffé, Aniela 37
Janouch, Gustav 152, 153
Jaspers, Karl 10
Journal of Analytical Psychology 73
Joyce, James 26, 46, 47, 49, 67
Jung, Carl G.: as artist 44–48; *Black
Books* 41, 43, 54; creative illness
of 41–42; break with Freud 30, 41;
Liber Novus/Red Book 37, 42, 54, 56;
paradoxical thoughts on creativity
93–94; psychological art and visionary
art, delineation between 11, 48–50;
shamanic sensibility of 20, 55–57; Taoist
sensibility of 31, 51, 53, 75, 78, 88; *see
also* alchemy; artist; daimon; Freud,
Sigmund; Hillman, James; Read, Herbert;
von Franz, Marie-Louise; psyche
Jungian archetypes 8, 45, 70, 79
Jungian hypotheses 67
Jungian psychology 6, 62, 85
Jungians 47, 49, 55, 73; 21st-century 75
Jungian self 72
Jungian scholars 11, 63, 76, 80
Jungian symbol 77–79, 90, 93

Kafka, Franz 10, 152–153; "dark rainbow"
of 13; Neumann's essays on 65
Kali (goddess) 8, 127, 129–130

164 Index

Kandinsky, [Wassily] 26
Kant, [Immanuel] 7, 26
kathochos (the spellbinder) 124
Keats, John 26, 88, 101, 112–113, 143; "negative capability/capacity" 74, 108, 149
Kirtimukha 133
Kunitz, Stanley 5, 6; on creators as "representative human beings" 150; on "dark angel" 38, 111–112; on dreams and dream images 92; on "incantation and sense" 106; personification of the unconscious as a wilderness 47; *poesis*/making associated with 92; on social imperative of art 109; on the unconscious life 152; on vulnerability and openness 107

Lakota people 146
Lao Tzu/Laozi 7, 51
Lascaux, cave paintings at 18; *see also* cave paintings
Lawrence, D.H. 5, 114–115, 147, 152
Lears, Jackson 5, 47
Lennon, John 5, 143, 149
Leonardo da Vinci 26, 65
Little Bear, Leroy 126, 146, 149
Legba 8, 126
Le Guin, Ursula K. 5, 107, 121
Lejeune, Claire 148
Lévi-Strauss, Claude 138n36, 142–143, 157
Lommel, Andreas 19–20
Lopez, Barry 120–121, 137
López-Pedraza, Rafael 85, 133–134
Lorca, Federico García 132

magic and magician 4; archetypal manifestation of 8; artist as 150; artmaking as 147; shamans and 6; gift of 56; as mythic creators 12; Paleolithic artists as 19; psychology of 79; revelation and 65–66; seriousness of role of 73; shaman as 16, 131; tricksters and 123–127, 129; universal path of 3
Magician, the 147
magic power: artistic creation as possessing 66, 146

May, Rollo 7, 130, 148
McConeghey, Howard 7
McEvilley, Thomas 7, 12, 16–17, 86, 131
McGuire, William 80n18
McLean, Margot 93, 107–108
Meade, Michael 154n28
Meister Eckhart 26, 39, 113
Meier, C.A. 51
Menuhin, Yehudi 110
Michelangelo 26
Milton, [John] 88
Miranda, Lin Manuel 5, 147
Moltzer, Maria 43
Monet, [Claude] 104
monotheism 77
mundus imaginalis 85, 104
muses, the 72–73
myth 8, 20; archetypal eye attuned to 87; Armstrong's history of 122; creation 77, 94; denial of 21; dreams and 135; Egyptian 31; Freud's work with 30–31; Greek 21–22, 123, 134; Le Guin's understanding of 121; logic and 23; mytho-poetic disclosure without 22; ritual and 69; shared 9; symbol-creating power of 66; *see also* Narcissus; Oedipus; Psyche; Eros
mythical thinking 106
mythic wounding 132
mythmakers and mythmaking 10, 17; artmaking and 120–123, 136
Myth of Er (Plato) 38, 110
mythological project: artist as carrier of 10, 136
mythological studies 7
mythology 6, 27, 29; human nature understood via 85; Jung's knowledge of 40; psychology substituted for 70; value of 83; *see also* Campbell, Joseph
mythopoesis 10, 12, 120–137; ur-domain of 144
mythopoetic imagination 44
mythos and logos 79

narcissism 94
Narcissus 30

Index 165

Native American stories 126; *see also* Changing Woman; Coyote; Raven
Native peoples 39
Nelson, Benjamin 29
Nerval, Gérard de 26, 49, 50
Neumann, Erich 6, 7, 11, 25; on artist as bisexual being 65, 74, 133; on the artist and the numinous 63–65; on artist as shaman-like figure 68, 69; on creative principle as crossroads 143; on curative power as creative power 132; Eranos conferences, participation in 67; essays on creativity 65; importance of Psyche and Eros story to 134; on "unitary reality" 65, 66, 146; on the "wounded healer" 65–66
neurosis 28, 31
Newton, [Isaac] 27
Nietzsche, Friedrich 7, 26, 48–50; as cautionary tale 43; as Dionysius 128
Nin, Anaïs 5, 9, 143–144
Noë, Alva 6
numinosity 64, 77
numinosum, the 64, 65
numinous, the: creativity and 4, 94; myth and 121; Neumann and 11, 63–64, 70, 146; the self and 70
Nut (Egyptian figure of) 8

Odysseus 131
Oedipus 30, 131
Oliver, Mary 152; on "the Miraculous" 2, 5, 47, 52; poems about dogs 104; three lessons for living a life 96, 150
onieros (god of the dream) 124
Orpheus 131
Osiris 125, 129

Paglia, Camille 7, 9, 147
Paracelsus 56, 149
Paris, France 42; Sorbonne 83
Paris, Ginette 7, 32, 123
Parvati (East Indian goddess figure of) 8, 129, 133
Paz, Octavio 5, 123, 130, 147, 152
Persephone 130–132
Philemon 41

Picasso, Pablo 26, 46, 47, 65, 67, 110; on creation and destruction 130
Plato 1, 7; *anamnesis* 72; *anima mundi* in thought of 145–146; archetypal psychology, as ancestor of 18, 85; *daimonion* 112; *eidos* 22; Ficino as translator of 86; Freud's familiarity with 30; Jung's reading of 39; Myth of Er 38, 110; Persia prior to 17; on poets and prophets 26; primacy of soul in thought of 113; *Republic* 38, 110; shamans in time of 16; soul in the thought of 22–25, 30, 54; *theia mania* (divine madness) 24–25, 31, 45, 64
Platonic cosmos 146
Platonic Forms 45
Platonic soul 23, 54
Platonic thought 23
Platonists and Neoplatonists 11, 86, 91
play *see* creative play
Plotinus, Plotino 7, 26, 86–87; *anima mundi* in thought of 145–146; archetypal psychology, as ancestor of 18; primacy of soul in thought of 113
p'o, Chinese concept of 51
poesis 3, 20, 92, 96, 109, 116; act of 143; *aesthesis* and 148; *see also* mythopoesis; psychopoesis
polis 109
Pollock, Jackson 110
portal, symbol of 77
Portmann, Adolf 91–92
Positivism 27
prayer: art akin to 10, 153; artmaking as act of 146; effective 24; strands of magic and 19; *via aesthetica* and 96
psychagogue 41
psyche: aesthetic nature of 84; ancient meaning of 96; anima, soul, and 52–55, 105; as archetypal first principal 18; artists as servants to 48; Carus's model of 51; as collective unconscious 49; Complex Psychology in reference to 45; as consciousness and "the unconscious" 27; creative 128, 151; creative process and 5; dream language of 153; embodied 78; Freud's theories of 29, 30; Hillman's

166 Index

research into 83, 115; human 87–88,
146; Jung's inquiries into 38, 39, 41, 57,
62, 70, 145; as image and imaginer of
reality 84, 88–92, 113, 148; as image
maker 101; as imaginative process
(Jung) 2; as image 6, 11; matter and 78,
79, 135; individual 150; mimesis and
122; multiple and relational 133; myths
emerging from 120, 142; Neoplatonist
approach to 86; polyvalent 76; primal
shaping energies of 8; as soul 104;
transpersonal and autonomous 44; "third
area of" 75; as type of
self-consciousness 23; universal 87
Psyche and Eros 95, 133–135
psyche and logos 106
psyche-soma split 23, 25, 77
psychic life 53
psychic images 86, 145
psychic reality 20, 94
psychic state 20
psycho 84
psychopoesis (soul making) 4, 97, 114
psychopomp (guides of souls) 2, 9, 134;
anima as 105; artist as 108, 115, 150,
153; shaman as 16, 56
puer 132, 133, 134, 150
puer aeternus 94
puritan 23
Puritanism 147
Pythagoras 21, 22, 39

Ra (god) 129
Raven (Native American trickster figure)
8, 126
Read, Herbert (Sir): alchemy and
alchemists, views on 68, 71, 73; on
artists and the unconscious 6; on
artists as "field of operation" 143;
consciousness, understanding of 68,
73, 76; Jung and 67–72; Jung's letter
writing to 57; on muses 2, 70, 72–73
Renaissance 1, 26, 27, 86
Renaissance man, Renaissance spirit:
Hillman as 83; Jung as 56, 63, 67
Riklin, Franz 42–43
Rilke, Ranier Maria 145, 147, 148

ritual 3, 7; art as form of 11; artistic
work as 114; Christian 25; creative
expressions such as 32; culture and 85;
dying and creating 74; image as 93;
myth and 69; pagan 25; sacred invoked
through 21
Romanticism 27
Rossi, Safron 154n28
Rowland, Susan 7, 11, 62–63, 76–80

sacrifice 3, 44; artist's fantasy requiring
114; artmaking and ego control linked to
115; Jung's recognition of the necessity
of 56; of life 124; selfless 49;
self-sacrifice 28, 55; shamanic
sensibility and 109; suffering and 74
Saint Augustine 26
Saint Teresa of Avila 26
saman 16; *see also* shaman
Sandywell, Barry 91
Sartre, Jean-Paul 69
Schopenhauer 26, 39
Salmacis 133
Seele, die and *seelisch* (Freud) 31, 54
seers 17, 18, 25, 124, 133
Sekhmet/Sakhmet 129
self 23; as archetype of wholeness 70;
dissolution of 128; Jungian concept of
72; loss of 24; orientation to world and
to soul 115
self and other, theories of 27
self-consciousness 23
self-dedication 4
self-sacrifice 28
self-transformation 6
Semele 129
senex (father image) 94, 134
Set (god) 129
Shakespeare, William 26, 108; on art as a
mirror, as referenced by Campbell 136;
Freud's passion for 29; Herbert Read,
influence on 72; Jung's view of 46
Shakti (goddess) 133
shakti/sakti 129
shaman: alertness associated with 71;
apprenticing of 49; as archetypal
ancestor of artist 3, 12, 143; artist as

Index 167

46, 66, 68, 79, 127; artist, *sourcier*, and 9–10, 153; Campbell's understanding of 143; "creative illness" associated with 28, 30; Eliade's understanding of 16; Jung as 55–57; multidimensional 16, 20; multifaceted 65, 131, 143; pre-differentiated figure of 26; prehistoric representations of 18–19, 26; *saman* and 16; seriousness of role of 73; *sophos* and 17; unified figure of 17

"Shaman, The" (cave painting at Lascaux) 18

shamanic master 30

shamanic patterns. . .: of disorientation, descent, death, and rebirth 41; of initiation 11

shamanic practices 32; Dodd's understanding of 22–23

shamanic sensibility 9, 75, 109, 146; artist as one who expresses 150; "creative illnesses" linked to 115; of working in the middle 104

shamanic soul 114–116

shamanic spirit 9, 56, 144

shamanic traditions 1

shamanism 16

Shamanism: The Beginnings of Art (Lommel) 19

shamanistic practices 10

shaman-like healers 6, 124

Shamdasani, Sonu 42, 43

Shelley, [Percy Bysshe] 26

Schelling 18

Shiva or Siva 8, 95, 126, 127–130

Shiva Nataraja 133

Shiva/Shakti 133

Slater, Glen 90, 117n31, 154n28

Slattery, Dennis Patrick 7

Society of Analytical Psychology 73; *Journal of Analytical Psychology* 73

sol and luna 106

Sophocles 26, 30, 133

sophos (human pursuit of wisdom) 17

soul: aesthetic 100–101; anima, psyche, and 52–55, 105; archeology of 16–32; as archetypal artist 142; artist and 142–153; as artist 12; artistic continuum

of 26; body and, split between 23; creativity and 1–2; definition of 16; crossroads, as resident of 142–144; depth psychology's valuing of 6, 20; Ficino's views on 86; as focus of Jungian and archetypal psychologies 10; Greek myth and 21–22; Heraclitus' views of 18; human maker and 114; kaleidoscopic 101–102; loss of 72; image and/as 90–91, 113, 148; making of 116; Neoplatonic 87; new science and 27–28; Plato's thoughts regarding 22–25, 30, 54; Plotinus's views on 87; psychology and 16–18; as root metaphor (Hillman) 8; science of 32; spirit and 102–103; as symbol and prism 104–105; writers concerned with 88

soul as maker 109–112

soul force 20

soulfulness 78, 84

soul guide 41; *see also* psychagogue; psychopomp

soul journeying 22

soul-making: artists as models of 150; Hillman's concept of 4, 7, 11, 57n5, 92, 95, 97, 98n43, 132, 150; image-making and (Hillman) 100–119; mythopoetics and 135–137; *psychopoesis* as 4, 97, 114

soul of the world 146

soul retrieval 22

soul-stones 39

soul therapy 84

soul-to-soul connection 121

soul work 57

sourcier 9–10, 12, 153

spirit: all creation as 126; creative 3, 11, 31, 37–57, 67, 150, 153; free 114; female 129; guardian 110; matter and 143; shamanic 9, 56, 65, 144; soul and 102–103; tortured 133; universal 144

spiritual facts 40

spirit guides 50

spirit of curiosity 63

spirit of the age 56

spirit of the depths 62

168 Index

spiritualism 27, 40
spirit world 25, 56, 108, 132, 146
Surrealism 42
symbol 1, 2; archetype and 45, 50; art
    and 78–79; bird as 47; bridge as 143;
    bridging 7, 8; conceptual 62; crossroads
    as 142, 143; function of 10; Jungian 78,
    93, 121; psychic experience of 20; soul as
    2, 104–105; sun as 47; synchronicity and
    78–79; synchronous 11; threshold as 77
symbol as portal 77–78
symbol-creating forces 66
symbolic discourse 68
Symbolism 42
symbolization 75, 122
symbolizing function 76, 108
synchronicity 7, 53, 62; alchemy and 79;
    Jung's work with 79; symbol and
    78–79
syzygy 105–106

talisman 147, 157
talismans of transformation 12
Tao and Taoism 31, 51, 53, 78; *Chinese Book
    of Life* 88; interplay of yin and yang in 75
Tarnas, Richard 7, 26–27
Teresa of Avila 26
theia mania (divine madness) (Plato)
    24–25, 31, 45, 64
Thomas, Dylan 72
Thoth 123, 125, 129
threshold: initiatory 20; soul as 55; as
    symbol 77; time as 25
Tiresias 133
transcendentalism 17
transcendent forms 24
transcendent functions 44, 75–76
trickster 8, 12, 62, 123–127, 129;
    archetypal artist as 153; as archetype
    131; creator as 136; as
    worldbuilder 134
transdisciplinarity 7, 32, 75–76
Tucker, Michael 12, 18, 19, 131, 144

"unaddressed appearances" (Portmann)
    91–92
unitary consciousness 27
unitary reality (Neumann's concept of) 65,
    66, 146; *see also* numinous, the
universali fantastici 86
unus mundus 78

van de Berk, Tjeu 78–79
via aesthetica (path of beauty)(Hillman)
    94–97, 148
via regia 44
Vico, Giambattista 7, 18, 26, 113;
    influence on Hillman 85–86; influence
    on Read 69; universal images
    of 86
vitalism: animalism and 77; Dylan
    Thomas' understanding of 72; primal
    68; Read's notion of 11, 71
vitality 91, 112; principle of
    70–72
von Franz, Marie-Louise 7; on Jung's
    daimon 38; on *emotio* principle 135;
    on Jung's *compassio* and empiricism
    40–41; on Jung as *hermeneut* 56; on
    Jung's sensitivity to beauty 46; on
    Jung's Taoist philosophy 51; on role of
    the creative artist for the
    collective 151

Wagner, [Richard] 49
Watkins, Mary 154n28
Wheelwright, Philip 17, 120
Wilder, Thornton: "Angel that Troubled
    the Waters" 130–131
Wotan 95
wounded healer 8, 12, 65–66, 153; oracles
    and 130–133
wounding, woundedness 20, 115, 143

Yeats, William Butler 136–137
yin and yang 31, 51, 75, 106

Printed in the United States
by Baker & Taylor Publisher Services